Ads, Fads, and
Consumer Culture

Ads, Fads, and Consumer Culture

Advertising's Impact on American Character and Society

FIFTH EDITION

Arthur Asa Berger
With illustrations by the author

ROWMAN & LITTLEFIELD
Lanham • Boulder • New York • London

Published by Rowman & Littlefield
A wholly owned subsidary of The Rowman & Littlefield Publishing Group, Inc.
4501 Forbes Boulevard, Suite 200, Lanham, Maryland 20706
www.rowman.com

Unit A, Whitacre Mews, 26-34 Stannary Street, London SE11 4AB, United Kingdom

British Library Cataloguing in Publication Information Available

Library of Congress Cataloging-in-Publication Data
Berger, Arthur Asa, 1933–
  Ads, fads, and consumer culture : advertising's impact on American character and society /
Arthur Asa Berger. — Fifth edition.
    pages cm
  Includes bibliographical references and index.
  ISBN 978-1-4422-4124-4 (cloth : alk. paper) — ISBN 978-1-4422-4125-1 (pbk. : alk.
paper) — ISBN 978-1-4422-4126-8 (electronic) 1. Advertising—United States. 2. Popular
culture—United States. 3. Consumer education—United States. I. Title.
  HF5823.B438 2015
  659.1'0420973—dc23

                                                                    2014030143

Printed in the United States of America

Some measure of greed exists unconsciously in everyone. It represents an aspect of the desire to live, one which is mingled and fused at the outset of life with the impulse to turn aggression and destructiveness outside ourselves against others, and as such it persists unconsciously throughout life. By its very nature it is endless and never assuaged; and being a form of the impulse to live, it ceases only with death.

The longing or greed for good things can relate to any and every imaginable kind of good—material possessions, bodily or mental gifts, advantages and privileges; but, beside the actual gratifications they may bring, in the depths of our minds they ultimately signify one thing. They stand as proofs to us, if we get them, that we are ourselves good, and full of good, and so are worthy of love, or respect and honour, in return. Thus they serve as proofs and insurances against our fears of emptiness inside ourselves, or of our evil impulses which make us feel bad and full of badness to ourselves and others.

—Joan Riviere, "Hate, Greed and Aggression"

CONTENTS

Foreword by Fred S. Goldberg   *xi*

Preface to the Fifth Edition   *xv*

Acknowledgments   *xxiii*

1   Advertising in American Society   *1*

Advertising as a Puzzlement   *1*

Defining Advertising   *5*

Advertising Agencies   *7*

Max Weber on Religion and Consumer Cultures   *9*

Advertising and Politics   *10*

A Psycho-Cultural Perspective on Advertising   *12*

Running It Up a Flagpole to See If Anyone Salutes   *13*

Commercials as Mini-Dramas and Works of Art   *15*

Teleculture and the Internet   *23*

The Super Bowl   *27*

The Global Nature of Advertising Agencies   *28*

Conclusion   *29*

2   Consumer Cultures   *33*

A Cultural Critique of Advertising   *33*

Consumer Cultures Defined   *34*

Taste Cultures and Advertising   *37*

The Postmodern Perspective   *38*

The Problem of Emotions Overcoming Rationality   *43*

Consumer Culture and Privatism   *44*

Neiman Marcus and "Couthification"   *45*

Needs Are Finite, Desires Are Infinite   *47*

Are There Four Consumer Cultures, Not Just One?   *49*

National Character and Consumer Cultures   *55*

3 **Advertising and the Communication Process**   *59*
    The Lasswell Formula   *59*
    Focal Points and the Study of Media   *61*
    Roman Jakobson's Model of the Communication Process   *62*
    Run It Up a Flagpole   *64*
    Metaphor and Metonymy   *65*
    Myth and Marketing   *67*
    Integrated Marketing Communication   *69*

4 **Running It Up a Flagpole to See If Anyone Salutes**   *73*
    Lisa's Morning: A Fiction   *73*
    Lisa Greatgal's and Johnny Q. Public's Daily Media Diet *74*
    Television Viewing and Exposure to Commercials   *75*
    A Note on "Hauls"   *77*
    The Price We Pay for "Free" Television   *77*
    The Illusion of Control   *78*
    Being a "Branded" Individual   *82*
    Selling Oneself   *87*
    Selling One's Body for Brands   *89*
    The Problem of Self-Alienation   *90*
    We Can Choose as We Please, but Can We Please as We Please? *91*
    The Agony of Choice   *93*
    Nonadvertising Forms of Advertising   *94*

5 **Sexuality and Gender in Advertising**   *99*
    Sex and Gender in Advertising   *100*
    Sex in Advertising   *101*
    Sexploitation and Anxiety   *107*
    The Peach That Became a Prune: A Cautionary Fable   *111*
    The Pseudopoetic Appeal to the Illiterati   *114*
    Sex Appeal and Gender Appeal   *116*
    Sex and the Problem of Clutter   *118*

6 **Political Advertising**   *125*
    The Cost of Presidential Campaigns   *129*
    The Cost of the 2012 Presidential Election   *130*
    Questions Raised by the Election Campaigns   *131*
    A Note on the California Campaign for Governor in 2010 *132*
    The Code of the Commercial (and Other Political Advertising) *133*
    The Emotional Basis of Partisan Politics   *134*

7 **The Marketing Society**   *139*
   Statistics on Advertising   *139*
   More Comments on the Illusion of Freedom   *140*
   The Marketing View   *142*
   The VALS 1 Typology   *144*
   Using the VALS 1 Typology: A Case Study   *147*
   VALS 2: A Revision of the VALS 1 Typology   *147*
   ZIP Codes and Kinds of Consumers   *149*
   The Claritas Typology   *151*
   Magazine Choice as an Indicator of Consumer Taste   *153*
   Types of Teenage Consumers   *155*
   Blogs and Marketing   *158*
   A Typology for Everyone in the World   *159*
   A Comparison of the Different Typologies   *161*
   A Conclusion to This Discussion in the Form of a Question   *163*

8 **Analyzing Print Advertisements or: Six Ways of Looking
   at a Fidji Perfume Advertisement**   *167*
   Lotman's Contributions to Understanding Texts   *167*
   What's There to Analyze in an Advertisement?   *168*
   Analyzing the Fidji Ad   *169*
   A Semiotic Interpretation of the Fidji Advertisement   *171*
   A Psychoanalytic Interpretation of the Fidji Advertisement   *173*
   A Sociological Interpretation of the Fidji Advertisement   *176*
   A Marxist Interpretation of the Fidji Advertisement   *177*
   The Myth Model and the Fidji Advertisement   *178*
   A Feminist Interpretation of the Fidji Advertisement   *179*
   Conclusion   *180*

9 **Analyzing Television Commercials**   *183*
   The Macintosh "1984" Commercial   *183*
   A Synopsis of the Text   *185*
   The Background   *186*
   Testing the "1984" Macintosh Commercial   *186*
   George Orwell's *1984* and Ridley Scott's "1984"   *188*
   The Image of the Total Institution   *189*
   The Prisoners' Boots   *189*
   The Blond as a Symbol   *190*
   The Brainwashing Scenario   *190*
   The Big Brother Figure   *191*

The Brainwasher's Message   *191*
The Big Explosion   *192*
The Inmates' Response   *193*
The Macintosh Announcement   *193*
The Heroine as Mythic Figure   *194*
Psychoanalytic Aspects of the Commercial   *195*
The Blond as Mediator   *196*
Alienated Proles   *197*
The Big Blue   *198*
A Clever Marketing Strategy   *199*
The "1984" Commercial and a Bit of Scholarly Research   *200*

10 **Where Next?**   *205*
Drug Advertising   *205*
Children and Advertising   *209*
Battling for People's Attention   *211*
Smart Phones, Social Media, and Advertising   *211*

Glossary   *215*

Annotated Bibliography   *233*

Bibliography   *237*

Index   *243*

About the Author   *251*

FOREWORD

Fred S. Goldberg

I spent thirty-four years in advertising: the first fifteen at what was then, arguably, the finest of the large traditional Madison Avenue agencies (Young & Rubicam, New York); the next nine years at arguably the finest creative agency in the country at the time (Chiat/Day, Los Angeles); and the last ten founding and managing my own agency (Goldberg Moser O'Neill, San Francisco). This experience provided me with a unique overview and insight into the business of advertising.

When you study advertising and advertising's impact, it helps to understand the context within which advertising messages are developed, produced, and aired. Many of the print ads and commercials that consumers ultimately see could have been demonstrably different were it not for the conflicting interests that went hand in hand with their development.

In theory, advertisers hire advertising agencies to create ads that will break through and impact their customers and potential customers. They hope to maximize the effectiveness of often limited media and promotional dollars, achieve a competitive edge, and gain extra mileage from each advertising message.

Yet, because of the nature of the industry and the agency and client relationship, a series of conflicts often prevents this from happening as frequently as it should. And this explains, at least in part, why there is so much advertising that is spurious, curious, muddled, and jumbled. The impact that it all has on the American character and culture, as explained in this book, is partially the result of the conflicting way advertising gets developed. One can only wonder what the ads—and their effect—would be if self-interest were removed along the way.

These conflicts have a numbing consequence on the impact of clients' advertising dollars and the subsequent success they have in the marketplace selling their products or positioning their companies or causes. The advertising business is unique and particularly difficult because it is fraught with these conflicts, which very often result in a dumbed-down final product.

Trying to represent what is best for the client while still trying to make a profit is sometimes a challenge for an advertising agency. It's easy to profess, as advertising agencies are prone to do, that their recommendations are impartially formulated only to drive a client's business, but that is not always the case. In fact, they are influenced by the existence of various agendas operating at different levels of management in an agency and in different departments. Similar agendas may exist on the client side.

Advertising executives may believe that they are providing complete objectivity, but at the end of the day, they can be often prejudiced, partial, and biased. One example that Arthur Berger observes in this book is that, for various reasons, it is important that the advertising agency recommend only one campaign. It must be made to seem to be the only answer to the company's problems. This practice provides fertile ground for conflicts of interests and less-than-complete objectivity.

Why does this happen? One reason is conflicts between departments. On the one hand, account management representatives may be trying to support the client's view and interest within the agency, while other departments are developing recommendations that may or may not reflect the client's actual needs. Or vice versa. The account planners are supposedly trying to represent the consumer, the creative people are representing their ad, and the client is concerned about his brand. This leads to internal agency debate, to compromises, and ultimately to a finished product that often depends on who made the strongest argument or had the most authority.

This is all further complicated, as Berger accurately points out, in that people in advertising agencies need to sell both themselves and the products they have been engaged to advertise. This can, in and of itself, create a conflict.

There is another conflict where many advertisers rely on creative testing to help them make a decision. They rely heavily on the often-spurious conclusions, and this conflicts directly with implementing work that can truly break through and impact the consumer in a highly competitive manner. In client organizations, testing is a political tool as often as it is a learning device. It helps protect people's decision making, particularly in the context of a large organizational framework, as much as it determines the worth of a particular message or idea. When a test shows an idea to be normative, then the decision to use it can be more easily justified. In other words, one's backside is adequately covered in the event of a failure.

Finally, there is the conflict in trying to develop truly unique and creative solutions to business and communication problems. It is my experience that, generally, opposition to a creative solution grows greater in direct proportion to its uniqueness and lack of familiarity. This is true for people within an ad agency, the client organization, and even potential customers, all of whom are asked to judge things that are new and different.

I was personally involved in what may have been one of the great advertising lessons of all time, exhibiting all of these various conflicting forces. It was for Apple Computer—a commercial known as "1984." This was the introductory commercial for Apple's Macintosh and was one of the most memorable, most persuasive, most effective commercials ever created.

However, the commercial, after being fully produced, was rejected by then–Apple CEO Steve Jobs after it was inordinately criticized by Apple's board of directors just prior to airing. They argued that it was an extravagance and did not appropriately communicate Apple's persona as a serious business computer company to stockholders, investors, and the consumer. They worried that Apple would look "insane" and "out of control" if the commercial aired.

A test of the commercial supported the board somewhat, although members never saw the results. It indicated that the commercial was well below established averages in its "effectiveness," scoring only a 5 against a norm of 29 for thirty-second business-directed commercials. The commercial was actually sixty seconds and should have scored all that much higher.

The commercial was to air during the Super Bowl. Because the advertising agency was not able to resell the media time it had purchased for it, Steve Jobs ultimately gave his approval to run the commercial in lieu of forfeiting the money for the time that had already been committed. This was done despite internal protestations at Apple.

History was made. The personal computer industry is entirely different today because of this single "conflicted" advertising decision. The commercial was recalled the day after it ran by 78 percent of viewers; Apple sold $3.5 million worth of Macintosh computers within six hours the next business day and $155 million over the next one hundred days. Today, Apple's revenues are $25 billion, and it has a market capitalization of $59 billion, arguably because of the airing of one single commercial.

This is but one eye-popping example of why advertising is such a unique business among businesses.

The manner in which advertising is developed and implemented—and the incredible influence it has on our culture and consumers—is profound. *Ads, Fads, and Consumer Culture* delves into this and other matters. Arthur Berger provides fresh insights and explanations on various aspects and issues of the industry and the ads and the impact on all of us. On the very first page, he identifies one of the critical issues: "Advertising agencies are forced to talk out of both sides of their mouths at the same time."

When one considers the enormous impact advertising has on millions of people every day and on our culture, it is mind-boggling that so many arbitrary factors and self-interests can shape the communication development process. Reading Mr. Berger's book in this context makes many of his analyses and conclusions that much more surprising, insightful, thought provoking, and entertaining.

The author specifically discusses and analyzes the Apple "1984" commercial in depth in the last chapter. It's amazing that this advertising had such a profound impact on products and people's lives when one considers the agony and irony involved in giving birth to a genuinely new idea.

On the other hand, maybe it's not so amazing. Maybe most advertising works, whatever the development process, just because all advertising works.

PREFACE TO THE FIFTH EDITION

It is a great pleasure for me to offer this new edition of *Ads, Fads, and Consumer Culture* to my readers. The advertising industry is one in which there is constant change, as new technologies develop, new products are created, and new services are offered. For example, the Internet and social media are major sources of advertising revenue, as anyone who has used search engines, such as Google, or social media, such as Facebook, knows. Blogging remains important, even as tweets and interactive posting gain ground.

Advertising companies are extremely interested in what bloggers say about new movies, video games, and other products to gain added insights into consumer behavior and are using "loyalty cards" to create brand advocates and mining data about consumer preferences wherever they can find it. There is a good deal of debate in academic circles and in the government about the role of advertising in American society. Does advertising for fast foods and junk food play a role in the rapid growth of obesity in America and in a number of other countries? If so, how big a role has it played, and what should be done to remedy this situation? Has advertising for expensive consumer drugs had a negative impact on the medical profession and on the health of Americans? Many people believe this to be the case, and this had led to changes in the rules that drug advertisers follow. Are young children being taught to be self-indulgent and materialistic as they are "branded" by advertising? If so, how do we counter this development? Has advertising shaped, in important ways, the way individuals perceive themselves and the way we perceive one another? If this is the case, how can people defend themselves against the way they are being affected or even "manipulated" by advertisers? These are only a few of the topics I deal with in this book.

HIDDEN PERSUADERS

Whatever else it might be, advertising is a form of mass persuasion, and we must wonder about the social, psychological, and cultural impact of this industry that plays so large a role in our media and everyday lives. In 1957, Vance Packard wrote a book, *The Hidden Persuaders*, that alerted his readers to the role advertising was playing in American society. He wrote (1957:3),

> This book is an attempt to explore a strange and rather exotic new area of American life. It is about the way many of us are being influenced and manipulated—far more than we realize—in the patterns of our everyday lives. Large-scale efforts are being made, often with impressive success, to channel our unthinking habits, our purchasing decisions, and our thought processes by the use of insights gleaned from psychiatry and the social sciences. Typically these efforts take place beneath our level of awareness; so that the appeals which move us are often, in a sense, hidden.
>
> Some of this manipulating being attempted is simply amusing. Some of it is disquieting, particularly when viewed as a portent of what may be ahead on a more intensive and effective scale for us all. Co-operative scientists have come along providentially to furnish some awesome tools.

The impact of this use of psychoanalytic and other methods has led advertisers to more effectively sell us (1957:3) "products, ideas, attitudes, candidates, goals or states of mind." Packard wrote his book more than fifty years ago. Since then, the advertising industry has developed incredible new means of understanding our thought processes and ways of shaping our behavior.

It has also extended its reach and now uses "product placements" to put certain products in television shows and films and now shows commercials on smart phones. In some cases, one product placement in a television show or film can lead to huge increases in the sales of that product. In addition, since films with product placements in them are widely distributed abroad, it gives products placed in films a global reach. Sometimes, products sold in a foreign country are substituted for the original product placements in films. Thus, in *Spider-Man 2*, Dr. Pepper was shown in the film in the United States, but Mirinda was shown overseas.

We can say, without stretching the truth too much, that, with few exceptions, wherever in the world there are flat surfaces, such as sides of buildings, cars, buses, and screens of all kinds and sizes, advertisers will find a way to use them for their purposes.

BRAIN SCANS AND CONSUMER BEHAVIOR

For a number of years, there has been experimentation in using brain scans to see which parts of the brain are activated by exposure to advertisements. Advertisers have moved beyond surveys, focus groups, and depth interviews and now are experimenting with bypassing people's explanations of why they do things to see, more directly, how specific images, bits of dialogue, and music passages stimulate certain parts of our brains. An article by Carmen Nobel in the February 22, 2013, issue of *Forbes* deals with the power of neuromarketing. Nobel quotes Uma R. Karmarkar, who teaches in the Harvard Business School (http://www.forbes.com/sites/hbsworkingknowledge/2013/02/01/neuromarketing-tapping-into-the-pleasure-center-of-consumers):

> "People are fairly good at expressing what they want, what they like, or even how much they will pay for an item," says Uma R. Karmarkar, an assistant professor at Harvard Business School who sports PhDs in both marketing and neuroscience. "But they aren't very good at accessing where that value comes from, or how and when it is influenced by factors like store displays or brands. [Neuroscience] can help us understand those hidden elements of the decision process."
>
> To be sure, there is a clear difference between the goals of academia and the goals of a corporation in utilizing neuroscience. For Karmarkar, her work falls into the category of decision neuroscience, which is the study of what our brains do as we make choices. She harbors no motive other than to understand that process and its implications for behavior, and draws on concepts and techniques from neuroscience to inform her research in marketing.

If advertisers are able to figure out how to bypass our consciousness by using information learned by studying brain scans, they will be even more powerful than they already are. Sigmund Freud, the father of psychoanalytic theory, had suggested that material stored in the unconscious elements of our psyches, areas we cannot access and of which we are unaware, is often responsible for our actions.

Many advertising agencies use this notion to convince us to purchase the goods and services they are selling. The Russian psychologist Pavlov showed how dogs could be trained to salivate on command by being given certain stimuli, and some advertisers have attempted to use this stimulus–response theory to attempt to shape our consumption behavior. Now, advertising agencies, using information derived from neurological studies of brain activation, may move beyond Freud's theory and develop strategies that can be described only as Orwellian in their implications.

I hope that you will find that this new edition of this book helps you understand the role advertising plays in American culture and society and advertising's role in giving you notions about who you are, what is important in life, and what role you should play in society. Advertising pervades our everyday lives. How advertising affects our psyches, our society, and our culture is a question that demands continual study and attention. This book will help you learn how to analyze print advertisements and television commercials as a means of gaining a bit of control over this subtle and all-pervasive force in American culture and other societies as well.

THE GOALS OF THIS BOOK

I wrote this book to do a number of things:

1. To teach you something about how advertising works.
2. To suggest how advertising has affected American society and culture.
3. To help you learn to analyze and interpret advertisements and commercials in more interesting and profound ways. This should help you learn to resist them better.

Since advertising is so pervasive in our culture, this book deals with a number of different topics—sexuality, politics, market research, consumer culture, and many other things. I hope that you, my reader, will find it interesting and useful and that it will help you see the role advertising has played—and is playing—in your life.

There was a great deal of interest before the 2014 Super Bowl in the commercials that were going to be shown during the game, for that's when companies, paying $4 million for thirty-second spots, which is what it cost for a thirty-second advertisement then, usually show their best ones. After the game, the general consensus was that the 2014 Super Bowl commercials weren't very good, for the most part. Why did that happen? Are the agencies running out of ideas? Are they trying too hard? Are our expectations too high? The high point in Super Bowl advertising occurred in 1984 when the classic "1984 Macintosh" commercial was shown. Since then, it has been mostly downhill for Super Bowl commercials, as a rule, and no commercial since then has elicited so much interest as the "1984" commercial.

I devote a chapter in this book to that commercial and show how it worked and how it drew on information most of us knew to achieve its effects. Fred Goldberg, who wrote the foreword to this book, was intimately involved in that commercial and played a key role in getting it aired despite the desire of some people who worked for Apple that it not be used. I also deal with a classic advertisement for Fidji perfume in my chapter on analyzing print advertisements. I wrote these two chapters, on methods of analyzing commercials and print advertisements, to enable my readers to make their own analyses of various kinds of advertising. By learning how specific texts (the term we use in academic discourse for advertisements, commercials, and other works in any medium) function, you will be able to understand their appeals and insulate yourself from them.

Advertising plays a major role in American life. Paco Underhill offers an interesting factoid about advertising in his book (2009:152) *Why We Buy: The Science of Shopping*: "The average four year old American child can identify more than one hundred brands," he writes, which is probably because American children watch so much television and because so much marketing is directed toward children and teenagers. That's because older people recognize that buying things isn't going to change their lives and become more adept at ignoring advertising. As Underhill explains (2009:152), "The older we get, the more we recognize that the ownership of any product, no matter what it is, isn't transformative. That dress, that lipstick, the iPod nano is not going to change you or anyone's opinion of you."

Teenagers, Underhill suggests, still believe in the power of brands to shape their lives and perceptions others have of them. As he writes (2009:163),

> Teenagers are still young enough to be total suckers for image, for all the blandishments of advertising, identity marketing, media messages, trends and labels. They still believe in a brand name's power to confer status, cool, charisma, knowledge. They construct their identities by the shopping choices they make—they're a lot like adults were back in the '50s, before we all became so wise in the way of image hucksters.

I would argue that many young adults and adults are also "suckers," to use Underhill's term, for the appeals of advertising and believe that their brand

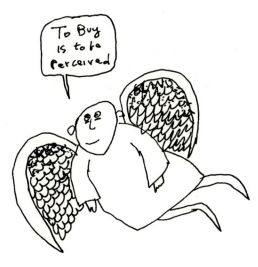

choices are transformative. That is because, in part, we are bombarded by advertising of all kinds all day long. We swim, like fish, in a sea of billboards, newspaper ads, magazine ads, television commercials, and ads on our smart phones and on the Internet, so it is very difficult to avoid being affected by all these messages. We have the illusion that we can shield ourselves from advertising and are not affected by it. It is analogous to fish believing that though they swim in water, they don't get wet.

We are also very interested in advertising and its impact on our society. This is reflected in the many sites devoted to advertising and various aspects of the industry on Google. If you go to Google search and look for sites that deal with advertising, this is what you will find:

	Dec. 5, 2012	April 8, 2014
Advertising	834 million	885 million
Advertising New Developments	614 million	642 million
Internet Advertising	1,750 million	1,690 million
Advertisements	68 million	74 million
Advertising Techniques	214 million	262 million
Advertising Agencies	247 million	202 million
Ads, Fads and Consumer Culture	29,000	26,000

If you go back a few years, you find the number of sites about advertising have increased a great deal, which suggests that people are now much more conscious of the role advertising is playing in American culture and their lives.

To my surprise, there were 26,000 sites on Google (as of April 8, 2014) that deal with or mention this book. Most of them involve stores that sell the book. One site that I found particularly interesting (and a bit distressing) was Campus Book Rentals (on Amazon.com), which rents books and wanted more than $15 to rent my book. Nobody knows what kind of impact companies that rent textbooks and electronic books will have on the publishing industry and whether students will be reading this book and most of their textbooks on electronic book readers such as Kindle, iPads, the Internet, computer monitors, or whatever.

WHAT'S NEW IN THIS EDITION

I've added new material to many of the topics I've dealt with in previous editions of the book and added new discussions of topics such as the following:

- Advertising and religion
- Psychoanalytic theory and sexual development
- Stuart Hall on "The Cultural Turn"
- Neuromarketing
- Myth and advertising
- Virginia Woolf and social change
- Social class and consumption: A learning exercise
- Lifestyles and consumption: A learning exercise
- Integrated marketing communication (IMC)
- National character and consumption
- Sex and gender
- Race and ethnicity

In addition, professors may now access the images and illustrations highlighted in the book as slides for use in teaching presentations. Contact textbooks@rowman.com for more details.

I hope that you will find this book helpful in understanding the way advertising works and the role that advertisements and commercials and the advertising industry in general play in your life and American culture and society as well. I have worked hard to make this book entertaining as well as informative and have reproduced a number of advertisements and drawn many illustrations to make the book more visually interesting. I would be happy if you think that two slogans from commercials that appeared many years ago apply to this book: "Try it! You'll like it!" and "I ate (read) the whole thing!"

A NOTE ON THE ADVERTISEMENTS USED IN THIS BOOK

Advertising campaigns come and go so quickly that it is impossible to keep up with the newest ads and commercials, and there is really no need to do so. Most advertising is undistinguished, at best. And the "life expectancy" for any advertisement or commercial or campaign is, generally speaking, not very long. One exception to this fact is the Absolut campaign, which lasted for twenty-five years before the company decided on a new campaign. The "Got Milk" campaign changed after a number of years, but most campaigns don't last very long.

Thus, for my chapters on analyzing print advertisements and television commercials, I have chosen texts of great interest and ones that are considered classics. They are also very useful since they are extremely rich in symbols and cultural significance and allow for a great deal of analysis.

The Fidji advertisement was the main subject of a major study of perfume advertising at INSEAD, the European Institute of Business Administration, one of the most important business schools in the world. I didn't know about the INSEAD study when I wrote my analysis of the advertisement. I was captivated by the complex symbology in the advertisement. The Macintosh "1984" commercial was voted the second-best advertisement in the 1980s (the first was the famous "fast talker" commercial for Federal Express by Ally & Gargano) by The One Club for Art and Copy, an organization that evaluates advertising in the advertising industry. Many people consider the "1984" commercial to be the best one ever made.

So I have selected texts for these two chapters (and in a number of other places) that are extremely interesting and useful for analysis. Choosing more up-to-date advertisements and commercials for my chapters on methods of analyzing print advertisements and television commercials, from my perspective, would serve no useful purpose, for it is the application of the techniques of interpreting and analyzing advertisements and commercials that is critical, not the texts themselves. However, I have inserted new advertisements in various places in the fifth edition, though what is really important is the degree to which the reproduced advertisement can be connected to some topic of interest dealt with in the book, not when it was made.

So now, I invite you to investigate, with my help, advertising—a fascinating industry and one that plays a role in our lives of considerable importance.

ACKNOWLEDGMENTS

My list of topics to consider on print advertising and television commercials draws on, but is a modification and enhancement of material in my book *Seeing Is Believing: An Introduction to Visual Communication* (1998). In *Ads, Fads, and Consumer Culture*, I focus on a more general analysis using some of the basic critical techniques. The interpretive techniques I use in the Fidji analysis are dealt with in more detail in my books *Media Analysis Techniques, Cultural Criticism, Seeing Is Believing: An Introduction to Visual Communication* and *Signs in Contemporary Culture: An Introduction to Semiotics*. They offer more amplified discussions of the various methodologies and concepts I will be using here, and they also have bibliographies for those interested in pursuing these interpretive methodologies in more depth. The glossary is an adaptation, revised and tied to advertising, of my glossary in *Essentials of Mass Communication Theory*.

I am grateful to Transaction Publishers for giving me permission to reprint my article on the "1984" commercial and to Sage Publications for giving me permission to reprint my analysis of the Fidji advertisement. I have revised both of these articles considerably for this book. I also want to thank the Advertising Education Foundation for granting me a visiting professorship in 1999 that enabled me to spend three weeks at Goldberg Moser O'Neill advertising in San Francisco and Fred Goldberg and all his colleagues for making my stay there so enjoyable and useful and for allowing me to use a number of their advertisements in this book. I also want to thank my editor, Leanne Silverman, for suggesting I write a new edition of this book; my copyeditor Bruce Owens for his help; Rhonda Baker for the layout; and three professors, whose names I do not know, for their reviews of the fourth edition of this book and suggestions for the fifth edition.

Is the advertiser the magician of modern times working out spells to entrap and subjugate desire, or is he merely a modest, honest intermediary investigating public requirements and broadcasting the discovery of new, exciting products to be launched shortly on the market in answer to such requirements? No doubt the answer lies between these two extremes. Does advertising create the need; does it, in the pay of capitalist producers, shape desire? Be this as it may, advertising is unquestionably a powerful instrument; is it not the first of consumer goods and does it not provide consumption with all its paraphernalia of signs, images and patter? Is it not the rhetoric of our society, permeating social language, literature and imagination with its ceaseless intrusions upon our daily experiences and our more intimate aspirations? Is it not on the way to becoming the main *ideology* of our time, and is not this fact confirmed by the importance and efficiency of propaganda modelled on advertising methods? Has not institutionalized advertising replaced former modes of communication, including art, and is it not in fact the sole and vital mediator between producer and consumer, theory and practice, social existence and political power?

—Henri Lefebvre, *Everyday Life in the Modern World*

Advertisements sanctify, signify, mythologize, and fantasize. They uphold some of the existing economic and political structures and subvert others. Not only does advertising shape American culture, it shapes Americans' images of themselves.

—Katherine Tolland Frith, *Undressing the Ad:*
Reading Culture in Advertising

1

ADVERTISING IN AMERICAN SOCIETY

ADVERTISING AS A PUZZLEMENT

Advertising is really quite puzzling. In 2014, it was a $144-billion-a-year industry (down from around $200 billion in 2006) in the United States. In 2010, eMarketer reported that we spent $142.5 billion for advertising in the United States and $467 billion on advertising worldwide. In table 1.1, I offer statistics on the projected growth of advertising in the United States. Note how rapidly Internet advertising is growing—doubling from 2011 to 2016—while television is growing modestly and print advertising is static. Global advertising expenditures in 2012 were $557 billion and American advertising expenditures for 2012, according to Statistic Brain, were $136 billion.

A department store merchant, John Wanamaker, is reputed to have said, many years ago, that "half of the money I spend on advertising is wasted . . . but I don't know which half." Also, advertising agencies are forced to talk out of both sides of their mouths at the same time. They have to convince clients that advertising is really effective—in generating sales, holding on to the customers a company already has, or attracting new customers. But when governmental agencies or consumer groups ask advertising agencies about what they do when it comes to advertising products such as cigarettes and alcohol, the advertising agencies argue that they have very little impact on people. The situation seems to be that although nobody in the business world

Table 1.1. Projected Growth of Advertising in the United States (billions of dollars)

Date	Online	Print	Television
2011	32	36	60
2012	39	33	64
2013	46	33	65
2014	52	33	67
2015	57	33	68
2016	62	32	72

Source: eMarketer.

Insights from Advertising Agencies

The psychological profile of people in advertising is that they love the drama involved in working in agencies and the excitement generated by making ads and commercials. Also, planning is about demonstrating that it's not just about logic. It's not a linear process. In the United States, businesspeople are rewarded for being extremely logical and having statistics to back themselves up. This produces dreadful advertising that often fails to make any impact. Advertising agencies are refuges for people who don't think only in a linear fashion and who recognize that other people—consumers of advertising—don't think that way, either.

is certain how advertising works, there is a consensus that it is necessary and that campaigns are worth the enormous amount of money they often cost.

Thus, for example, commercials broadcast during the 2005 Super Bowl cost $2.4 million for thirty seconds, and the cost of the commercials during the 2006 Super Bowl was $2.5 million for a thirty-second spot. By 2010, it was $3 million, and for 2014, it was almost $4 million. This is a great deal of money, but there are reasons why companies pay that amount of money to show commercials during the game—because it has an audience advertisers want to reach. I will discuss Super Bowl advertising in more detail shortly. We must always keep in mind the difference between the cost of making a nationally broadcast television commercial and the cost of purchasing airtime to show a commercial.

The cost of making a standard thirty-second nationally broadcast television commercial is between $300,000 and $400,000 now, though some commercials can cost a good deal more than that. A typical "Got Milk" commercial costs around $370,000. After many years, this campaign has been discontinued, and a new milk campaign has been launched. Purchasing the airtime might run into the millions of dollars. Naturally, advertisers want to run effective commercials, so it's worth spending a bit more money for a commercial that will work. The campaign for "Got Milk" attracted an enormous amount of attention and has spawned many "Got Milk" imitations. Of course, advertisers and advertising agencies never know which commercials will be effective and why they are effective. Though there is often an enormous amount of data about target audiences "behind" a given commercial, all the data in the world doesn't mean anything when it comes to making a commercial that is effective.

The Cost of a Typical Commercial

These figures represent a breakdown on the cost of a thirty-second "Got Milk" commercial made a number of years ago. They were supplied by a former student of mine who works at the advertising agency that created the commercial. A typical thirty-second spot costs between $300,000 and $400,000; this spot cost $363,000. We also have to consider the cost of purchasing time to air the commercials on television networks and stations.

$281,000	Television production
$45,000	Television postproduction (editing)
$6,000	Music (usually much higher)
$1,000	Sound effects search/narration
$11,000	Talent fees (three principal actors, five extras, including voice-over)
$1,000	Tapes and dubs
$1,000	Legal clearances (often much higher)
$1,000	Shipping
$16,000	Agency travel, casting, callbacks, pre-pro edit
$363,000	Total

If we believe what advertising agencies (and the companies they make advertisements and commercials for) tell us, we have to conclude that advertising works in strange and mysterious ways and that although nobody is sure precisely how it works, it does have an impact—though its power to shape any given individual's behavior is (or seems to be) really quite minimal.

We each like to think that we (perhaps "uniquely") can resist advertising and that it has no impact on us. This notion, which I will discuss in more detail in chapter 3, makes light of the power of advertising and helps us preserve our sense of autonomy. Others are brainwashed by ads and commercials, but not us, we think—as we find ourselves purchasing products that we feel, somehow, we must have. Thus, we play into the hands of advertisers who use our illusion that we are not affected by advertising against us. As the president of a large advertising agency once told me, "Even lousy advertising works!"

We cannot show that a given commercial or campaign makes a given individual buy a product or service being advertised—or is the primary force in shaping that person's behavior—but we can see that advertising has a collective impact; that is, it affects people in general. Corporations don't spend hundreds of billions of dollars a year because they are Good Samaritans who want to make sure that radio stations and television networks are very profitable. And politicians, who spend millions of dollars on their election campaigns, aren't Good Samaritans either. In their book *Social Communication in Advertising: Consumption in the Mediated Marketplace*, by William Leis, Stephen Kline, Sut Jhally, and Jacqueline Botterill, we find an assessment of the role of advertising in society. They write (2005:3–4),

> It is their prominent discussion of consumption that leads some commentators, such as James Twitchell (1996) to compare advertising to a religion for its honest celebration of consumer goods as the key to contemporary American life-ways. We agree with Twitchell that no other discursive practice in modern society exemplifies the tension underlying the expansionary phase or market society. Since the 1950s, these tensions have provoked a growing debate about the role that advertising plays in the marketplace. Celebrated by the enthusiasts of marketing as the informational tool that empowered the consumer and critiqued by mass culture gurus for turning consumers into dupes, the advertising agency seemed to embody all that was both good and bad in the changing relationships between producers and consumers. Some styled it a mirror, reflecting back to us our deep-seated material visions of well-being. Others felt it was a persuasive force articulating new consumption patterns which impacted on the ongoing social, economic and cultural practices of the consumer society. Advertising thus became the lightning rod for critics who accused it of all manner of evil from accelerating environmental destruction to breeding a generation of super-sized children.

I believe that advertising is a very powerful force, one that plays a major role in the economy and in our culture. It has replaced Puritanism in motivating people to work hard so that they can earn money and be able to buy things.

Advertising employs a goodly number of the brightest and most creative people in American society and other societies as well (often at very high salaries to boot). Curiously, people who work in the industry have difficulty proving that it works—especially in the long term. The word "advertising" means "to make known" and generally is understood to refer to public—now we would say mass-mediated—announcements of products and services that are for sale. The Latin root of the word is "advertere," which means "to pay attention to." This word can be broken down further: "ad" means "toward," and "vertere" means "to turn." So advertising attempts to turn our attention toward something—namely, the announcement of some product or service. There is logic, then, to the first rule of advertising, which is to attract attention. If people aren't paying attention to a print advertisement or a radio or television commercial, you can't persuade them to do anything.

DEFINING ADVERTISING

This is the way the advertising industry works, most of the time:

1. Advertising agencies purchase space for print advertisements in newspapers, magazines, or other kinds of publications or time to broadcast commercials made for companies selling products or services on radio and television stations. Some organizations and corporations do their own advertising, but this is not usually the case. There are other ways of advertising, such as putting ads on billboards, in bus shelters, or on buses and taxicabs (figure 1.1); using the Internet; sponsoring events; and placing products in films and television shows.

2. These commercials or print advertisements are generally designed to attract the attention of people with suitable demographics and the proper psychographics—values and lifestyles—for some product or service. Advertising agencies tend to concentrate on people, roughly speaking, from ages eighteen to forty-nine—assuming they are the ones who buy most of the products and services advertised. Certain products are aimed at children and others at older people,

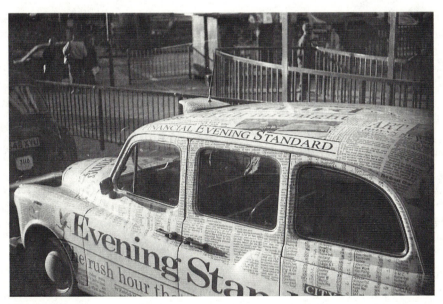

Figure 1.1

but most advertising is aimed at the eighteen- to forty-nine cohort, give or take a few years on either end.

3. Advertising tries to attract attention to, create the desire for, and stimulate action that leads to the purchase of products and services advertised on the part of those reading print advertisements, listening to radio commercials, or watching and listening to television commercials. That is, advertisers hope to convince, to persuade, to motivate, and, most important, to get people to act, to do something. This something generally involves moving from the desire for products and services to the actual purchase of the products or services.

There are, as I pointed out earlier, a number of different forms and genres of advertising. Advertising pervades the American media and our lives—from the billboards on our highways to the print ads in the publications we read, the commercials on radio and television, and the designer logos on T-shirts and other kinds of clothes we wear. Advertising is also used by charities, labor unions, and organizations of all kinds to get their messages to the public. In consumer cultures, it seems fair to say that just about everyone is advertising, which creates a major problem—clutter. There are so many messages being sent to us that sometimes, as the result of information overload, we get them all mixed up.

If you look at the advertising for such products as athletic shoes, razors, perfumes, beer, and automobiles, you find advertising agencies fighting, desperately, to hold on to their segment of the market and, if possible, to gain market share. They use every editing technique they can think of to make their commercials visually more memorable and every trick of language and narrative structure to gain our attention and divert our attention from the advertising of competitors.

One of the problems advertisers face is that of clutter—the enormous number of advertisements we are exposed to on a given day, which leads to information overload and, in many cases, paralysis. So advertising agencies knock themselves out to differentiate their campaigns from other campaigns and get the attention of the target audience they are attacking. A remarkable Honda commercial, made in England, cost $6 million to make, involved 606 takes, and took three weeks, shooting nonstop day and night, to film and three months to make. It is two minutes long as well, which means it costs an enormous amount of money to air the commercial on television. But the commercial has attracted an enormous amount of attention and interest, and thus, Honda no doubt believes, it was worth doing.

Many Americans report that they are annoyed by all the advertising to which they are exposed. A 2004 survey by Yankelovich Partners, done for the American Association of Advertising Agencies, reported the following:

- Sixty-nine percent expressed interest in products that would block advertising.
- Sixty-six percent felt they are constantly bombarded by advertising.
- Sixty-one percent described the amount of advertising to which they are exposed as out of control.
- Sixty percent felt their opinion of advertising is more negative than before.
- Fifty-four percent said they avoid buying products that advertise too much. (http://www.medialiteracy.com/stats_advertising.jsp)

So there was—and there still is, I would add—a good deal of hostility in the American public about the amount of advertising to which they are exposed, and that is an additional problem the advertising industry faces. This hostility has manifested itself in Americans purchasing time-shifting devices for recording television programs that enable them to skip commercials with relative ease.

ADVERTISING AGENCIES

Advertising agencies, we must remember, are media businesses, and like all businesses, they have human resource departments, accounting departments, production departments, and various levels of management (such as chief executive officers, chief financial officers, executive vice presidents, senior vice presidents, and ordinary vanilla vice presidents). They also have huge account management departments, with account supervisors, account directors, and many, many account executives. The job of account executives, generally speaking, is to look after the agency's clients. Some cynics have suggested that what account executives do best is take clients out to lunch.

In a typical full-service advertising agency, according to William Wells, Sandra Moriarty, and John Burnett in their book *Advertising: Principles and Practices* (7th ed., 2005) we find the following:

Account management departments
Account planning and research departments
Creative development and production departments

Internal agency services departments
Media planning and buying department

We see, then, that many people who work in large advertising agencies are not involved in marketing research and the creation of advertising; they could be working in another industry.

The most important employees of advertising agencies, I would suggest, are what are generally called the "creatives." The creatives are the creative directors and their teams of copywriters and art directors (and sometimes others) who turn all of the data provided by the marketing researchers into print ads and radio and television commercials. The creatives think up campaigns like "Got Milk" or the Absolut vodka advertisements and are the "stars" in any agency—the people who bring fame and fortune (in the form of new billings) to their agencies. Like all important creative artists, they are given a great deal of freedom. There are numerous awards given by organizations in the advertising industry, and some creatives have dozens of awards to their credit.

Interestingly enough, for an industry seen as glamorous by most people, advertising doesn't always pay that well. The top management of big advertising agencies make a great deal of money, and the creatives do well, but most of the other people in advertising agencies aren't always well paid, and some don't make as much as a good secretary (who can make $50,000 to $75,000 a year). Entry-level positions in advertising are very low because there is a great deal of competition for what are thought to be "glamour" jobs. There are many women working in advertising, and, as we know, women everywhere are generally paid considerably less than men for doing the same job, though that is changing slowly.

Salaries are also affected by the size of the agency one works in and the location of the agency. Thus, in a major market such as the San Francisco Bay Area, account executives might earn around $75,000 and art directors around $115,000 or more, and workers in smaller agencies in smaller markets would earn considerably less. Salaries in big New York agencies are also considerably higher, while salaries in small, southern agencies are a good deal lower than those in the North or in big cities. But there are also bonuses that people who work in agencies get and other rewards as well.

During my three weeks at Goldberg Moser O'Neill, I interviewed people involved in every aspect of the advertising business, and everyone intimated that it was their job that was absolutely crucial and that without them, the place would fall apart. I found the people in these agencies to be, as a rule, very intelligent and extremely hardworking. The work is so demanding that advertising agencies have very high turnover rates; I was told by the GMO human resources director that the average advertising agency loses something

Insights from Advertising Agencies

The salary numbers for advertising agency salaries found in *Advertising Ages* are terribly misleading and have never reflected the reality of the workplace. These numbers have always been way understated. For example, an average Art Director would easily make $75K, a good one $150. Associate Creative Directors make upwards from $150K. Creative Directors make far more money than indicated. This data does not include bonuses, which could be up to 50 percent, and other rewards like stock, etc. One of the reasons this data is distorted is because it is not a proper statistical sample and tends to reflect the smallest agencies with the fewest people. The larger and medium-sized agencies don't bother to respond. If you're in advertising and if you're good, you can make a lot of money. You do have to work your ass off and you do tend to be underpaid at the start for a fair amount of time. (Fred Goldberg, retired chairman and CEO of Goldberg Moser O'Neill)

like a third of its employees from burnout and other factors in a given year. In some cases, people move to better jobs in other agencies, and others leave advertising for another career.

MAX WEBER ON RELIGION AND CONSUMER CULTURES

Max Weber (figure 1.2), one of the greatest sociologists of the nineteenth century, wrote a classic study of the relationship between Puritanism and capitalism, *The Protestant Ethic and the Spirit of Capitalism*. In this book, he pointed out that John Calvin, an important theologian, argued that the possession of wealth was to be taken as an indicator of God's blessing. The Puritans believed that the impulse toward acquisition was, Weber writes (1958:171), "directly willed by God." These religious beliefs did two other important things for wealthy businessmen (1958:177):

> The power of religious asceticism provided him with sober, conscientious, and unusually industrious workmen, who clung to their work as to a life purpose willed by God. Finally, it give him the comforting assurance that the unequal distribution of goods in this world was a special dispensation of Divine Providence, which in these differences, as in particular grace, pursued secret ends unknown to men.

Thus, wealth is a sign of being blessed and poverty a sign of not being blessed, and nothing humans can do will change things. In the last part of his

Figure 1.2. Max Weber was a German sociologist who did much work on the relationship between Protestantism and capitalism.

book, Weber talks about the ideas of a different Puritan minister, Richard Baxter, who believed that (1958:181) "the care for external goods should only lies on the shoulders of the 'saint like a light cloak which can be thrown aside at any moment.' But fate decreed that the cloak should become an iron cage." Weber lamented that the desire for material goods had become a kind of obsession with people and that this desire had reached its highest development in the United States. He wrote (1958:182),

> In the field of its highest development, in the United States, the pursuit of wealth, stripped of its religious and ethical meaning, tends to become associated with purely mundane passions, which often actually give it the character of sport.
>
> No one knows who will live in this cage in the future, or whether at the end of this tremendous development entirely new prophets will arise, or there will be a great rebirth of old ideas and ideals, or, if neither, mechanized petrification, embellished with a sort of convulsive self-importance. For of the last stage of this cultural development, it might be truly said: "Specialists without spirit, sensualists without heart; this nullity imagines that it has attained a level of civilization never before achieved."

Weber's critique is a moral one; he is highly critical of the way a passion for consumption can take hold of individuals and, in his comments about the United States, whole countries. It would be interesting to know what he would of said about contemporary China, where the rage to succeed and consume has transformed that country, in just a few generations, from a Third World, poverty-stricken land into a world power.

ADVERTISING AND POLITICS

Increasingly, in recent years, advertising is used more and more in the political sphere. Advertising has the power, I believe, to influence and, in some cases, shape people's behavior, broadly speaking. For example, in the

1994 campaign by forces against the Clinton health care plan, the "Harry and Louise" commercials, broadcast by groups opposed to the plan, are credited with eroding support for the plan by approximately twenty percentage points. In these commercials, Harry and Louise criticized the Clinton plan for making major changes in the medical system and lamented the way big government would be telling them who their doctor had to be and would be depriving them of their freedom to make decisions about medical matters. The passage of the health reform bill in 2010 represented a remarkable achievement in the face of enormous sums of money spent on advertising by groups that opposed the measure. Since its passage, there has been a great deal of money spent by conservative political forces attacking it.

I'm not suggesting that campaigns always work or that they always work the way advertisers and advertising agencies imagine they will. But if we take a broad look at human behavior in the long run, it seems quite obvious that advertising exists and has been flourishing because, somehow, it works—that is, it works a good deal of the time the way those paying for the advertising want it to work. And this is particularly the case when it comes to political advertising. This matter will be discussed more in chapter 6.

This book focuses on print advertisements and television commercials and the role they may play in stimulating the consumption of products and services by people. Traditionally, we call sales messages in print "advertisements" and sales messages on electronic media that use sound effects, music, and actors "commercials." Originally, most of the sales messages on the Internet were little more than print advertisements. Now, with new technological developments, we find pop-up screens, cartoon animations, and other ways of attracting the attention of people using the Internet. Internet advertising has grown a great deal in recent years. In 2008, almost $18 billion were spent on this form of advertising, and it is estimated that it will be around $60 billion by 2016. A friend of mine who works in a major advertising agency in San Francisco told me, "The focus now is on the Internet and social media. That's where all the energy in our agency is going. Print media are no longer that important." The methods of analysis I discuss can be used on all forms of advertising.

It is worth noting some of the ideas mentioned in the most common definitions of advertising. We find such terms as "arouse" and "desire," which suggest there are very powerful "affective" and perhaps even unconscious or "irrational" elements at work in advertisements.

In his book *Visual Persuasion: The Role of Images in Advertising*, Paul Messaris suggests that there may be certain kinds of hardwired responses in human beings that function as a result of visual cues to which they are exposed. He discusses the work of a number of researchers in this area and writes (1997:4),

When we look at the world, we are strongly predisposed to attend to certain kinds of objects or situations and to react in certain kinds of ways. These predispositions reflect the influence of culture, but . . . they have also been shaped to a certain extent by biological evolution. In short, real-world vision comes with a set of built-in response tendencies. Consequently, to the extent that a picture can reproduce the significant visual features of real-world experience, it may also be able to exploit the response tendencies that are associated with those features.

Messaris offers as an example of these "response tendencies" the use in magazine ads and other kinds of advertising of having someone—spokespersons in television commercials and models in magazine advertisements—look directly at the viewer or reader. In real life, we have a natural tendency to look back at someone who looks at us, and advertising agencies can exploit this in attracting our attention to their advertisements and generating emotional responses to them.

Later in the book, I will quote from an article that makes an even stronger argument, namely, that the famous experiment in which Ivan Pavlov was able to train dogs to act in certain ways when special cues were given to them is the basic metaphor for understanding how advertising works. That is, advertising conditions us—as individuals and as members of society—in the same way that Pavlov was able to train dogs.

A PSYCHO-CULTURAL PERSPECTIVE ON ADVERTISING

The model that many social scientists have used in studies of the impact of advertising is a psychological one (or perhaps a social-psychological one). People are tested to see whether they recall advertisements or whether their attitudes or opinions have been changed by having been exposed to advertisements.

This approach, which often is quite sophisticated in terms of research design, frequently indicates that advertising has little or no effect on respondents—or, to be more precise, none that can be detected or measured or, in some cases, no long-term effects that can be measured.

I would like to suggest a different model (see figure 1.3), one that focuses not on attitude or opinion change but rather on the effect of advertising on society and the culture of advertising in general and, in some cases, of a particular campaign.

Figure 1.3 focuses not on opinion or attitude change but instead on two different matters. One can broadly be defined as cultural behavior and the other on the collective unconscious. Focusing on individuals or groups

Exposure to ad or commercial	People's psyches exposed to ads
↓	↓
Recall, attitude or opinion change	Cultural behavior of people
Social-Psychological Model	**Psycho-Cultural Model**

Figure 1.3.

of individuals in test studies frequently concludes that advertising plays no significant role in decision making. An examination of advertising as a cultural phenomenon, on the other hand, suggests something quite different, a conclusion that might explain why revenues for advertising keep growing and why businesses continue to advertise. In the introduction to his book *Representation: Cultural Representations and Signifying Practices*, Stuart Hall, a British scholar, describes why so many scholars are interested in culture. He writes (1997:2–3),

> What has come to be called "the cultural turn" in the social and human sciences, especially in studies and the sociology of culture, has tended to emphasize the importance of meaning to the definition of culture. Culture, it is argued, is not so much a set of things—novels and paintings or TV programmes and comics—as a process, a set of practices. Primarily, culture is concerned with the production and exchange of meanings—the "giving and taking of meaning"—between the members of a society or group. . . . It is participants in a culture who give meaning to people, objects and events. Things "in themselves" rarely if ever have one, single, fixed and unchanging meaning.

It is because meaning is so central to the advertising industry, because advertisers want their target audiences to interpret the advertisements and commercials they receive correctly, that semiotics, the science of meaning, is of such interest to advertising agencies. The problem is, as Hall points out, people often don't interpret advertisements or commercials the way they were supposed to interpret them.

RUNNING IT UP A FLAGPOLE
TO SEE IF ANYONE SALUTES

Corporations and organizations that advertise are not irrational; they do not spend money "running flags up flagpoles to see if anyone salutes" out of idle curiosity. (On the other hand, while companies that advertise may not be irrational, they assume that people are irrational. More precisely, they assume that people respond to messages that avoid ego-dominated "rational" decision making but have an effect on unconscious elements in their psyches that often shape their behavior.)

In his structural hypothesis, Sigmund Freud suggested that the human psyche was composed of three elements: the id, which represents drives (and says "I want it now"); the superego, which represents moral sensibilities and conscience (and says "don't do it"); and the ego, which has the task of perceiving and adapting to reality and mediating between the id and the superego. Freud described the id in his *New Introductory Lectures on Psychoanalysis* (quoted in Hinsie and Campbell [1970:372]):

> We can come nearer to the id with images, and call it a chaos, a cauldron of seething excitement. We suppose that it is somewhere in direct contact with somatic processes, and takes over from them instinctual needs and gives them mental expression, but we cannot say in what substratum this contact is made. These instincts fill it with energy, but it has no organization and no unified will, only an impulsion to obtain satisfaction for the instinctual needs, in accordance with the pleasure principle.

Thus, advertisements appeal to id elements in our psyches and our desires for gratifications of all kinds ("I want it now") and seek to avoid the strictures of the superego ("you can't afford it and you don't need it") and the mediating efforts of the ego ("maybe you ought to think a bit before buying it").

The devaluation of the power of advertising by advertising agencies and by businesses that use advertising is generally an attempt to escape from regulation by governmental agencies and to escape from criticisms of being manipulative and, in some cases, antisocial by consumer groups and other interested parties. Communication scholars, I might point out, have wavered in their assessments of the power of media. Thirty years ago, scholars concluded that the media were powerful; then they changed their minds and concluded that they are weak. (A famous scholar said something to the effect of "Some media sometimes have some effects on some people.") Now, it seems, the notion that the media are powerful is once again gaining acceptance.

Given this situation, when the media were seen as weak, advertisers could argue that advertising was relatively trivial—a service to inform or entertain the public but little more than that. Yet at the macro level, when we look at collective behavior, it seems that advertising does have power. It is advertising's role as a cultural and political force that is significant. We may lack the tools in the social sciences to show how advertising affects specific individuals or small groups of people in tests, but when we look at advertising as a social and cultural phenomenon, the situation is strikingly different.

One argument that advertising people use to defuse criticism is the post hoc, ergo propter hoc argument. Just because something happens after something doesn't mean it was caused by it. That is, just because Y follows X does not mean that X caused Y. Thus, if Lisa sees a beer commercial on television and then drinks a beer, it does not mean the commercial caused Lisa to drink the beer. Nobody can argue with this. But when you move to the collective level and have lots of people drinking beer after having seen lots of beer commercials, there is good reason to believe that the beer commercials might have played some role in the behavior of the beer drinkers.

That is, commercials for alcoholic beverages may not be the sole causative factor responsible for people drinking, but they may play an important contributing role. Since the public airways are held "in trust," so to speak (and are supposed to broadcast "in the public interest"), by television stations, the question we must ask is whether this trust is being abused. One reason it is so difficult to establish via experimental methods a direct causal link between television commercials and consumption is that television is so ubiquitous that it is very difficult to find a "control" group, a group of people who are not exposed to television. That is why I think the anthropological model, which focuses on cultures, is more useful than the social-psychological model.

COMMERCIALS AS MINI-DRAMAS AND WORKS OF ART

Commercials—in my opinion the most interesting and powerful form of advertising—should be seen as works of art that have their own conventions; they might best be thought of as mini-dramas that employ all the techniques of the theater and the cinema to achieve their aims. At their best, they use language brilliantly, they are dramatic, they employ the most sophisticated techniques of lighting and editing, they have wonderful actors who use body language and facial expressions to get their messages across, and they often cost enormous amounts of money, relatively speaking, to produce—many times, the production costs (on a per-minute basis) outstrip those of the programs during which they are shown.

The power of the human voice is well known. When it is added to strong narratives, music, sound effects, and superb writing, it is easy to see why the commercial is such an incredible means of persuasion. Commercials (and advertisements in print and other media, to an extent) also make use of many of the concepts discussed in the following sections.

Heroes and Heroines

Young people often identify with heroes and heroines and try to emulate their behavior, their "style," or their images—if not in the real world, then in the world of consumption. Some of these heroic figures are show-business personalities—singers, dancers, comedians, actors, and athletes. As Carl G. Jung explains in his book *Man and His Symbols* (1968:111),

> In the developing consciousness of the individual the hero figure is the symbolic means by which the emerging ego overcomes the inertia of the unconscious mind, and liberates the mature man from a regressive longing to return to the blissful state of infancy in a world dominated by his mother.

For Jung, then, heroes play an important role in our psychological development. And as many psychoanalysts have explained, identification and imitation (of heroes and heroines) are powerful forces that can shape our behaviors in ways of which we are generally unaware. We find these heroes and heroines in our myths but also in popular culture, where we can follow the exploits of heroes and heroines like Superman, Batman, Wonder Woman, the Fantastic Four, ad infinitum in comics and now in films, as well as in elite culture, where we can follow the adventures of Leopold Bloom in James Joyce's *Ulysses* and countless other heroes in novels, plays, operas, and other forms of elite culture.

Sexuality and Gender

Many commercials overtly connect sex and consumption (figures 1.4 and 1.5). These commercials often feature extremely beautiful women; they are shown as an integral part of the consumption experience. One hopes, in one's unconscious, that by purchasing the product, one will get the beautiful woman (or some beautiful woman) as well—or, in some cases, an attractive man. In recent years, advertising has used homoerotic appeals for gay men and lesbians. I talk at length about sexuality in advertising in chapter 5. The "sexploitation" of women and their bodies continues to be a problem in advertising, even though feminist media critics have complained about the matter, and that is because sexually exciting images are effective. As Lee Eisenberg writes in his book *Shoptimism: Why the American Consumer Will Keep on Buying No Matter What* (2009:52),

> Just a few years ago, a large-scale eyeball tracking study indicated that men do pay greater attention to ads featuring female sexual imagery. It found that breasts, legs and exposed skin serve to raise a man's *intention* to buy products featured in ads oozing female pulchritude.

Figure 1.4

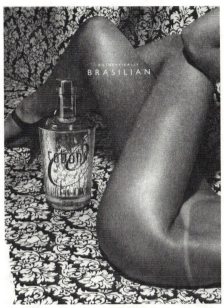

Figure 1.5. This advertisement for a Brazilian liquor, Cabana Cachaca, is very erotic, but it doesn't show anything except a woman's knees and elbows. How do we explain its power?

He discusses research carried on by the motivation researcher Ernest Dichter, whose research indicated "that when men look at pictures of nudes . . . their pupils open wide," which makes them "more attentive to visual stimuli." Dilated, that is, enlarged, pupils are a sign of sexual arousal, and many print advertisements show pictures of women with artificially dilated pupils, which, it is assumed, may turn on or excite men who see the dilated pupils, even though the men viewing these ads are not aware of the dilated pupils. This process works on the unconscious level. In recent years, scholars have become interested in gender, which is not the same as sexuality. It is commonly held that gender is socially constructed, which means our attitudes toward gender are taught to us by the societies in which we live, and some societies construct gender differently than we do in the United States.

Race and Ethnicity

The models in advertising, years ago, tended to be white, and racial and ethnic minorities, along with older people, were underrepresented. That explains why bell hooks could write, in her book *Black Looks: Race and Representation* (1992),

If we compare the relative progress African Americans have made in education and employment to the struggle to gain control over how we are represented, particularly in the mass media, we see that there has been little change in the area of representation. Opening a magazine or book, turning on the television set, watching a film, or looking at photographs in public spaces, we are most likely to see the images of black people that reinforce and reinscribe white supremacy. Those images may be constructed by white people who have not divested of racism or by people of color/black people who may see the world through the lens of white supremacy—internalized racism.

Fortunately, things have changed, and now we see many African Americans and other people of color in our advertisements. Race and ethnicity still remain an issue in American society, but over the years American society has become much more multicultural, and thus it is understandable why our advertising would reflect these changes in American society and be more multicultural as well.

Humor

At one time, advertisers were afraid of humor. Now they realize that humor sells, and many commercials are extremely funny (figure 1.6). This

Figure 1.6. This Fendi ad has a whimsical quality.

humor generates what might be called a "halo effect," a feeling of well-being that becomes attached to the products being advertised. Since there is so much hostility toward advertising in the general public, many companies that use advertising are turning to humor as a means of entertaining viewers of their commercials and thus eliciting some goodwill. Mirthful laughter generates endorphins in our brains that make us feel good, and some of this may also rub off on the product being advertised. Humor also is a way of establishing relationships with others, so there is a value in using humor as long as it doesn't offend people and get in the way of the persuasive part of the advertisement.

A number of years ago, I did some research on the techniques that generate humor in plays and other texts. I found that the techniques I discovered formed four different categories of humor. The list appears in table 1.2; you can use it to analyze humor in print advertisements and commercials and all kinds of other works. There is considerable disagreement among scholars about the definition of some of these terms, such as satire and parody, but most of them are more or less self-evident.

Table 1.2

Language	*Logic*	*Identity*	*Action*
Allusion	Absurdity	Before/after	Chase
Bombast	Accident	Burlesque	Slapstick
Definition	Analogy	Caricature	Speed
Exaggeration	Catalogue	Eccentricity	
Facetiousness	Coincidence	Embarrassment	
Infantilism	Comparison	Exposure	
Insults	Disappointment	Grotesque	
Irony	Ignorance	Imitation	
Misunderstanding	Mistakes	Impersonation	
Over-literalness	Repetition	Mimicry	
Puns and wordplay	Reversal	Parody	
Repartee	Rigidity	Scale	
Ridicule	Theme and variation	Stereotype	
Sarcasm	Unmasking		
Satire			

Fun

Jean Baudrillard (figure 1.7), a French sociologist, argues that in modern consumer societies, we now feel obliged to have fun. He writes in *The Consumer Society: Myths & Structure* (1998:80),

Figure 1.7. Jean Baudrillard was an influential French sociologist whose theories about simulations have been very controversial.

The Fun System of Forced Enjoyment

One of the strongest proofs that the principle and finality of consumption is not enjoyment or pleasure is that that is now something which is forced upon us, something institutionalized, not as a right or a pleasure but as the duty of the citizen. . . . Consumerist man . . . regards enjoyment as an obligation; he sees himself as an enjoyment and satisfaction business. He sees it as his duty to be happy, loving, adulating/adulated, charming/charmed, participative, euphoric and dynamic.

This represents a reversal, Baudrillard adds, of the old Puritan ethic of hard work and abstention for the glory of God. It is now our "duty" to have fun, and we do this, to a great degree, by being a member in good standing (and good purchasing) of our contemporary consumer culture.

Success

In many commercials, we see (and, it is suggested, we emulate) people who use a given product or service and who are successful (figure 1.8). One aspect of being successful is knowing what to consume—having "product knowledge," which has replaced regular knowledge in all too many people in America. They don't know history, are not well read, have no appreciation of art, music, philosophy—you name it. But they have incredible product knowledge; that is, all they know is what they can buy.

I used to play a learning game in which I asked students to determine what products Americans would likely purchase based on their class makeup. I used a well-known classification system by sociologist W. Lloyd Warner, elaborated fifty years ago, that suggested we have six classes in America (table 1.3).

These percentages still apply, generally speaking, with minor modifications. The percentage of wealth of the top 1 percent has increased considerably over the years, and the number of people falling into poverty has also increased.

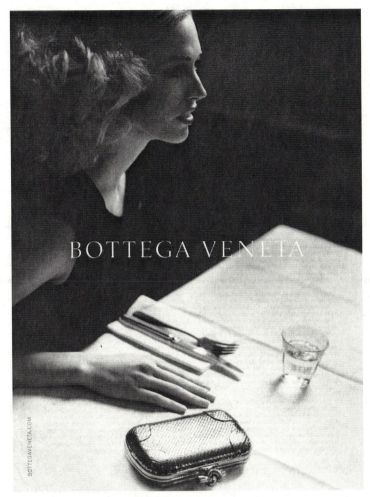

Figure 1.8. This Bottega Veneta ad plays upon the aesthetic codes of elite classes: simplicity is tied to upscale taste. For downscale taste, see supermarket ads.

Table 1.3

Class	Percentage of Population
Upper-upper	1.4
Lower-upper	1.6
Upper-middle	10
Lower-middle	25 (common man and woman level)
Upper-lower	35 (common man and woman level)
Lower-lower	25

Table 1.4. Brands, Models, and Socioeconomic Class Consumption Game

Class	Automobile	Smart Phone	Beer
Upper-upper			
Lower-upper			
Upper-middle			
Lower-middle			
Upper-lower			
Lower-lower			

The top 1 percent of Americans own around 33 percent of the wealth in America, the same amount as the bottom 90 percent.

What I discovered is that my students were able to make a large number of very subtle distinctions about which products people in the various class levels might consumer. There was a considerable debate among them about whether lower-upper-class people would or should purchase a BMW or a Mercedes and which particular model of each car they would buy. They debated endlessly whether an entry-level BMW had more status than an entry-level Mercedes. What this demonstrated to me is that my students had an enormous amount of "product knowledge," based on their constant exposure to advertising in print and electronic media.

The learning game shown in table 1.4 should be played in groups of three students, with one student, the "scribe," writing down the answers that the members of the group decide on but also participating in the game. What is interesting to see is the degree to which the different groups come up with similar brands and models for the products they deal with.

Rewards

Purchasing various products—such as soft drinks and automobiles—is often shown as a "reward" for people who have worked hard and who therefore "deserve" their drinks, gadgets, sport-utility vehicles, and anything else. This appeal works at both the blue-collar and the white-collar level. The rewards one gets are fun, comradeship, pleasure, and sex—especially sex, as I explained above. Our print advertisements and television commercials are pervaded by sex, and most Americans live in a sexually saturated media environment, where men and women are used as sex objects to sell everything from trucks to cruises.

Insights from Advertising Agencies

We try to make ads that evoke an emotion—humor is often useful in this respect. We brainstorm together about ideas that might be used for an ad. Usually, we come up with three or four ideas for a spot. We're looking for the single most compelling idea to communicate.

TELECULTURE AND THE INTERNET

The term "teleculture" suggests that our culture is, to a large degree, shaped by television. Thus, television is not a simple medium for entertainment, which merely reflects the culture in which it is found. Television does, of course, reflect culture, but the important thing to keep in mind is that it also profoundly affects culture. It does this, in part, by focusing attention on certain aspects of culture and not paying attention to others, by creating certain kinds of heroes and heroines and neglecting other kinds. We must add the Internet to teleculture, which occupies more and more of our time, as also having a profound effect on individuals and society. In my opinion, television and the Internet are the most powerful socializing and enculturating forces in society. They not only entertain us but also instruct us, even when they are not trying to do so. Thus, they have usurped the roles formerly played by other actors who used to be dominant figures in the socialization process. Let me list them below.

Parents

With the changes that have taken place in the family structure and the breakdown of both the family (due to the high numbers of divorces) and parental authority in America, the role of the parents in socializing young people has greatly diminished. Many children are now raised in one-parent families or in blended families or in gay families, especially now that gay marriage is legal in many states.

Priests, Ministers, Rabbis, and Imams

Nowadays, the clergy also has a diminished role in our socialization, though some of the priesthood has discovered television and now uses it for its various purposes. The use of television by the clergy, however, tends to be associated with fundamentalist sects (and, in some cases, charlatans) and is not, in large measure, found in mainstream religious organizations.

Professors

At one time, teachers and other academics played a significant role in socializing young people, and in many cases they still do. But this role has also been diminished. This is because teachers cannot compete with popular culture and in fact have to spend a good deal of their time doing what they can to counter the corrosive effects of the media and popular culture.

Peers

It is widely known that children and adolescents are particularly susceptible to peer pressure, and at various stages in their developmental cycle, peer pressure is much more significant to young people than parental pressure. What about these peers? Who or what, may we ask, socializes peers? Where do these peers get their values and attitudes? They, too, like the opinion leaders who allegedly affect the beliefs of older generations of people, are socialized by the media. Now that many adolescents send as many as a hundred messages a day to their friends, the influence of peers is probably considerably stronger.

Pop Culture

It is, of course, simplistic to claim that popular culture and the mass media are the only determinants of behavior, but it probably is correct to argue that the media play a major role (or, at least, an increasingly important role) in the socialization of young people. And it is television that is of major significance here—for it is television that broadcasts (and affects as well) much of our popular culture. The most important genre on television is, of course, the commercial. Teleculture is, in large measure, commercials and thus plays an important role in creating and maintaining consumer cultures. Baudrillard devotes the last section of his book *The System of Objects* (figure 1.9) to advertising. He makes an interesting point in his analysis (1968:167):

> Neither its rhetoric nor even the information aspect of its discourse has a decisive effect on the buyer. What the individual does respond to, on the other hand, is advertising's underlying leitmotiv of protection and gratification, the intimation that its solicitations and attempts to persuade are the sign, indecipherable at the conscious level, that somewhere is an agency . . . which has taken it upon itself to inform him of his own desires, and

Figure 1.9. Jean Baudrillard's book deals with material culture and contemporary consumer culture.

to foresee and rationalize these desires to his own satisfaction. He thus no more "believes" in advertising than the child believes in Father Christmas, but this in no way impedes his capacity to embrace an internalized infantile situation, and to act accordingly. Herein lies the very real effectiveness of advertising, founded on its obedience to a logic which, though not that of the conditioned reflex, is nonetheless very rigorous: a logic of belief and regression.

This is an important insight to keep in mind. Baudrillard thinks that advertising works not by use of conditioned reflexes but by regressing people to infantile states. It may be that advertising uses both conditioning (think of Pavlov here) and regression (think of Freud here) in accomplishing its mission. Freud explained that individuals go through a number of different stages as they grow up: oral, anal, phallic, and genital. In L. Eidelberg's *The Encyclopedia of Psychoanalysis*, we find a useful description of the four stages of our sexual development (1968:210–11):

> The mouth represents an erotogenic zone for the infant. Sucking and later eating represent the gratification of oral needs. The fact that the infant often sucks a pacifier indicates that he is not only concerned with the incorporation of calories. When the infant begins to have teeth, the need to bite expresses his sadistic desires. The second stage of development is usually referred to as the sadistic-anal, and is characterized by the infant's interest in excreting or retaining his stools. Finally, the third stage is referred to as

the phallic, in which the boy is interested in his penis and the girl in her clitoris. The boy's interest in his penis appears to be responsible for his positive Oedipus complex, which is finally dissolved by the fear of castration. The girl reacts with penis envy, if she considers her clitoris to be an inferior organ to the penis.

Freud pointed out that the stages are not clear-cut and that the fourth stage, the genital phase, is achieved only with puberty.

According to Freud, our sex lives are rich but dissociated and unfocused during infancy; the focusing takes place at puberty. Regression involves, then, people going back, psychologically speaking, to earlier stages in their development.

In 1951, Marshall McLuhan wrote a pioneering book, *The Mechanical Bride* (figure 1.10), which was devoted to understanding the role that popular culture, the media, and, in particular, advertising played in shaping people's consciousness. The book analyzes the symbolic and cultural significance of comic strips and the front pages of newspapers, but most of *The Mechanical Bride* is devoted to advertisements that McLuhan mines for their cultural importance.

He explains the problems caused by entertainment and pop culture and his method of operation in the preface to the book (1951:v):

> Ours is the first age in which many thousands of the best-trained individual minds have made it a full-time business to get inside the collective public mind. To get inside in order to manipulate, exploit, control is the object now. And to generate heat not light is the intention. To keep everybody

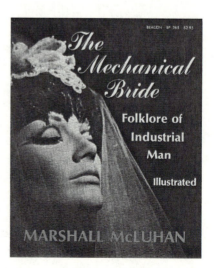

Figure 1.10. Marshall McLuhan's *The Mechanical Bride* deals with the social, psychological, and political content of comics and advertisements.

in the helpless state engendered by prolonged mental rutting is the effect of many ads and much entertainment alike. . . . The present book likewise makes few attempts to attach the very considerable currents and pressures set up around us today by the mechanical agencies of the press, radio, movies, and advertising. It does attempt to set the reader at the center of the revolving picture created by these affairs where he may observe the action that is in progress and in which everybody is involved. From the analysis of that action, it is hoped, many individual strategies may suggest themselves.

It is McLuhan's aim to waken people from the collective dream in which they find themselves by using the methods of art criticism and literary analysis to show how advertising agencies manipulate people and strive to obtain the effects they seek—shaping consumer taste and behavior. Each of the short chapters in the book contains an image—usually of some advertisement—and some elliptical questions and his analysis, often written in a rather jazzy style, of the social, psychological, and cultural significance of the language and images in the advertisement.

THE SUPER BOWL

The 2006 Super Bowl, held on February 5, attracted an audience of something like 90 million people in the United States and hundreds of millions of people in more than 200 other countries. In 2014, around 110 million people watched the Super Bowl. There are a number of reasons why companies advertise during the Super Bowl, even if the cost of doing so is very high in dollar terms. First, there is a good deal of prestige connected with having a commercial shown during the game. Companies recognize that having a commercial during the Super Bowl attracts a great deal of interest in the media as well as the general public.

In addition, because Super Bowl commercials are "showcase" advertisements, which are specially designed for their entertainment value, people watching the game—especially the hard-to-reach males between eighteen and forty-five—tend to also watch the commercials rather than zapping them. The audience for the game wants to see which commercials are outstanding, and having a commercial that is successful is an important plus for advertisers and the agencies that make the commercials. A highly successful commercial helps "make" a brand by attracting the attention and entertaining members of the Super Bowl audience. Commercials on the Super Bowl can help companies that are relatively unknown make a name for themselves.

One company, Budweiser, advertises a great deal on the Super Bowl. Budweiser prepares for the broadcast by having advertising agencies create something like fifty different spots that might be used in the game. It then pares the list down to the final ones it will use just before the game. It is in a battle with other advertisers, such as Burger King and Pepsi, to create memorable commercials. A number of these commercials will be humorous, some will have celebrities, and others will feature animals—and all of them will attempt to become the subject of positive commentary by those who watched the game. Super Bowl commercials that "bomb" and that fall flat, for one reason or another, are a disaster. Not only do they turn off members of the audience, but they are likely to be ridiculed in media reports on the Super Bowl commercials. So the stakes are very high, and there is a great deal of competition among the advertising agencies that make the commercials shown during the Super Bowl to create "winning" commercials.

THE GLOBAL NATURE OF ADVERTISING AGENCIES

Over the past twenty years or so, there has been a great deal of consolidation in the advertising industry, and now there are just a small number of dominant advertising holding-company super-agencies or mega-agencies, such as Omnicom, Interpublic (USA), WPP (UK), and Publicis (France). Each of these mega-agencies owns many smaller agencies that are located all over the world. For example, it is estimated that Omnicom owns around 1,500 agencies. The relationship that exists between individual or "subsidiary" agencies and their holding companies is often a source of considerable friction, and the movement toward gigantic multiagency mega-advertising agencies has been countered by the development of small, so-called boutique agencies that are independent and in many cases are freer to create more imaginative advertising.

It is important for companies with global campaigns to take into consideration the different belief systems and cultural values of the countries where advertisements and commercials will be shown. That is why holding-company advertising agencies, with branches in various countries, are useful to advertisers planning global campaigns. The advertising has to fit with the cultural values and beliefs of people in the countries who will be exposed to the advertisements, and branches in each country can help advertisers avoid making mistakes. The infamous Chevrolet campaign for its Nova automobile in Latin America was a disaster since the word "Nova" sounds like "no va" in Spanish, which means, roughly speaking, "doesn't go."

CONCLUSION

Let me offer here a summary of the main points I have made and a summary of the conclusions I draw from these points.

First, advertising is a huge industry that plays an important role in the socialization of men and women, young and old, in American society. It provides what might be called "product knowledge," and research evidence suggests that even young children, at five or six years of age, know a great deal about many of the products advertised on television (and are often able to sing the jingles from commercials).

Second, corporations advertise because it is effective in a number of different ways. Advertising campaigns often have as their primary goal, we are told, holding market share, but it is reasonable to suggest that these campaigns also attract new users. People who are exposed to commercial campaigns may not be able to recall the commercials they have seen or provide evidence that their opinions and attitudes have been affected, but advertising campaigns leave a certain kind of feeling with people and generate a certain kind of sensibility.

In addition, I have suggested that television commercials, in particular, are extremely complicated and powerful texts (or artworks) that work a number of different ways. I list, later in the book, some of the factors to be considered in analyzing commercials. This complexity, the fact that works of art affect people in strange and complicated ways, makes it difficult to measure their effects. But the fact that corporations continue to advertise and often increase their advertising budgets each year leads us to conclude that advertising does work. We have only to look around us and observe the way people behave (in supermarkets, at work, at parties) to see the power of advertising.

Finally, I have suggested that commercials are part of what I call "teleculture," which is now probably the most important enculturating and socializing force operating in society. It is naive to think of television (or any of the mass media) as simply an entertainment that does not have a profound impact on the people who watch it. For one thing, we know that the average person watches television more than four hours per day. If television does generate "culture," as I've argued, that is a tremendous amount of time for it to enculturate people.

Television along now with the Internet and social media have usurped the place that used to be occupied by parents, the clergy, teachers, and other institutions as socializers of the young. We learn from all of our experiences, a phenomenon called incidental learning (though we may not be conscious of the fact that we are learning), and since television and the Internet are such a large part of our experience, they must play an important role in "teaching" us about life. And commercials are the most ubiquitous genre on television and quite probably the most powerful one. In this book, you will not only learn how to analyze print advertisements and television commercials but also learn about the impact of the advertising industry on you, on the political order, and on American society and culture. I hope that as a result of reading this book, you will be better able to resist "saluting" when some advertising agency creates an advertisement or a radio or television commercial and "runs it up a flagpole."

STUDY QUESTIONS, APPLICATIONS, AND ASSIGNMENTS

1. What was said about the role of advertising in American society and culture?
2. How do advertisers deal with the problem of clutter?
3. How do Americans avoid being exposed to advertising?
4. Investigate the global nature of advertising. How is organization of the industry changing?
5. What was Max Weber's theory about religion and capitalism?
6. Investigate the role of advertising in a political campaign.
7. What's the difference between social psychological approaches to advertising and the psycho–cultural approach?
8. What did Hall say about the "cultural turns" in the humanities and social sciences?
9. What did Freud say about the "id"? What roles does the id play in our lives as consumers?
10. What does "post hoc, ergo propter hoc" mean? How is it relevant to our behavior as consumers?
11. In what ways are some television commercials mini-dramas?
12. Videotape a humorous television commercial and use the forty-five-techniques chart to analyze how the humor was created. Do you think the humor was effective in the ad?
13. What is the difference between sexuality and gender? Analyze a print advertisement where sexuality and gender are important.

14. What was said about socioeconomic class in America? Does socioeconomic class always influence our behavior as consumers?
15. What did Eidelberg say about the four stages of sexual development? What role does our sexual development play in our consumption behavior?
16. What was said about the Super Bowl and advertising? Do a study of critiques of the Super Bowl advertising for the most recent Super Bowl.

Advertising transfers its breadth of experience and calculation to its target groups. It treats its human targets like commodities, to whom it offers the solution to their problem of realization. Clothes are advertised like packaging as a means of sales promotion. This is one of the many ways in which commodity aesthetics takes possession of people.

The two central areas in which advertising offers, by means of commodities, to solve the problems of "scoring hits" and sales are, on the one hand, following a career of the labour market and, on the other, gaining the respect of and attracting others. "How is it that clever and competent people don't make it in their careers?" was the question put by a wool advertisement in 1968. "Don't call it bad luck if it is only a matter of 'packaging.' You can sell yourself better in a new suit! And that is often what counts in life." A woman whose romance has failed and who is looking for a new partner was recommended by Teen magazine in 1969, as "step 9" in its advice, to "become overwhelmingly pretty. . . . Why not try what you've never tried before? If you want to scour the market, you've got to show yourself in your best packaging." Where love succeeds, brought about by this fashionable packaging, and leads to encounters which under existing conditions appear in the form of a commodity-cash nexus, the cost of clothes can be interpreted as "capital investment."

—W. F. Haug, *Critique of Commodity Aesthetics:*
Appearance, Sexuality, and Advertising in Capitalist Society

2

CONSUMER CULTURES

Students who take courses in critical thinking learn about a major fallacy in reasoning called the post hoc, ergo propter hoc fallacy, which I discussed earlier. Just because someone sees a commercial for some product, such as a Norelco electric razor, and then purchases a Norelco razor doesn't mean that the commercial necessarily was the prime factor or the only factor leading to the purchase decision. There could have been any number of other factors or combinations of factors, such as the person's old razor breaking down, a terrific sale on Norelco razors, word of mouth from a friend who has one, and so on. It is important that we don't oversimplify matters in dealing with advertising. But we also must not underestimate or neglect advertising's influence on us as individuals and its influence on our society and culture. Advertising now permeates American culture and has affected, in profound ways, everything from our food preferences and our body shapes to our politics.

A CULTURAL CRITIQUE OF ADVERTISING

The discussion of the impact of advertising on American personality, culture, and society that follows is best understood as an example of cultural criticism. Cultural criticism makes use of psychoanalytic theory, literary theory, Marxist theory, sociological theory, semiotic theory, and various other theories, methodologies, and disciplines that can be used as means of interpreting texts and understanding social and cultural behavior. What I offer here is my interpretation of the impact of advertising on a number of important aspects of American culture and society. My analysis will also draw on critiques and interpretations of advertising made by other scholars in America and elsewhere. Although my focus is on advertising in the United States, the concepts I use and techniques I explain can be used to analyze advertising in other countries as well.

Advertising has been of interest to scholars in many disciplines because these scholars see advertising as one of the central institutions in American

33

society. Americans, we must keep in mind, are exposed to more advertising than people in any other society. This is because of the amount of television we watch and the amount of time we spend listening to the radio and because our media tend to be privately owned and financed by advertising. Our media institutions are mostly private, for-profit ones; public television and public radio attract relatively small (though generally highly influential) audiences in America.

David Potter, in his classic work *People of Plenty,* points out that advertising not only has economic consequences but also shapes our values. As he writes (1954:188),

> The most important effects of this powerful institution are not upon the economics of our distributive system; they are upon the values of our society. If the economic effect is to make the purchaser like what he buys, the social effect is, in a parallel but broader sense, to make the individual like what he gets—to enforce already existing attitudes, to diminish the range and variety of choices, and in terms of abundance, to exalt the materialistic virtues of consumption.

Potter makes an important point. Advertising, as an industry, is often quite avant-garde and bold in the techniques it uses, but, ironically, its impact tends to be a conservative one—to maintain, as much as possible, the status quo. One of the main things companies that advertise try to do is maintain their market share; if they can increase it, all the better. But they don't want to lose share at any cost. And advertising must be examined not only in terms of its economic impact but also in terms of its influence on American beliefs and values. In this chapter and the ones that follow, I discuss topics such as consumer cultures and consumer "lust," the use of sexuality to sell products and services, political advertising, and related matters.

CONSUMER CULTURES DEFINED

Consumer cultures, as I understand them, are those in which there has been a great expansion (some might say a veritable explosion) of commodity production, leading to societies full of consumer goods and services and places where these consumer goods and services can be purchased. In consumer cultures, the "game" people play is "get as much as you can." Success is defined as being the person "who has the most toys." This leads to a lust for consuming products—and conspicuously displaying them—as a means of demonstrating that one is a success and, ultimately, that one is worthy. And the very act of consumption has now also become aestheticized and sexualized and is itself the source of a great deal of pleasure. America has long been an important consumer culture and has recently been joined by China as a major consumer culture.

In *Consumer Culture and Postmodernism*, Mike Featherstone explains the importance of "lifestyle" in contemporary consumer societies. He writes (1991:86),

> Rather than unreflexively adopting a lifestyle, through tradition or habit, the new heroes of consumer culture make lifestyle a life project and display their individuality and sense of style in the particularity of the assemblage of goods, clothes, practices, experiences, appearance and bodily dispositions they design together into a lifestyle. The modern individual within consumer culture is made conscious that he speaks not only with his clothes, but also with his home, furnishings, decoration, car and other activities which are to be read and classified in terms of the presence and absence of taste. The preoccupation with customizing a lifestyle and a stylistic self-consciousness are not just to be found among the young and the affluent; consumer culture publicity [advertising] suggests that we all have room for self-improvement and self-expression whatever our age or class origins.

And, of course, it is advertising that "teaches" us about the world of consumer goods—what is fashionable and "hot" or, maybe even better for some people, "cool" (figure 2.1). Semioticians tell us that everything we do is read as a "message" and that we are always sending these messages to other people—just as they are always sending messages to us. These messages are sent by our lifestyle decisions—our clothes, hairstyles, cars, homes, and other material goods—as well as our bodies, facial expressions, and body language. For example, serving the right brand of wine shows that we are sophisticated and have good taste. The advertisements for expensive wine must also be elegant and reflect a sense of refinement (figure 2.2).

Along with the growth of the supply of material objects, there is also a growth of leisure—which must be filled with the right kind of activities, depending on one's social class and status. Thus, upscale (those with high incomes and an appreciation of elite culture) people also consume high-art cultural products—operas, plays, works of sculpture, paintings, and so on—while those in a lower class tend to consume more ordinary products—inexpensive

Figure 2.1. Detail from a Saint Laurent ad. This ad is extremely simple and understated, in line with upscale aesthetic codes.

Beringer Wine Estates

Figure 2.2. Beringer wine estates.

clothes, drive-to vacations, and fast food, for example. It doesn't always work exactly that way; some people with limited incomes love opera and ballet, but, generally speaking, there is a connection between socioeconomic status and taste level. More elite elements in society (socioeconomically speaking, that is) take expensive vacations, drive expensive cars, and go to trendy and generally expensive restaurants, for example.

TASTE CULTURES AND ADVERTISING

Sociologist Herbert Gans suggested that there are a number of what he called "taste cultures" in the United States. As he writes in his book *Popular Culture and High Culture: An Evaluation of Taste* (1974:x),

> I suggest that America is actually made up of a number of taste cultures, each with its own art, literature, music, and so forth, which differ mainly in that they express different aesthetic standards. . . . The underlying assumption of this analysis is that all taste cultures are of equal worth. . . . Because taste cultures reflect the class and particularly education attributes of their publics, low culture is as valid for poorly educated Americans as high culture is for well-educated ones, even if the higher cultures are, in the abstract, better or more comprehensive than the lower cultures.

These five taste cultures are high culture, upper-middle culture, lower-middle culture, low culture, and quasi-folk culture. This classification system is similar, in many respects, to the six socioeconomic classes that W. Lloyd Warner found when he analyzed American society. To give you an idea of how these taste cultures differ, table 2.1 shows a chart with some of each taste culture's purchasing preferences during the 1970s, when Gans's book was published.

Table 2.1

Culture	Taste Preferences
High culture	Primitive art, abstract expressionist paintings
Upper-middle culture	*Time, Newsweek, The New Yorker*
Lower-middle culture	*Life, Look, Reader's Digest*
Low culture	Tabloids, westerns, Lawrence Welk
Quasi–folk culture	Comic books, old westerns, Mexican soap operas

If Gans is correct and there are these five different taste cultures, this poses a problem: it means advertising agencies have to figure out how to direct messages that will resonate with the various taste cultures. One way that advertising agencies have addressed this problem is by targeting different audiences. That is, advertising agencies look for ways of reaching specific audiences for particular products and services, which means, for example, that they have to determine who will most likely be watching a certain television program. The larger the audience, the more difficult it is to find ways of reaching all the different taste cultures in print ads and radio and television commercials.

Gans offers some comments about advertising in his book that are worth thinking about (1974:35–36):

> Unknown numbers of children and adults are . . . taken in by the puffery and exaggeration of advertising, and ought to be protected against it; but part of the attractiveness of the ads is that people want the offered goods and it is not at all certain that the ads themselves initiate the wants. Nor is it wrong that people should want things that are useful or provide pleasure. Moreover, studies of advertising impact and the complaints of advertising executives suggest that most people retain little of the ad content they see and misinterpret much of the message. Successful ads produce sharp increases in sales curves, but often these reflect the behavior of only a few hundred thousand people and no one yet knows the relative impact of ad and product on buying decisions.

These comments reflect notions about advertising that were rather common some thirty years ago, when it was generally held that the impact of the media was weak. Today, there is less ambivalence about the power of the media and of advertising.

THE POSTMODERN PERSPECTIVE

We often see the term "postmodern" in newspapers and magazines, generally referring to buildings that blend a number of different styles together. For example, Philip Johnson's AT&T building has Roman colonnades at the street level and a Chippendale pediment at the top. But postmodernism is broader than architecture and has been used by some philosophers and cultural theorists to characterize contemporary societies in which pastiche and a mixing of styles is dominant. The term means, literally, coming after or moving beyond modernism—the period covering (approximately) from 1900 to 1960, which was characterized by a sense that we could know reality and that there were valid rules that governed politics and society

Figure 2.3. Jean-François Lyotard is a French scholar who did important work on postmodernism.

LYOTARD

An influential postmodernist theoretician, Jean-François Lyotard (figure 2.3), described postmodernism as "incredulity toward meta-narratives," by which he meant a lack of acceptance of the great philosophical systems that had ordered our lives in the past. He writes (1984:xxiv), "Simplifying to the extreme, I define "postmodernism" as incredulity toward metanarratives. This incredulity is undoubtedly a product of progress in the sciences; but that progress in turn presupposes it." Later in the book, he discusses one of the more important aspects or signifiers of postmodernism, its embrace of eclecticism (1984:76):

> Eclecticism is the degree zero of contemporary general culture: one listens to reggae, watches a Western, eats McDonald's food for lunch and local cuisine for dinner, wears Paris perfume in Tokyo and "retro" clothes in Hong Kong; knowledge is a matter for TV games. It is easy to find a public for eclectic works. By becoming kitsch, art panders to the confusion which reigns in the "taste" of the patrons. Artists, gallery owners, critics, and public wallow together in the "anything goes," and the epoch is one of slackening. But this realism of the "anything goes" is in fact that of money; in the absence of aesthetic criteria, it remains possible and useful to assess the value of works of art according to the profits they yield.

What Lyotard is describing is the world in which we live, in which—without any rules that everyone accepts—we all create and change our lifestyles and identities whenever we feel like doing so. Postmodernism also doesn't accept that there are significant differences between elite forms of art and popular or mass-mediated forms and isn't concerned about narratives having the traditional beginning, middle, and end, in which everything is resolved. In the

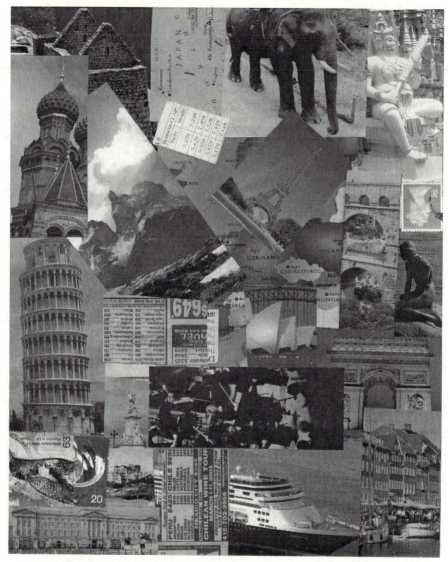

Figure 2.4. The pastiche is considered a postmodern art form.

postmodern world, simulations are dominant, and everyone is playing games with everyone else. In the postmodernist world, remember, anything goes. The pastiche, which combines elements from many different sources into an image, is considered a quintessential postmodern art form (figure 2.4).

Douglas Kellner, who has written many books on postmodernism, offers this description of it in his article "Postmodernism as Social Theory: Some Challenges and Problems" (*Theory, Culture and Society* 5, nos. 2–3 [June 1988]: 239):

As opposed to the seriousness of "high modernism," postmodernism exhibited a new insouciance, a new playfulness, and a new eclecticism embodied above all in Andy Warhol's "pop art" but also manifested in celebrations of Las Vegas architecture, found objects, happenings, Nam June Paik's video-installations, underground film, and the novels of Thomas Pynchon. In opposition to the well-wrought, formally sophisticated, and aesthetically demanding modernist art, postmodernist art was fragmentary and eclectic, mixing forms from "high culture" and "popular culture," subverting aesthetic boundaries and expanding the domain of art to encompass the images of advertising, the kaleidoscopic mosaics of television, the experiences of the post holocaust nuclear age, and an always proliferating consumer capitalism.

Kellner's analysis has the advantage of naming some of the works that reflect postmodernist culture and specifically links advertising to postmodernism.

One important theorist of postmodernism, Fredric Jameson, has argued that what we call postmodernism is, in reality, the form that capitalism takes in advanced capitalist societies. In his book *Postmodernism or, The Cultural Logic of Late Capitalism* (1991:xii), he writes that postmodernism is not the cultural dominant of a wholly new social order (the rumor about which, under the name of "postindustrial society," ran through the media a few years ago) but only the reflex and concomitant of yet another systematic modification of capitalism itself. His point is that what we describe as postmodernism can be thought of as the sheep's clothing hiding the wolf of capitalism; postmodernism is, then, a disguise by which a new form of capitalism manifests itself—though the impact on our culture of postmodernism has been substantial. I should add that not all theorists of postmodernism would agree with Jameson. The most widespread and eclectic art form in our day, I would suggest, is the advertisement, which helps us decide on what to consume to create our "eclectic" lifestyles. Madison Avenue and the advertising world have been quick to adopt the postmodern sensibility, and now we see television commercials that don't seem to make any sense. Things happen, but they don't seem to mean anything. What's important in these commercials is their "look." Jack Solomon describes a postmodern television commercial for a perfume. He writes in *The Signs of Our Time* (1990:229),

> Traditional commercials often set up a narrative situation of some sort, which, though trivial, has a beginning, middle, and an end—as when Mrs. Olson saves her young neighbors' marriage by introducing them to Folger's Coffee. But in Calvin Klein's postmodern campaign for Obsession perfume, it's virtually impossible to tell just what is going on. A tormented woman seems to be torn between a young boy and an older man—or does the young boy represent a flashback to the older man's youth? Maybe it's her kid brother? Her son? She touches his face for an instant but he refuses to

be touched and glides away. Tears run down her glacial Art Deco face, but it isn't clear what she's crying about.

It may very well be the confusion created by this commercial that is part of the sell, but it also may be wrong to look for logic and rationality in a postmodern television commercial. The assumption has to be made that people with a postmodern sensibility will "get" whatever message the Obsession commercial is delivering to them.

One essential attribute of postmodernism as it relates to advertising involves what has been described as "de-differentiation." In their book *Consumer Behaviour: A European Perspective*, Michael Solomon, Gary Barmossy, and Soren Askegaard describe this phenomenon (2002:560):

> Postmodernists are interested in the blurring of distinctions between hierarchies such as "high and low culture," or politics and show business. Examples would be the use of artistic works in advertising and the celebration of advertising in artistic works. Companies such as Coca-Cola, Nike and Guinness have their own museums. Another clear example is TV programmes featuring advertising for themselves (in order to increase viewer ratings) and TV commercials [that] look like "real" programming, as the ongoing soap opera with a couple spun around the coffee brand Gold Blend. The blurring of gender categories also refers to this aspect of postmodernism.

The authors add fragmentation, by which they mean the ever-growing brand extensions and categories of products, and hyperreality, involving simulations and a loss of an ability to distinguish between the authentic and simulations, as other important aspects of postmodernism. In postmodern societies, where there are no all-encompassing and dominating philosophical and ethical belief systems, the notion of a coherent identity is not valued, and people are constantly changing their identities and "looks," and all these changes are tied to purchasing the right products. Postmodern societies are consumption societies in which people are always looking for the next craze—whether it is iPods or iPhones or iPads or a new brand of sneaker. If the postmodern theorists are correct, postmodernism represents an important change in our culture, a "cultural mutation" that has taken place, which explains why American culture is the way it is and why our young people behave the way they do.

Many years ago, Virginia Woolf wrote an essay, "Mr. Bennett and Mrs. Brown," that dealt with a similar mutation in culture—except that Woolf was describing how modern society replaced Victorian culture. She wrote,

> On or about December, 1910, human character changed. I am not saying that one went out, as one might into a garden, and there saw a rose had

flowered, or that a hen had laid an egg. The change was not like that. But a change there was, nevertheless, and since one must be arbitrary, let us date it about the year 1910. When human relations change, there is at the same time a change in religion, conduct, politics, and literature.

She noted that relations between masters and servants, husbands and wives, and parents and children had changed. We can say, imitating Woolf, that according to postmodern theorists, sometimes in the 1960s, maybe on or about December 1960, American culture and society changed and that there were major changes to societies all over the world. The debate about postmodernism and its influence on American culture, character, and society continues in our universities. Some culture theorists argue now that postmodernism has run its course and that we live in a post-postmodern era, but there's no agreement on what to call it—if, in fact, that is the case. Marxists like Fredric Jameson would argue that if we are, in fact, living in a post-postmodernist era, it still really is only a new form of capitalism.

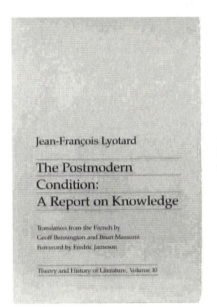

Figure 2.5. The cover of Lyotard's widely read book on postmodernism.

THE PROBLEM OF EMOTIONS OVERCOMING RATIONALITY

Many people have illusions about the way people act when they purchase things. This illusion suggests that people consider alternatives and think carefully about their projected purposes. The truth of the matter is that consumers generally act in a nonrational way when making purchases. According to Gerald Zaltman, a professor of marketing at the Harvard Business School, consumer behavior is not well reasoned or linear in nature. As he explains in his book *How Customers Think: Essential Insights into the Mind of the Market* (2003:8–9),

> The selection process is relatively automatic, stems from habits and other unconscious forces, and is greatly influenced by the consumer's social and physical context. . . . In reality, people's emotions are closely interwoven with reasoning processes. Although our brains have separate structures for processing emotions and logical reasoning, the two systems communicate with one another and jointly affect our behavior. Even more important, the emotional system—the older of the two in terms of evolution—typically exerts the first force on our thinking and behavior. . . . Ninety-five percent of our thinking takes place in our unconscious minds—that wonderful, if messy, stew of memories, emotions, thoughts and other cognitive processes we're not aware of or that we can't articulate.

What Zaltman suggests is that consumer cultures are built on appeals to our emotions. He adds, later, that we are not aware of the role the unconscious plays in our thinking, and writes (2003:40),

> According to most estimates, about 95 percent of thought, emotion, and learning occur in the unconscious mind—that is, without our awareness. As important as it is, consciousness is the end result of a system of neurons processing information in largely unconscious ways.

Later, he adds (2003:50), "At least 95 percent of all cognition occurs below the level of awareness in the shadows of the mind while, at most 5 percent occurs in higher-order consciousness." Thus, the notion that consumers are always rational in their decision making is fallacious. Zaltman sounds very Freudian here, though we don't find Freud in his book's index.

CONSUMER CULTURE AND PRIVATISM

One of the most important critiques scholars and social critics make of the consumer culture is that it is privatistic; the focus is on personal consumption, not social investment for the public good. Governments spend also, but if a governmental agency helps build up the infrastructure in some city, that spending yields jobs and increased productivity and is really a form of investment. Personal consumption, on the other hand, is based on private desires and the satisfaction of individual wishes. It may have a marginal benefit to society because the money spent on personal consumption "drips down" to other people, but economists generally find the amount of money dripping down to be quite minimal.

A number of years ago, a company that manufactured eyedrops suggested that using its product was the solution to smog and polluted air. Rather than fix the quality of air for everyone, this company suggested that everyone use its eyedrops instead. When you push the argument to its most extreme end, society is an abstraction, and there are only individuals inhabiting the same territory, each of whom pursues (and should pursue) his or her private destiny. From this perspective, the worse things are, the more opportunities there are to sell products to people, so the market economy may have an implicit stake in social disorganization and the neglect of the public sphere.

Advertising, since it is paid for by private entities, does not generally have a social investment message to it but instead focuses on individuals pursuing their private passions. "The hell with everyone else" is the subtext of many of these messages. And as American society becomes more and more split into two classes, one that is increasingly wealthy and one that is increasingly poor, the social tensions and possibilities for serious class conflict become stronger. People can retreat to gated communities to avoid crime, but they end up prisoners of those communities. My point, then, is that advertising often distracts us from paying attention to the need for social investments, from a concern for the public sphere, and thus, by its very nature, tends to be politically conservative. The argument about "Obamacare" in the fall of 2013 can be seen in the light of this discussion. Many Republicans believe that the law intrudes on personal freedom and liberty, while many Democrats stress the importance of providing health insurance to millions of people who don't have it or can't afford it.

NEIMAN MARCUS AND "COUTHIFICATION"

There is a great deal of pressure on people to show taste and discrimination, suitable to their place in the great chain of being (that is, to their socioeconomic status), in the products and services they consume. Neiman Marcus, for example, was useful to oil millionaires who had plenty of money but no sense of style adequate to their financial resources. What Neiman Marcus did was what I would describe as "couthification." The salespeople at Neiman Marcus made sure that nouveau riche oil millionaires purchased the right clothes for themselves and their families and bought the right home furnishings. (Stanley Marcus provided this insight to me when we appeared on a radio program

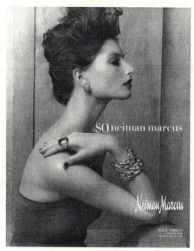

Figure 2.6. Notice the long neck, the profile, and the pose of this model for the Neiman Marcus company. How does this image suggest sophistication and an elite status?

together.) The famous Neiman Marcus catalogs, with their absurdly expensive "his" and "hers" gifts, generated a great deal of publicity for the store and also generated a halo effect for items purchased at Neiman Marcus. Anything bought there was, Neiman Marcus suggested, by definition stylish and in good taste (figure 2.6). For people with no taste, Neiman Marcus—and the legion of other stores like it—provided an escape from the anxiety of showing poor taste. Neiman Marcus was expensive, but it was worth it.

On the radio program we were on, I suggested to Stanley Marcus that department stores, such as Neiman Marcus, reminded me of medieval cathedrals. One can find interesting parallels between the two. These similarities are reflected in table 2.2.

We can see from the parallels between department stores and cathedrals that there is something holy, something of the sacred, connected to purchasing objects—the things we buy are signs, it can be surmised, that we have been blessed. And so we consume, often with religious fervor—even though we may not recognize the sacred dimension of our activities.

In his book *The Waning of the Middle Ages*, the historian Johan Huizinga explains how the two realms—the sacred and the secular—merged into one another. He writes (1924:156),

> All life was saturated with religion to such an extent that the people were in constant danger of losing sight of the distinction between things spiritual and things temporal. If, on the one hand, all the details of ordinary life may be raised to a sacred level, on the other hand, all that is holy sinks to the commonplace, by the fact of being blended with everyday life.

Table 2.2. Department Stores as Functional Alternatives to Cathedrals

Department Store	Cathedral
Modern	Medieval
Paradisal: Heaven on Earth now	Paradisal: Heaven in the future
Merchandising	Passion: salvation
Sales: save money	Prayer: save souls
Sacred texts: catalogs	Sacred texts: Bible, prayer books
Clerks	Clergy
Sell: products	Sell: God
Possessions as signs of spiritual election	Holiness as a sign of spiritual election
Big sales	Religious holidays
Sale of an expensive product	Conversion of a sinner
Buy incredible gifts	Experience miracles
Pay taxes	Pay tithe
Muzak	Religious music
Lighting to sell	Lighting to inspire reverence
Bad credit	Penance
Advertising	Proselytizing
Cash register	Offering plate
Brand loyalty	Devotion

Our lives, in contemporary consumer cultures, are saturated with commercials and other forms of advertising. And beneath these advertisements and fueling our desire to consume more and more products is, I would suggest, a sense that our actions have an unconscious and ultimately religious dimension to them; they are a means of showing our "election" (a good Puritan term) and that we are the worthy beneficiaries of God's grace.

NEEDS ARE FINITE, DESIRES ARE INFINITE

In America, as the quintessential consumer culture (not that many Western European, Asian, or Latin American countries are far behind us), what you can afford becomes the means of determining who you are—or who people think you are. In earlier days, consumption was more or less limited to a small percentage of fabulously wealthy industrialists and entrepreneurs. America's great genius has been to spread consumer lust to the middle classes and, for some items, to the lower classes. One problem with consumer cultures is that people become too caught up in consuming things as a means of validating themselves and proving their worth (there is a religious dimension to this, ultimately, as my discussion of department stores and cathedrals suggests). In consumer cultures, all too often people don't think about what they have but concern themselves only with what they don't have. And that is, in part, because advertising constantly reminds them of what they don't have. Needs are finite, but desires are infinite, and thus, as soon as our needs have been taken care of, we become obsessed with what we don't have but want—or, more precisely, one might suggest, with what advertising tells us we should want.

What advertising does, among other things, is manufacture desire and shape it and thus create people who are insatiable and who have been conditioned to continually lust for more things. And the more we have, the more we want because the things we buy—the sport-utility vehicles, the expensive vacations, and the trophy wives and husbands—are evidence that we believe in our intelligence, industry, potency, and, ultimately, our worth (in man's and God's eyes).

Paco Underhill, a "retail anthropologist" who studies shoppers for a living, has noticed this in his work (2000:116–17):

> At that exalted level, shopping is a transforming experience, a method of becoming a newer, perhaps even slightly improved person. The products you buy turn you into that other, idealized version of yourself. That dress makes you beautiful, this lipstick makes you kissable, that lamp turns your house into an elegant showplace.

The subtitle of Underhill's book, in its updated and revised version, published in 2009, is *The Science of Shopping* (figure 2.7). There is also a banner saying "Updated and Revised for the Internet, the Global Consumer and Beyond," which indicates, first, that shopping in now a "science" (in that it is studied in scientific ways) and, second, that the Internet is now playing an increasingly important role in advertising and that many of the insights that

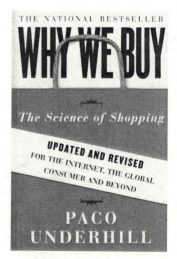

Figure 2.7. *Why We Buy* **was a best-selling book that discusses what motivates shoppers.**

Underhill offers in the book now have relevance to everyone. That is because shopping is a global passion. His book is filled with fascinating factoids about the amount of time people spend shopping in supermarkets and department stores and information he has to offer about how consumers behave in various settings where they purchase goods and services and ideas he offers about how to facilitate their purchasing things.

The British novelist and critic John Berger has a different perspective on advertising and consumer cultures. In his influential book *Ways of Seeing* (also a British Broadcasting Company television series), he offers what is, in essence, a Marxist critique of advertising or "publicity." He writes (1972:131, 132),

> It proposes to each of us that we transform ourselves, or our lives, by buying something more.
>
> This more, it proposes, will make us in some way richer—even though we will be poorer for having spent our money.
>
> Publicity persuades us of such a transformation by showing us people who have apparently been transformed and are, as a result, enviable. The state of being envied is what constitutes glamour. And publicity is the process of manufacturing glamour. . . . Publicity is never a celebration of pleasure-in-itself. Publicity is always about the future buyer. It offers him an image of himself made glamorous by the product or opportunity it is trying to sell. The image then makes him envious of himself as he might be. Yet what makes this self-which-he-might-be enviable? The envy of others. Publicity is about social relations, not objects.

This is an important point. What Berger suggests is that advertising takes advantage of the desire we have for a better life for ourselves and our loved ones and uses our envy of others and of ourselves—as we might be if we purchase the right things—against us.

ARE THERE FOUR CONSUMER CULTURES, NOT JUST ONE?

When we talk about consumer cultures, we use the term to describe the fact that the private consumption of objects and services is a cultural dominant in many different modern societies. But it may be a simplification to say that there is just one consumer culture. It can be argued that there are actually four different consumer cultures found in democratic societies, based on certain beliefs and values (tied to the strength or weakness of group affiliations and adherence to few or many rules by people in these groups that members hold in common).

Insights from Advertising Agencies

Bianca Jagger would be a good person to associate with the wine we're trying to advertise, since she's one of the new aristocracy or celibritocracy. They are the opinion leaders and style setters thrown up by the world of pop culture, who set trends and influence a number of "hip" people.

This analysis draws on the cultural theories of a political scientist, Aaron Wildavsky, and a social anthropologist, Mary Douglas. Wildavsky suggested that cultural theory tries to help people answer two basic questions—the question of identity: Who am I? and the question of action: What should I do? Wildavsky writes, in his chapter "A Cultural Theory of Preference Formation" (1989:25),

> The question of identity may be answered by saying the individuals belong to a strong group, a collective that makes decisions binding on all members, or that their ties to others are weak in that their choices bind only themselves. The question of action is answered by responding that the individual is subject to many or few prescriptions, a free spirit or tightly constrained. The strength or weakness of group boundaries and the numerous or few, varied or similar, prescriptions binding or freeing individuals are the components of their culture.

We find, then, that there are four political cultures—and, by extension, so Douglas argues, consumer cultures—that arise from this situation. Wildavsky calls his four political cultures hierarchical or elitist, individualist, egalitarian, and fatalist. These cultures are created by the strength and weakness of group boundaries and the numbers and kinds of rules and prescriptions. Social scientists Michael Thompson, Richard Ellis, and Aaron Wildavsky point out, in their book *Cultural Theory*, how the four cultures are derived (1990:6–7):

> Strong group boundaries coupled with minimal prescriptions produce social relations that are egalitarian. . . . When an individual's social environment is characterized by strong group boundaries and binding prescriptions, the resulting social relations are hierarchical [sometimes known as elitist]. . . . Individuals who are bounded by neither group incorporation nor prescribed roles inhabit an individualistic social context. In such an environment all boundaries are provisional and subject to negotiation. . . . People who find themselves subject to binding prescriptions and are excluded from group membership exemplify the fatalistic way of life. Fatalists are controlled from without.

The basic characteristics of these four political and consumer cultures are described below.

Hierarchical/Elitists

Hierarchical/elitists believe in the need for hierarchy in societies—to make them run efficiently and to motivate people—but feel a sense of obligation to those below them.

Individualists

Individualists feel that individuals are basic and that the role of government should be minimal—protecting against crime and invasions and maximizing possibilities for individuals in the business world. They have little sense of obligation to others since they believe that we're all responsible for ourselves.

Egalitarians

Egalitarians believe that everyone has certain needs that have to be looked after by government; they try to "raise up" the fatalists and look after the needs of people in general. Egalitarians are critics of the status quo and, in particular, of elitists and individualists. They stress the importance of voluntary consent.

Fatalists

Fatalists are at the bottom of the totem pole and have little economic, purchasing, or decision-making power. They depend on luck (such as winning lotteries) to escape from their fatalist status. Over the course of time, Wildavsky changed the names of some of his cultures, I should add, in an attempt to clarify things. But the changes were relatively minor. Mary Douglas, the British social anthropologist who did most of the pioneering work on grid-group theory, used the term "lifestyles" for the four groups.

We can use these four political/consumer cultures/lifestyles to understand why people consume the things they do, like certain books and television programs and so on. Some examples are shown in table 2.3.

This chart can be extended and can deal with many other categories of purchases, and it's an interesting project to consider how people in the four political/consumer cultures make the choices they make (see table 2.4). We can play a learning game in which we try to determine which products people in the four cultures of lifestyles would purchase. This game should be played in

Table 2.3. Lifestyles and Preferences

Category	Elitist	Individualist	Egalitarian	Fatalist
Songs	"God Save the Queen"	"My Way"	"We Are the World"	"Anarchy in the UK"
Fashion	Uniforms	Suit	Blue jeans	Thrift shop
Books	*The Prince*	*Looking Out for Number One*	*I'm OK— You're OK*	*1984*
Restaurants	French	Cafeteria	McDonald's	Food kitchen
Automobiles	Rolls Royce	BMW	Civic	Yugo

Table 2.4

Lifestyle	Vacations	Smart Phones	Beer
Elitists			
Individualists			
Egalitarians			
Fatalists			

groups of three, with one member of the group being the "scribe" who writes down the results but also participates in the deliberations. The aim of playing the game is to see whether the different groups come to the same conclusions.

Wildavsky adds an important point—there are only four political cultures possible in any democratic society, and individuals make political decisions on the basis of their allegiance to whichever political culture they find themselves in and not on the basis of self-interest since people generally don't often know what is in their self-interest. In table 2.5, I list the four consumer cultures and their relation to groups, boundaries, and prescriptions. Members of these four political cultures or consumer cultures don't recognize that they are members of one of these groups; that is, they probably aren't even aware of their existence. But they have certain values and belief systems connected to group affiliation and rule acceptance that Wildavsky and Douglas have identified as placing them in one of the political cultures.

Table 2.5

Culture	Boundaries	Prescriptions
Hierarchists	Strong	Numerous and varied
Egalitarians	Strong	Few and weak
Individualists	Weak	Few and weak
Fatalists	Weak	Numerous and varied

Mary Douglas, who collaborated with Wildavsky on a number of projects, argues that these four political cultures can also be seen as consumer cultures—which for her purposes she also describes as lifestyles. She substitutes the terms "isolates" for "fatalists" and "enclavists" for "egalitarians" and explains that membership in one of the four consumer cultures or lifestyles—each of which is antagonistic toward or in conflict with the three others—best explains people's consumer choices. As she writes in her essay "In Defence of Shopping" (1997:19),

> None of these four lifestyles (individualist, hierarchical, enclavist [egalitarian], isolated [fatalist]) is new to students of consumer behavior. What may be new and unacceptable is the point [that] these are the only four distinctive lifestyles to be taken into account, and the other point, that each is set up in competition with the others. Mutual hostility is the force that accounts for their stability. These four distinct lifestyles persist because they rest on incompatible organizational principles. Each culture is a way of organizing; each is predatory on the others for time and space and resources. It is hard for them to co-exist peacefully, and yet they must, for the survival of each is the guarantee of the survival of the others. Hostility keeps them going.

Douglas offers her theory of the four consumer cultures to counter the theories of consumption that come from a framework based on individualist psychology. She argues that "cultural alignment is the strongest predictor of preferences in a wide variety of fields" (1997:23). It is, then, our lifestyle group affiliations that shape our desires and our purchases.

Her theory argues, then, that there is an inherent logic behind the shopping that people do and, furthermore, that it is shoppers, or consumers, who ultimately dictate what will be sold. We can see this is the case if we examine the households of people from different consumer cultures. Members of the different consumer cultures may have similar incomes (except for the fatalists/isolates, who are at the bottom of the income ladder, generally speaking), but their patterns of consumption and the way they organize their households are affected by their membership in one of the four groups. Douglas concludes that it is cultural bias and membership in one of the four consumer cultures that is critical to understanding consumption. The notion that shopping is essentially the expression of individual wants is incorrect then. As she writes in the concluding section of her essay (1997:30),

> The idea of consumer sovereignty in economic theory will be honoured in market research because it will be abundantly clear that the shopper sets the trends, and that new technology and new prices are adjuncts to achieving the shopper's goal. The shopper is not expecting to develop a personal identity by choice of commodities; that would be too difficult. Shopping is

agonistic, a struggle to define not what one is but what one is not. When we include not one cultural bias, but four, and when we allow that each is bringing critiques against the others, and when we see that the shopper is adopting postures of cultural defiance, then it all makes sense.

If Douglas is correct, there are, in fact, four distinct and mutually antagonistic lifestyles or consumer cultures, even though people who are in each of them may not be aware of the matter. This would mean that it wouldn't be socioeconomic class and discretionary income that is basic in consumption decisions but, rather, lifestyles or membership in one of the four mutually antagonistic consumer cultures.

The comment by Douglas that shopping is "a struggle to define not what one is but what one is not" is similar in nature to Ferdinand de Saussure's writings about how language shapes the way we find meaning in life. In his classic work *Course in General Linguistics*, Saussure (figure 2.8) wrote (1966:120) that "in language there are only differences," and when it comes to concepts (1966:117), he added,

> It is understood that concepts are purely differential and defined not by their positive content but negatively by their relations with the other terms of the system. Their most precise characteristic is in being what the others are not.

What Saussure is suggesting is that nothing has meaning in itself; it is the relationships in language that are basic, and the most important relationship among words and concepts involves opposition. His book is one of the founding documents of semiotics, the science of signs. He divided signs into two parts—a *signifier* (sound or object) and a *signified* (concept or idea generated by the signifier)—and pointed out that the relationship between signifiers and signifieds is based on convention. A sign, we can say, is anything that can stand for something else. Hairstyles, facial expression, body language, clothes—just about everything we can think of—are signs and send messages to others who

Figure 2.8. Ferdinand de Saussure was one of the founding fathers of semiotics.

S aussure

interpret the signs we send and don't always do so correctly. I will use semiotics to analyze print advertisements and television commercials in chapters 8 and 9 of this book.

When we purchase things, Douglas argues, we do so to show who we are by showing who we are not. To simplify matters greatly, what we mean by "poor" is "not rich" and by "happy" is "not sad." That is why she argues that shopping is "agonistic." We want to demonstrate, she says, that we are not a member of the three other consumer cultures and are not guided by their aesthetic standards. From Saussure's perspective, everything has meaning by being opposite of something else. Douglas moves consumption decisions from psychology to membership in a consumer culture or lifestyle. Modern societies may be characterized as being consumer societies and "consumer cultures," but, if Douglas is correct, there are really four consumer subcultures, and they are of major importance when it comes to such things as individuals making decisions about what to buy or, to the extent that voting is a kind of consumption, whom to elect to public office.

There is the question, of course, of whether Douglas is correct and whether her typology of four consumer cultures is the best way to understand patterns of consumption. It is certainly worth keeping in mind when we consider the way advertising attempts to persuade people to buy various products and services. Later in the book, we will see that marketers have devised many different ways of breaking down American society into different target audiences. What we have to wonder about is whether each of these many different target audiences can be subsumed under one of the four consumer cultures Douglas writes about or whether her theory is, while intellectually elegant, too narrow. For example, marketers have focused a good deal of attention on how to reach children and make use of their notorious "pester power." (I'll deal with this subject in more detail at the end of this book.) How does Douglas's theory take into account the influence of children on the consumption patterns of their parents?

NATIONAL CHARACTER AND CONSUMER CULTURES

Americans aren't the only people living in consumer cultures, and, as one might expect, advertising in foreign countries, with different cultural values and beliefs, is often quite different from advertising in the United States. A fascinating book by Clotaire Rapaille, a French marketing consultant, *The Culture Code: An Ingenious Way to Understand Why People around the World Live and Buy as They Do*, argues that children in all countries are "imprinted" by the codes (which operate on us at the unconscious level) for their culture by the time they are seven years old and that these codes will shape their thinking and behavior for the rest of their lives. For example, we see cheese as "dead" in the United States and wrap it in plastic and keep in the refrigerator. The French see cheese as alive and keep it in a cloche (container) and not in a refrigerator.

He offers many interesting discussions of the way different cultures see a given product (and thus the way it is advertised). He gives the example of Chrysler's Jeep. He uses psychoanalytic approaches to find out how people feel about products rather than asking them for their preferences. He focuses on feelings and emotions. When Chrysler hired him, he did some work with respondents and told Chrysler that the code for Jeep in the United States was HORSE. The Chrysler executives were astounded, for they had many research studies that countered that notion. They asked for people's preferences but not how people felt about Jeeps.

Rapaille had Chrysler test his finding by changing the headlights of Jeeps from square to round lights since horses have round eyes. When they did that, the sales of Jeeps went up. It was also cheaper to make round headlights, so the Chrysler executives were pleased, and the Jeep got a new face. Since his advice was so useful and led to increased sales, Chrysler asked him to find out how to sell Jeeps in France and Germany. He writes (2006:3),

> Respondents in both France and Germany saw Wranglers as reminiscent of the Jeeps American troops drove during World War II. For the French this was the image of freedom from the Germans. For the Germans, this was the image of freedom from their darker selves. . . . I returned to Chrysler and told them that the Code for the Jeep Wrangler in both countries was LIBERATOR.

So Chrysler advertised the Jeep as HORSE in the United States and LIBERATOR in France and Germany. That is, they used images and appeal congruent with each of these codes in the countries where they advertised. He describes culture codes as (2006:5) "the unconscious meaning we apply to any given thing—a car, a type of food, a relationship, even a country—via the culture in which we were raised." So we are imprinted with codes, and these codes then play a role in the way we live and what we buy.

STUDY QUESTIONS, APPLICATIONS, AND ASSIGNMENTS

1. What is cultural criticism? What methodologies does it use?
2. What did David Potter say about advertising's role in American society?

3. How are consumer cultures defined? What are their basic characteristics?

4. What was said about semiotics? How does semiotics help us understand how advertising works?

5. What did Herbert Gans say about taste cultures? How do they relate to advertising?

6. What are the basic attributes of postmodernism? How did Douglas Kellner and Frederic Jameson characterize it?

7. According to Virginia Woolf, the world changed on December 10, 1910. What happened?

8. Investigate modernism and compare it to postmodernism. Make a chart showing their differences.

9. What did Gerald Zaltman say about emotions and rationality? What role does the unconscious play in our purchasing decisions?

10. What did Max Weber say about the relation between Protestantism and capitalism?

11. In what ways are department stores functional alternatives to cathedrals?

12. Compare Paco Underhill and John Berger on shopping.

13. What is grid-group theory? How does this theory explain the formation of four lifestyles in a country?

14. What did Mary Douglas say about consumer choice? Do you agree with her? If so, explain your reasons. If not, explain your reasons.

15. What is national character? How does Clotaire Rapaille explain the role of culture on children? What role do culture codes play in our daily lives and purchasing decisions?

For the semiotician, the contradictory nature of the American myth of equality is nowhere written so clearly as in the signs that American advertisers use to manipulate us into buying their wares. "Manipulate" is the word here, not "persuade"; for advertising campaigns are not sources of product information, they are exercises in behavior modification. Appealing to our subconscious emotions rather than to our conscious intellects, advertisements are designed to exploit the discontentment fostered by the American dream, the constant desire for social success and the material rewards that accompany it. America's consumer economy runs on desire, and advertising stokes the engines by transforming common objects—from peanut butter to political candidates—into signs of all the things that Americans covet most.

—Jack Solomon, *The Signs of Our Time:*
The Secret Meanings of Everyday Life

Any analysis of the system of objects must ultimately imply an analysis of discourse about objects—that is to say, an analysis of promotional "messages" (comprising image and discourse). For advertising is not simply an adjunct to the system of objects; it cannot be detached therefrom, nor can it be restricted to its "proper" function (there is no such thing as advertising strictly confined to the supplying of information). Indeed, advertising is now an irremovable aspect of the system of objects precisely because of its disproportionateness. This lack of proportion is the "functional" apotheosis of the system. Advertising in its entirety constitutes a useless and unnecessary universe. It is pure connotation. It contributes nothing to production or to the direct practical application of things, yet it plays an integral part in the system of objects not merely because it relates to consumption but also because it itself becomes an object to be consumed.

—Jean Baudrillard, *The System of Objects*

3

ADVERTISING AND THE
COMMUNICATION PROCESS

It is useful, at this point, to place advertising in the communication process—
so we can better understand how print advertisements and radio and television commercials (and other forms of advertising on the Internet and in other
media) function. To do this, I offer a brief overview of communication theory,
focusing on one of the most famous statements, the famous Lasswell formula
(and an amplification of this formula that I've made), and Roman Jakobson's
model. There are, of course, numerous models for understanding the communication process, just as there are many different ways of analyzing and interpreting advertisements and commercials and the role they play in our lives.

THE LASSWELL FORMULA

Harold Lasswell—an influential political scientist—said, in a 1948 article,
that to understand the communication process we should ask the following
questions:

Who?
Says what?

In which channel?
To whom?
With what effect?

In Denis McQuail and Sven Windahl's *Communication Models: For the Study of Mass Communication*, they suggest that this formula is (1993:13) "perhaps the most famous single phrase in communication research." They then discuss how this phrase offers a perspective on the communication process:

Who	**Says What**	**in Which Channel**	**to Whom**	**with What Effect**
Communicator	*Message*	*Medium*	*Receiver*	*Effect*

They point out in their comment on the Lasswell formula (1993:15):

> The Lasswell Formula shows a typical trait of early communication models: it more or less takes for granted that the communicator has some intention of influencing the receiver and, hence, that communication should be treated mainly as a persuasive process. It is also assumed that messages always have effects. Models such as this have surely contributed to the tendency to exaggerate the effects of, especially, mass communication. On the other hand, this is not surprising when we know that Lasswell's interest at the time was political communication and propaganda. For analyzing political propaganda, the formula is well suited.

It is also well suited, I would add, for analyzing advertising because what advertisers are interested in, to a great degree, are the effects of advertising.

In my model of the focal points and the study of media, I have offered an overview of the communication process that is somewhat similar to the Lasswell formula (table 3.1). I deal with four focal points in the study of communication and with their relation to media. These focal points are (1) the work of art, (2) the artist, (3) the audience, and (4) America (or the society in which the work of art is created or disseminated by the media).

Table 3.1. Comparison of the Lasswell Formula and Focal Points

Lasswell	*Berger*
Who?	Artists, copywriters, etc.
Says what?	Artwork (advertisements)
In which channel?	Medium
To whom?	Audience
With what effect?	America (society)

FOCAL POINTS AND THE STUDY OF MEDIA

We can see the relationships that exist among these focal points in figure 3.1. The arrows connect each focal point to every other focal point, either directly (for example, art and audience or art and artist) or indirectly (art/medium/America or artist/medium/audience).

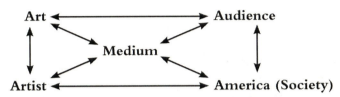

Figure 3.1. Focal points in the study of communication.

The work of art (or "text" in the jargon of communication scholars) is, in terms of our interests, a print advertisement or a radio or television commercial. It is important that we realize that print and electronic advertisements are works of art—even though their purpose is a commercial one—to convince people to use some product or service. Thus, we have to consider, among other things, aesthetic matters when dealing with advertising.

All advertising is directed toward a target audience—the people who are the most likely purchasers of the product or service being advertised. Copywriters and artists work hard to create advertisements and commercials that will interest and appeal to members of their target audience. Advertisers talk about upscale audiences, who have a considerable amount of money to spend (on things such as expensive cars and vacations), and downscale audiences, who are targeted for low-cost products. Research companies have elaborated various schemes and categories of purchasers, based on ZIP codes, racial and ethnic characteristics, values and lifestyles, and so on. A number of these matters are discussed later in the book. Advertising is a collaborative medium. So when we talk about artists in my chart of focal points, we really are talking about teams of copywriters, artists, directors, musicians, filmmakers, and numerous other creative artists in addition to researchers and others involved in the complicated process of making advertisements. Television commercials are the most complex form of advertising since they involve script writers, actors, musicians, cinematographers, and others.

The fourth focal point is America or the society in which advertisements are disseminated—either via print or via electronic media, such as radio, television, or the Internet. The term "society" is probably too broad since advertisements are traditionally targeted and directed to certain segments of the general

Insights from Advertising Agencies

A great ad is one that connects people to what you're selling and isn't too subtle. If it's too subtle people will see it but not remember it. But if it's too gimmicky, people will get bored with it once they've seen it. We conduct wear-out analyses to see how long an ad will last. Sometimes we put them on the shelf and then bring them back after a while.

population—based a good deal of the time on demographic factors, such as age, gender, sexual orientation, or socioeconomic standing.

Finally, there is the medium that is used to disseminate the advertisements. The medium used has a major impact on the creation of texts. Each medium—print (newspapers and magazines), radio, or television—has certain strengths and weaknesses. So although the medium may not be the message (the late Marshall McLuhan, a famous communication theorist, argued that "the medium is the message"), it has a lot of impact on the message. One of the problems advertisers face, now, is how to advertise on the Internet and reach and persuade the huge number of people with smart phones who use the Internet.

In figure 3.1, there are arrows pointing in all directions, which signifies that all of the focal points are connected to one another. The more focal points we consider, the more complicated the analysis becomes, which leads me to suggest that it is generally more productive to focus on fewer focal points. I developed my model of the focal points by extending one used by literary theorist M. H. Abrams. He was dealing with books and literature, so he didn't include media in his analysis. When I elaborated this model, I did not realize that my focal points were similar to the different elements found in the Lasswell formula. The similarities between the Lasswell formula and my focal points are shown in table 3. 1. The major difference between the two, aside from the fact that I've used alliteration as a mnemonic device, is that my focal point America (or society) doesn't concern itself directly with effects.

ROMAN JAKOBSON'S MODEL
OF THE COMMUNICATION PROCESS

Another well-known model of the communication process is similar, in certain ways, to the models discussed above but adds some new factors to understanding the communication process. The linguist Roman Jakobson elaborated a communication model (figure 3.2) that is useful for us because

Roman Jakobson

it uses many of the terms currently popular with communication theorists. In this model, someone, a sender, sends a message to someone else, a receiver, using a code such as the English language. The context helps us interpret the message better. The Jakobson model was explained in part by Robert Scholes, a literature professor, in *Structuralism in Literature: An Introduction*. As Scholes writes (1974:24),

Whether we are considering ordinary conversation, a public speech, a letter, or a poem, we always find a message which proceeds from a sender to a receiver. These are the most obvious aspects of communication. But a successful communication depends on three other aspects of the event as well: the message must be delivered through a contact, physical and/or psychological; it must be framed in a code; and it must refer to a context. In the area of context, we find what a message is about. But to get there we must understand the code in which the message is framed—as in the present case, my messages reach you through the medium of an academic/literary subcode of the English language. And even if we have the code, we understand nothing until we make contact with the utterance; in the present case, until you see the printed words on this page (or hear them read aloud) they do not exist as a message for you. The message itself, uniting sender and receiver, in the quintessentially human act of communication, is simply a verbal form, which depends on all the other elements of a speech event to convey its meaning. The message is not the meaning. Meaning lies at the end of the speech event, which gives the verbal formula its life and color.

One of the problems those who make advertisements and commercials face comes from the fact that audiences or receivers "aberrantly decode" the messages (advertisements and commercials) they are sent. In part, this is because communication is such a complicated process, but also this problem stems in a general sense from differences in education, socioeconomic class,

Figure 3.2. The Jakobson model of communication.

Table 3.2. Comparison of Models of Communication

Lasswell	Jakobson	Berger
Who?	Sender	Artist
Says what?	Message	Artwork (text)
In which channel?	Contact (medium)	Medium
To whom?	Receiver	Audience
With what effect?		America

and cultural level between the makers and senders of the messages and the receivers of the messages.

The Jakobson model uses different (and now common) terms from the Lasswell model and my focal points model, but there are also a number of similarities, as table 3.2 shows. What the Lasswell model doesn't deal with are codes and the importance of context in interpreting (decoding) messages. And the Jakobson model doesn't concern itself with effects, as the Lasswell model does. The Berger model indirectly involves context in that American society provides a background that helps people decode messages. With these models, we now have a better knowledge of the communication process and can understand how print advertisements and commercials function from a theoretical point of view. In this book, I use various aspects of communication theory, such as different focal points, codes, receivers and senders, and so on, from time to time as it suits my purpose, in my discussion of specific print advertisements or television commercials and advertising in general. Consider, for example, all those television commercials we watch. They all want to persuade us to do something—whatever the maker of the product or provider of the service being advertised (the advertiser) and the advertising agency that made the commercial want us to do.

RUN IT UP A FLAGPOLE

The phrase "run it up a flagpole to see if anyone salutes" actually is, in its own way, similar to the Lasswell formula. We can see this by comparing the flagpole phrase and the Lasswell formula:

Lasswell Formula	**Run It Up a Flagpole**
Who?	(Let us) run
Says what?	It (the advertisement or commercial)
In which channel?	Up a flagpole (to show in print or electronic medium)
To whom?	To see if anyone (some kind of audience)
With what effect?	Salutes (is affected by it)

In both the Lasswell formula and the flagpole phrase, most of the elements in the communication process are taken into consideration, though the advertising phrase is much more colloquial and doesn't seem to be concerned with the communication process, except in a rather vague manner.

But how do advertisers get us to salute? How do they manipulate us? How do they manufacture desire in us? How do they (when they do, that is) shape our desire and engineer our consent? One way is by wearing us down under a constant barrage of advertisements and commercials. The main way we resist—not on purpose, of course—is by decoding these advertisements and commercials aberrantly, that is, by not interpreting the advertisements the way the copywriters and artists who created them expect us to or want us to.

METAPHOR AND METONYMY

There are two rhetorical devices, metaphor and metonymy, that are commonly used by copywriters and artists to communicate with people. Jakobson argues that metaphor and metonymy are the two essential ways that people communicate meaning. Metaphor is a technique that uses analogy to create its effects. It explains or interprets one thing in terms of something else. "My love is a rose" is a metaphor. There is a weaker form of metaphor known as simile, which uses a "like" or "as." "My love is like a rose" is a simile. Metaphor, it turns out, is a very important means of communication. As George Lakoff and Mark Johnson point out in their book *Metaphors We Life By* (1980:3),

> Most people think they can get along perfectly well without metaphor. We have found, on the contrary, that metaphor is pervasive in everyday life, not just in language but in thought and action. Our ordinary conceptual system, in terms of which we both think and act, is fundamentally metaphoric in nature.

Figure 3.3. Metaphor and identity: I am a sea shell.

The concepts that govern our thought are not just matters of the intellect. They also govern our everyday functioning down to the most mundane details. Our concepts structure what we perceive, how we get around in the world, and how we relate to other people. Our conceptual system thus plays a central role in defining our everyday realities.

So metaphor is a crucial element in our lives because it shapes our thinking and our communicating—even if we don't recognize it as such or assume that metaphor is just a literary device.

Insights from Advertising Agencies

"Bad taste" is anything that keeps a person comfortable in his situation and reactions, anything that soothes rather than stimulates, anything dated rather than trendy, anything sentimental rather than sophisticated. This is the taste of more than 70 percent of the public, and it is this taste that dictates to advertisers. Advertising does not lead, it only follows. It's a service of communication, of selling, of a dialogue with consumers that is supposed to argue, cajole, or coax them into learning about goods for sale. It depends not on orders from manufacturers or retailers or providers of goods and services, but on dictation from the public. By a dictation from the public's instincts or habits of mind or mindlessness, too strongly entrenched for mere word-spinners and picture-makers to do anything about.

Metonymy uses associations to communicate information and attitudes that we all learn as we grow up. Thus, if we see a Rolls Royce in an advertisement, we know that the person who owns the car is very wealthy and can afford "the best." The person who drives a Rolls Royce is different from the person who drives a Ferrari, and they are both different from people who drive Honda Civics. Copywriters and art directors can use this information we all have (that is, certain associations or metonymies) to communicate, rather quickly, notions they want us to have. There is a form of metonymy in which a part stands for a whole (or vice versa) that is known as synecdoche. For example, when people say "The Pentagon," we interpret this to stand for the U.S. military services. When we see a Mercedes-Benz symbol, we know it stands for a car.

Metaphor, it turns out, is one of the basic ways human beings make sense of things, so metaphor and metonymy—which are often mixed together—turn out to be very powerful tools that advertisers use to provide information to us and to generate desired emotional responses in us. Table 3.3 compares

Table 3.3. Metaphor and Metonymy

Metaphor	*Metonymy*
Analogy	Association
meta = to transfer; *phor* = bear	*meta* = to transfer; *onoma* = name
"My love is a rose"	Rolls Royce associated with great wealth
Simile—analogy with "like" or "as"	*Synecdoche*—part stands for whole or vice versa
"My love is like a rose"	"The crown" stands for royalty
Spider-Man's costume	Royal seal on British marmalade jars
"Drive = Love"	Derby suggests English society

the two devices. We can see from this table that there are both verbal and graphic forms of metaphor and metonymy, and they are used to great effect in all kinds of advertising. For example, an image of a snake in an advertisement can be construed metaphorically as a phallic symbol and metonymically as alluding to the snake in the Garden of Eden. Later in the book, I will analyze the Fidji advertisement that uses a snake prominently, and we will see that it is a complicated symbol.

In a semiotics seminar I once taught, I played an interesting game. I asked my students to put simple objects that they thought reflected various aspects of their personalities in a brown paper bag and bring them to class. I also asked them to list the qualities that they thought the objects reflected and write them on a piece of paper that they were to put in the bag. That way, nobody could tell who submitted which object. I collected the brown paper bags and pulled out a sea shell from one of them. I asked the members of the class what the object, functioning semiotically as a sign, reflected about the person who had submitted the object. My students answered with terms such as "sterile," "empty," "dead." Then I pulled out the slip of paper which the student had submitted and read, "beautiful," "elegant," "natural." The moral is, we may think we are sending certain messages about ourselves by the way we dress and what we say when we talk, by our facial expressions and body language, but other people may not be interpreting those messages the way we thought they would. That's one of the main problems advertisers face—people don't "get" their messages.

MYTH AND MARKETING

Let me suggest here that many of the things we do and the things we buy are affected by certain myths found in Western culture. I got the idea of writing about myth and its relation to advertising after reading Mircea Eliade's book *The Sacred and the Profane.* In this book, he explains (1961:204),

The modern man who feels and claims that he is nonreligious still retains a large stock of camouflaged myths and degenerated rituals. . . . A whole volume could well be written on the myths of modern man, on the mythologies camouflaged in the plays that he enjoys, in the books that he reads. The cinema, that "dream factory," takes over and employs countless mythological motifs—the fight between hero and monster, initiatory combats and ordeals, paradigmatic figures (the maiden, the hero, the paradisal landscape, hell, and so on).

Myths are sacred histories—stories about heroes and heroines and gods and goddesses in ancient times. In the Western world, it is Greek and Roman myths that tend to be dominant. What I believe is that these myths still play a role in our lives, in the camouflaged rituals we observe. As Raphael Patai writes in his book *Myth and Modern Man* (1972:2), "Myth . . . is a traditional religious charter, which operates by validating laws, customs, rites, institutions and beliefs, or by explaining socio-cultural situations and natural phenomena." They take the form of dramatic stories.

After reading Eliade and Patai, I developed what I describe as a "myth model" that deals with the way myth informs (though we are generally not aware of the process) many aspects of our lives. The myth model involves stories from the Bible and Greek and Roman myths about such famous figures as Prometheus, Sisyphus, Medusa, Ulysses, and so on:

- *A Myth*, understood to be a sacred story that validates behavior
- *Historical Experience*, where various heroes can be tied to myths
- *Psychoanalytic Theory*, where the myth is found or used to describe something
- *Elite Culture*, which has plays, operas, novels, and other texts about the myth
- *Popular Culture and the Mass Media*, which employ myths in films, advertising, and so on
- *Everyday Life*, where myth subtly shapes our thinking, behavior and purchases

To show how the myth model affects our behavior as consumers, I will take one of the most important myths in the Western world—the myth of Adam and Eve. I will show not only that this myth is all-pervasive in American culture but also that it plays a role in shaping the things we buy and do:

- *Myth:* Adam and Eve in the Garden of Eden—innocent until they eat from the tree of knowledge

- *Historical Experience:* The Puritans come to America to escape corruption in Europe
- *Psychoanalytic Theory:* Repression or suppression? Escapism?
- *Elite Culture:* Adamic figures like Christopher Newman in Henry James's *The American*
- *Popular Culture: Shane* and other westerns involving restoring innocence to the frontier
- *Everyday Life:* Buy a house in the suburbs, away from "decadent" city centers

What I'm suggesting is that there may be camouflaged (or unconscious) myths, or residues of myths, that play a role in some of our decisions about what to consume. We are not aware of the way myths may be shaping our behavior because these myths are part of our cultural upbringing and operate at the unconscious level. Eliade suggests that New Year's Eve parties, festivities we take part in when we purchase a new house, celebrations at weddings (tying old shoes to car bumpers), and that kind of thing all have hidden mythic or sacred dimensions.

INTEGRATED MARKETING COMMUNICATION

Integrated marketing communication is defined on the Web page of the *Journal of Marketing Communication*, published at the Medill School at Northwestern University, as follows:

> IMC is a strategic marketing process specifically designed to ensure that all messaging and communication strategies are unified across all channels and are centered around the customer. The IMC process emphasizes identifying and assessing customer prospects, tailoring messaging to customers and prospects that are both serviceable and profitable, and evaluating the success of these efforts to minimize waste and transform marketing from an expense to a profit center.

What it does, as I understand it, is to make sure that the various platforms for sending messages to potential customers, such as general advertising, sales promotion, public relations, and direct response advertising, all work together to maximize the impact of each of these approaches. It sometimes turns out that in large, complex organizations like advertising agencies, the left hand doesn't know what the right hand is doing, and thus the different kinds of advertising work not in harmony but rather at cross-purposes.

Fred Goldberg offers an example:

> It means the adverting should be strategic when it was developed and then
> have its message integrated and compatible with all the other elements of the
> marketing mix. Integrated marketing communications is simply (at least as
> I knew it) making sure that all of the elements (advertising, publicity, sales
> promotion, point of sale, etc.) are working together and communicating
> the same single-minded primary message. For example, take our California
> Cooler campaign—"The Real Stuff." That's what the ads said. The outdoor
> boards said. The point of sale in the end aisle displays in the supermarkets
> said. The hang tags on the bottles said. The carton that held the bottles said.
> You get the idea.

Integrated marketing communications works, I would suggest, on the
principle of the "gestalt." Gestalt psychology argues that something that is
made of many parts is more than the sum of the parts, that the whole is different from the sum of its parts. Also, there is the matter of reinforcement, for
if all of the different kinds of advertising messaging make the same point, it
will make a stronger impact than a series of random and unrelated messages.

STUDY QUESTIONS, APPLICATIONS, AND ASSIGNMENTS

1. What is the Lasswell formula? What are its strengths and weaknesses?
2. Describe the Berger focal points model. What are the four focal
   points? In doing research on advertising, which focal points are
   most important? Explain your answer.
3. What the components of the Jakobson model?
4. If you were to make a communication model, what would it
   look like? Make one in the form of a diagram.
5. What similarities exist among the three models discussed in this
   chapter?
6. What was said about the Lasswell model and "Run It Up a Flagpole to See If Anyone Salutes"?
7. Define metaphor and metonymy and their subcategories simile
   and synecdoche. Find a print advertisement in which you find
   metaphor and metonymy and write a short paper about their role
   in the advertisement. Attach the advertisement to your paper.
8. Let us suppose metaphors have logical implications. If that is the
   case, what are the implications of the metaphor "love is a game"?

9. What was said about metaphor and identity? If you were asked to choose a simple object that reflected your personality, what would you choose?

10. What is the myth model? What are its components? What was said about how myth relates to marketing?

11. What are the basic elements in integrated marketing communication? Do a research project/case study that shows how it works with an advertisement and a campaign for some product or service.

In the second half of the twentieth century in Europe, or at any rate in France, there is nothing—whether object, individual, or social group—that is valued apart from its double, the image that advertises and sanctifies it. This image duplicates not only an object's material, perceptible existence but desire and pleasure that it makes into fictions situating them in the land of make-believe, promising "happiness"—the happiness of being a consumer. Thus publicity [advertising] that was intended to promote consumption is the first of consumer goods; it creates myths—or since it can create nothing—it borrows existing myths, canalizing signifiers to a dual purpose: to offer them as such for general consumption and to stimulate the consumption of a specific object.

—Henri Lefebvre, *Everyday Life in the Modern World*

The knowingness and skepticism of advertising audiences are now taken for granted by advertising professionals and media studies analysts. . . . The knowledge of the audience, and their indifference, pose problems both for the advertisers and for analysts of advertising. For the advertisers, the problem is getting around the skepticism, the knowingness, and the boredom, and still having an effect, or even using these responses for their own purposes. For the analysts, the skepticism and knowingness undermine simplistic critiques of advertising effects, in which people do what ads tell them, accept the roles offered in ads as representations of the world, and take up the positions offered by advertising texts. But if they know how advertising works, does this protect them against its effects? Or is their knowingness limited and ultimately deceptive?

—Greg Myers, *Ad Worlds: Brands/Media/Audiences*

4

RUNNING IT UP A FLAGPOLE
TO SEE IF ANYONE SALUTES

Let me start by offering a somewhat exaggerated account of a typical morning of a typical college student. The heroine of this story is Lisa Greatgal, but I could also use Johnny Q. Public or any number of other male or female figures of varying ages, ethnicities, racial groups, socioeconomic groups, subcultures, and so on.

LISA'S MORNING: A FICTION

Lisa Greatgal got up at 8:30 A.M. and got ready to go to the college, where she was a sophomore. She had a 9:10 class. She shared an apartment near the campus with another girl, Melanie Valleygirl, and a junior at her school, Johnny Q. Public. Lisa put on a Maidenform bra and panties from Nordstroms, a yellow Nike T-shirt with a green swoosh, a pair of faded Polo jeans by Ralph Lauren with torn knees, white Nike anklet socks, and a pair of thick-soled black Doc Martens boots that had become popular in England a few years earlier. She scrubbed her face using Dove soap and brushed her teeth with Colgate Total toothpaste and a Colgate Reach toothbrush. She rinsed her mouth with Listerine mouthwash. She dabbed a bit of Fidji perfume on her neck. Her hair was dyed blond with Loreal Preference hair color. Her eyeglass frames were by Guess?

For breakfast, she had a glass of Ocean Spray Ruby Red and Mango juice (which Martina Hingis says she loves), a bowl of Post Shredded Wheat cereal with Lucerne 1 percent milk, and a cup of Yuban coffee with Carnation evaporated skim milk. She made some toast with Wonder bread and spread Brummel & Brown margarine, made with yogurt, on it. She hastily dumped some textbooks into an L.L. Bean knapsack and rushed off to class, arriving only ten minutes late.

That afternoon, after she had a Boston Carver lunch—a double-sided meat loaf, corn bread, and salad—she got a telephone call from a marketing-survey company. She was asked whether she felt she was influenced by advertising.

"I'm aware of advertising," she replied, "but I'm not influenced by it."

LISA GREATGAL'S AND JOHNNY Q. PUBLIC'S DAILY MEDIA DIET

Lisa Greatgal and Johnny Q. Public are both students, but let's assume their media diet is typical of the American public. According to data from eMarketer, we find the following information about media usage per day:

Medium	2010	2013
Digital	3:14	5:09
Television	4:24	4:31
Radio	1:36	1:26
Print	0:50	0:32
Other	0.42	0:14
Total	10:46	11:52

Source: eMarketer, July 2013.

In 2013, this totals more than eleven hours per day, but because of multitasking, the average number of hours per day is smaller.

Maybe, since they're students, Lisa and Johnny spend a bit more time than around thirty minutes a day reading newspapers and magazines, though on the basis of teaching for almost forty years, I wonder how much time students actually spend reading anything, especially in this era of ever-changing technology. Many students now work, and school is something they have to fit into their busy schedules, and nowadays students and the general population alike read articles and get much of their news online.

We see, then, that Americans spend an enormous amount of time involved in the media of all kinds. It's important to keep in mind that if children watch something like twenty hours of television per week, they are exposed to an enormous number of television commercials. A report on television viewing at http://www.livestrong.com/article/222032-how-much-tv-does-the-average-child-watch-each-day offers the following information:

In 2009, the Nielsen Co. reported that children's television viewing had reached an eight-year high. Children ages 2 to 5 watched TV for more than the product or service being advertised. It used to be a rule of thumb, a few years ago, that the average thirty-second television spot cost around $350,000 to make. If it costs, say, $500,000 now to make a thirty-second commercial, this means that a thirty-minute program, if it cost as much per second as a television commercial, would cost $15 million—which is more than the price of making a low-budget movie.

A NOTE ON "HAULS"

A friend of mine who has his own advertising agency called me recently and said, "Have you seen any of the hauls on YouTube? You might find it interesting." I immediately went to YouTube and typed in "hauls" and found a number of videos, made by young women, who introduced themselves and then displayed clothes that they had recently purchased in stores. Some of them showed their garments and other products with the price tags, but most just showed what they had bought. They often made comments such as "this blouse is really cute. I like it so much I may go back and get another one in a different color." One women complained she didn't think the lipstick she bought looked good on her.

The term "hauls" for this genre of video tells us that these women had "hauled" the things they purchased back to their homes or apartments but distances the process from a word such as "purchased" or "bought." What these videos do is focus on the importance buying clothes has for women. If 93 percent of teenage girls report that shopping is their favorite activity, then the "hauls" show how they spend their money. They reflect a combination of materialism and narcissism: shopping is a word that means looking for things to buy, and making videos for YouTube showing what they have purchased reflects a kind of innocent narcissism. It may also reflect an attempt to escape from a sense of anonymity that many people feel and attempt to assuage by purchasing things. As I explained earlier, playing on Bishop Berkeley's statement, "To buy is to be perceived." Now, with hauls, people can move from being perceived by sales clerks and perhaps a few people in a store to thousands of people on YouTube.

THE PRICE WE PAY FOR "FREE" TELEVISION

The price we pay for "free" television is being exposed to countless commercials. The impact of these commercials is not to be measured only in terms of the pressure they put on us to purchase things; commercials (and advertising in general) have a much more profound impact than we imagine on our consciousness, our identities, our belief systems, our private lives, and our societies and culture in general. It is to these subjects that I now turn in this chapter on what might be generally described as the cultural consequences of the commercial and of the advertising industry in general.

THE ILLUSION OF CONTROL

In May 1998, I received a telephone call from a reporter from the *New York Daily News*. She asked me to comment on a survey that found that many young men and women reported that they were aware of print advertisements and radio and television commercials but felt that they weren't influenced by them. Since the average person watches almost four hours of television per day (it's a bit less for teenagers) and listens to the radio for an hour or so, it's impossible to be unaware of advertisements and commercials.

Insights from Advertising Agencies

When I'm having a hard time thinking something up, I run through the seven deadly sins—sloth, envy, and so on—to look for ideas.

But is it possible to be immune to their influence? That's the question. And is it not likely that the illusion many young people have—that they aren't affected by advertising—contributes to their seduction by the advertisements and commercials to which they are exposed?

We must keep in mind the insight provided to us by Carl Jung, the great Swiss psychologist. Jung wrote in *Man and His Symbols* (1968:22), "Many people mistakenly overestimate the role of willpower and think that nothing can happen to their minds that they do not decide or intend. But we must learn carefully to discriminate between intentional and unintentional contents of the mind." Freudians would make the same point. Sigmund Freud (figure 4.1) argued that there were three levels to the human psyche. One level is consciousness, in which we are aware of what is in our minds. Just below consciousness is a level Freud called preconsciousness, a level we generally don't think about but one we can access if we put our minds to it. And below this level, at the deepest level and one that is not accessible to us, is what Freud called the unconscious.

Figure 4.1. Sigmund Freud is considered to be the father of modern psychoanalytic theory. He is one of the most influential thinkers of the nineteenth century.

Freud explained his notions about the unconscious in his pioneering essay "Psychoanalysis," first published in 1922 (Rieff 1963:235–36):

> It was a triumph of the interpretive art of psychoanalysis when it succeeded in demonstrating that certain common mental acts of normal people, for which no one had hitherto attempted to put forward a psychological explanation, were to be regarded in the same light as the symptoms of neurotics: that is to say, they had a meaning, which was unknown to the subject but which could easily be discovered by analytic means. The phenomena in question were such events as the temporary forgetting of familiar words and names, forgetting to carry out prescribed tasks, everyday slips of the tongue and of the pen, misreadings, losses and mislayings of objects, certain mistakes, instances of apparently accidental self injury, and finally habitual movements carried out seemingly without intention or in play, tunes hummed "thoughtlessly," and so on. All of these were shorn of their physiological explanation, if any such had ever been attempted, and were shown to be strictly determined and were revealed as an expression of the subject's suppressed intentions or as a result of a clash between two intentions one of which was permanently or temporarily unconscious. . . . A class of material was brought to light which is calculated better than any other to stimulate a belief in the existence of unconscious mental acts even in people to whom the hypothesis of something at once mental and unconscious seems strange and even absurd.

According to Freud, we are not aware of everything that goes on in our minds, and, in fact, only a small percentage of our mental activity is accessible to us.

This hypothesis can be best visualized by imagining an iceberg floating in the water. We know that the part of the iceberg floating above the water is only a relatively small part of the iceberg. This part of the iceberg represents our consciousness. We can also dimly make out part of the iceberg that is five

or ten feet below the water. It is accessible to us with a bit of work. That area
represents our preconscious. And the
rest of the iceberg, most of the iceberg,
that exists in the black depths of the
ocean, which we cannot see, represents
our unconscious. It is not accessible to
us unless we have the help of a psychologist or psychiatrist.

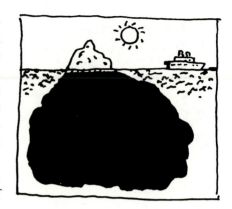

If Freud is correct, something can be
in our minds without our being aware of
it. We can make a preconscious thought
conscious by paying attention to it, and, conversely, something we are conscious
of is no longer so when we stop paying any attention to it. The important thing
about the unconscious is that it affects and in many cases determines many of
our actions, even though we are unaware that it is doing so. We have repressed
much of the material in our unconscious and thus find ourselves doing things at
the "command," so to speak, of forces in our unconscious.

Wilson Bryan Key expands on this point in his controversial book *Subliminal Seduction* (figure 4.2). Key takes Freud's notions about sexuality and
the unconscious and pushes them, some have argued, to ridiculous extremes.
Whatever the case, it is interesting to see how Key explains the power of advertising. He writes (1973:11),

> The basis of modern media effectiveness is a language within a language—one
> that communicates to each of us at a level beneath our conscious awareness,

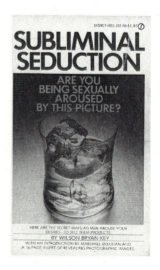

Figure 4.2. *Subliminal Seduction* **makes the argument
that advertising uses many subliminal means to arouse
individuals and get them to purchase things. The ice
cubes on the cover are alleged to have sexual symbols
inside them that affect us.**

one that reaches into the uncharted mechanism of the human unconscious. This is a language based upon the human ability to subliminally or subconsciously or unconsciously perceive information. This is a language that today has actually produced the profit base for North American mass communication media. It is virtually impossible to pick up a newspaper or magazine, turn on a radio or television set, read a promotional pamphlet or the telephone book, or shop through a supermarket without having your subconscious purposely massaged by some monstrously clever artist, photographer, writer, or technician. As a culture, North America might well be described as one enormous, magnificent, self-service, subliminal massage parlor.

Key's thesis—that advertising agencies are using subliminal means that we are not conscious of to persuade us to buy the products and services they are peddling—has never been proved. That is, the notion that certain symbols or phrases are hidden in many print advertisements and commercials (or even products like crackers) is highly questionable. But Key's point about our being susceptible to influences beyond our consciousness is an important one, especially since advertising is so ubiquitous and plays so big a role in our entertainment and our lives.

Insights from Advertising Agencies

You can think of me as an architect. I help translate the desires of the person who wants to have a house built into a plan for the house. Sometimes, of course, our clients don't know what they want. We have a number of groups of people involved in dealing with clients. The brand planner thinks "my consumer." The creative people think "my ad or commercial." The client of the agency thinks "my brand."

This notion is not only held by psychoanalytically oriented scholars. Those with a more behavioral orientation make the same point. This is made clear by an article in the *Wall Street Journal* that suggests that Ivan Pavlov rather than Freud may be the real founder of modern advertising techniques.

Do television commercials make people behave like Pavlov's dogs? Coca-Cola Co. says the answer is yes. In recent years, the Atlanta soft-drink company has been refining an ad-testing procedure based on the behavioral principles developed by the Russian physiologist. So far, Coke says, its new testing system has worked remarkably well.

In his classic experiment, Ivan Pavlov discovered he could get dogs to salivate at the ring of a bell by gradually substituting the sound for a spray of meat powder. Coca-Cola says that, just as Pavlov's dogs began to associate a new meaning with the bell, advertising is supposed to provide some new image or meaning for a product.

Although the specifics of Coke's test are a secret, the company says it attempts to evaluate how well a commercial "conditions" a viewer to accept a positive image that can be transferred to the product. During the past three years, Coca-Cola says, ads that scored well in its tests almost always resulted in higher sales of soft drinks.

"We nominate Pavlov as the father of modern advertising," says Joel S. Dubrow, communications research manager at Coke. "Pavlov took a neutral object and, by associating it with a meaningful object, made it a symbol of something else; he imbued it with imagery, he gave it added value." That, says Mr. Dubrow, "is what we try to do with modern advertising." ("Coca-Cola Turns to Pavlov," *Wall Street Journal*, January 19, 1984, 34)

So whether we buy something because of deep, hidden unconscious forces of the kind Freud and his followers discussed or because we've been "conditioned" like one of Pavlov's dogs to buy it, one fact remains all-important—we've bought something as a result of some process affecting our minds and some advertisement or commercial that an advertiser wanted us to buy.

BEING A "BRANDED" INDIVIDUAL

Lisa Greatgal might be a caricature of a "branded" individual—someone who has been led to purchase only brand-name products (and certain brand-name products, at that)—but she's probably much more representative of what goes on in American households than her opposite, someone who buys only store brands and consults *Consumer Reports* before purchasing most products and services. And, to make matters worse, many people delude themselves into thinking that they don't buy brand-name products, but they actually do. These brand-name products are used to help create an image of oneself for others and to reinforce this assumed identity. We can use clothes, eyeglasses, and other props to create identities for ourselves and to change these identities when we tire of them.

In an article I wrote, "The Branded Self" (*The American Sociology* 42, no. 2 [2011]: 232–39), I suggest that we use brands to obtain a sense of "self" and to provide others with our images of ourselves based on our brands:

This paper suggests that a self, at least a public identity, can be seen, semiotically speaking, as a kind of text that is constructed, in an intertextual way, out of other people's texts, or to be more specific, their branded fashion creations and other similarly branded commodities. Brands, for semioticians, are what Saussure called signifiers (yet they often are identified by icons) that companies use to help establish their identities. The essence of a brand is being "different" from other brands and from generic products. Brands use advertising to establish an image of what they are and who uses their products. Brands, we may say, are pure connotation. Saussure said "in language there are only differences." From a Saussurean perspective we can say "in brands, there are only differences." Brands compete with one another and with generic products or commodities. . . . It is semiotic theory more than anything else . . . that enables us to understand what brands are, how they work and the role they play in consumer decision making.

Branding claims distinctiveness—relative to other brands, that is. If three men or three hundred men wear the same brand of sunglasses, they cannot claim to be distinctive, except in relation to other brands.

It is advertising, more than anything else, that brands use to establish their identities and to portray the kind of people who use or should use that brand. Some brands use celebrities in their advertisement. In other cases, a celebrity or prominent person wears a product that becomes popular. What's important about brand-name products is that when we see a person wearing a certain brand or collection of brands, we get, that is, we believe, a sense of what the

Figure 4.3. This Hermes ad features a naked woman clutching her prized possessions: Hermes handbags.

person using the brands is like—if we have seen advertisements for the brand and know something about it. Branded objects are status symbols and help confer identity on those who use them. If a self is a kind of conversation we have with ourselves, what happens when we get tired of certain brands and switch to others? Is there a kind of dissociation that occurs as we take on a new self based on new brands that we find attractive?

The problem with using brands to shape our sense of self is that we are affected by changes in fashion, meaning that we find ourselves continually changing our "images," and, in the process, any sense of self we had becomes compromised. I would suggest this problem is a reflection of the postmodern sensibility that has so profoundly affected our culture and societies. The following comes from an article, "The Case of the Closet Target," by Martin Solow, who is a copywriter. (It was published in *Madison Avenue* magazine originally.) He describes being invited to a party in Long Island's Nassau County. When his hostess hears that he's in the advertising business, the following takes place (1988):

> "I'm sorry," [the hostess] says, "I never watch TV commercials, I can't stand advertising . . . any advertising." Chimes of approval and assent from the small group around us. I throw up a few defenses, because I know the syndrome: "How do you buy the products you buy?" I want to know. I get a patronizing smile. She buys what she considers best; what Consumer Reports tells her; what she knows (and how does she know, I murmur to myself) to be the best. I excuse myself and ask, since it is a large house, for a roadmap to the bathroom. Once in the large bathroom, the door safely locked, I open the medicine cabinet and survey the contents: Colgate toothpaste, L'Oreal hairspray; Trace II shaving cream and the new Gillette Trac II razor; Ban Roll-On Deodorant (for him, I guess) and Arid Extra Dry (for her—or maybe vice-versa); Bayer aspirins.

Solow goes on, at considerable length, listing the numerous brand-name products he found in the medicine cabinet. Bayer aspirin is significant because, according to *Consumer Reports*, all aspirin is the same, so people who use Bayer aspirin are paying two or three times as much for their aspirin as they would if they bought Rite-Aid aspirin; that is, they really are paying for Bayer's advertising.

It's the same story all the time, he says, which leads him to offer "Solow's First Law: Those who claim they don't watch TV are much more vulnerable to commercials than those who unashamedly do." And when he asks people who use brand-name products why they do, they invariably, as he puts it, "play back the message"—that is, repeat the claim, sometimes verbatim, made by the advertiser in the commercial. Many young children, who watch a great deal of television each day, can sing the lyrics of jingles found in countless commercials. Isn't that cute? we think. Is it possible that we have a subtle form of brainwashing going on here? Or is it that I'm taking something that's actually rather trivial too seriously?

In an unpublished paper, "Suspension of Disbelief as a Bridge between Media and Consumption," social scientist Norbert Wiley of the University of Illinois offers an interesting insight into the relationship between advertising and consumption. The term "the willing suspension of disbelief" was first used by the writer Samuel Taylor Coleridge to describe the way people attending plays and other theatrical productions (and, by extension, films, videos, and other similar kinds of productions) identify with the characters in these works. What happens is that we forget that we are watching a show and become involved in the drama as if we were actually part of it.

Wiley's thesis is that "the suspension of disbelief places customers in a relaxed and unguarded state, such that it is easier to sell them products" (undated:1). He suggests that the owners of stores and the manufacturers of the products in these stores have to infuse products with the suspension of disbelief. He writes,

> They have to get the aesthetic suspension of disbelief somehow into the products, so that people find themselves caught up in fantasy and identified with the things on the shelf. Once that is done, access to the wallet or pocketbook is almost automatic.
>
> A clue to how this might be done is what the shopper might do, or think they might do, with the product. Needs are pretty physical and body-based. We die, or at least languish, without needs. Wants are another matter. They get to be wants, not through elementary body drives, but through the action of the mind. That darling toy, or powerful fishing rod or adorable outfit became a want by thought and fantasy. The advertisers may have dinned us with temptation and suggestion, but at some point we give in to their blandishment. We begin to let the image enter the play of our minds.

Thus, the item we purchase becomes part of our fantasy life, and we suspend disbelief and, in most cases, the strictures of the ego and superego when we buy things.

Figure 4.4. Detail from United Airlines ad based on Freud's id/ego/superego model of the psyche.

As we've seen, Freud posited that our psyches have three components that are in constant conflict at the unconscious level:

> our ids, which represent desire and lust;
> our egos, which represent knowledge of reality;
> our superegos, which represent conscience and guilt.

It is the task of the ego to mediate between our ids and superegos, between our desires on the one hand and our sense of guilt on the other. Our ids provide energy, and our superegos provide restraint. When people have a balance between the id and the superego, all is well. When either the id or the superego is too dominant, we have problems. Much advertising seeks to evade the strictures of our superegos and the reasonableness of our egos and appeal directly to our ids. These contending forces represent those found in the dramas that Wiley talks about. As Wiley concludes, "Fantasying ourselves with the object was the performance and buying is the catharsis," the resolution of the drama with attendant emotional rewards.

Aristotle argued that theatrical performances led to a catharsis, an outpouring of emotion, in the audiences of these works. We need these commodities, Wiley argues, to complete the dramatic performances in which we are caught up. Many sociologists have used theater as a metaphor to explain various aspects of social life, and Wiley's notion that advertising helps us "suspend disbelief" and enter into fantasies in which we use the commodities we purchase for various satisfactions is an excellent example of how the theatrical metaphor can help explain consumer behavior and how people become "branded" and attached to certain products and services. Advertising agencies stress the importance of "branding," which means developing an emotional tie between some product or service and individuals. More precisely, it involves an emotional tie between individuals and the images they have of the product.

In his book *Provocateur: Images of Women and Minorities in Advertising*, Anthony J. Cortese offers a good description of branding. He writes (2004:4),

> Branding—the process of differentiation—is at the core of advertising. What distinguishes similar products is not ingredients but packaging and brand names. Most major shampoos, for example, are made by two or three manufacturers. . . . The major thrust of advertising is to remind shoppers to seek out and purchase a particular brand. Branding seeks to nullify or compensate for the fact that products are otherwise fundamentally interchangeable. Tests have shown that consumers cannot distinguish between their own brand of soap, beer, cigarette, water, cola, shampoo, gasoline from others. In a sense, advertising is like holding up two identical photographs and persuading you that they are different—in fact, that one is better than the other.

Figure 4.5

One of the reasons that we become attached to certain brands is that they help us form an identity. We use brands to differentiate ourselves from other people and to generate images of ourselves to others that we think are positive. We become, so to speak, the sum of our brands. It is the symbolic value of brands, not the functions of the products, that become most important.

And once established, it is relatively easy for brands to extend themselves. For example, the Mont Blanc pen company, which has a reputation for making outstanding fountain pens, now sells expensive watches (figure 4.5).

There is what might be called a "halo effect" that transfers from the Mont Blanc fountain pens to its watches. Once a brand becomes very popular, it is often the case that we find brand extension, and the brand is used to sell other products. At the core of branding is a sense of confidence people develop that the brands they use are good and reflect positively on them. Branding, we may say, sells the sizzle, not the steak.

SELLING ONESELF

In a marketing society like the United States, we learn to market ourselves, and using brand names gives anxiety-ridden people a sense of security that they believe will enhance the job of selling themselves that they feel they must do. Personality is the product, so to speak. The term "personality" has its root in the Latin word "persona," which means "mask." So our personalities are masks we wear to sell ourselves to others—to become popular, to market ourselves, to find a job or a mate, whatever. The matter is complicated because almost everyone we meet is in the same bind—we are always (with few exceptions) marketing ourselves to others, and they are marketing themselves to us. And much of this marketing—another term might be "manipulation"—is done by using products that announce to others our sense of who we are and, by implication, what our socioeconomic level is and what kind of taste we have. I knew someone who wanted to work in advertising. He wore Robert Hall cheapie suits in a world where, at the time, rather expensive Brooks Brothers and J. Press suits were what advertising people wore. The people in the advertising agencies took one look at him in his Robert Hall suit and thought, "Not one of us!"

Willy Loman, the hero of Arthur Miller's play *Death of a Salesman*, is an example of a person who thinks he can sell himself on the basis of his winning personality but who ends up, in fact, alienated and lonely. Literary scholars debate whether Loman (low man) is pathetic or tragic. Fritz Pappenheim, a Marxist scholar, has written a book, *The Alienation of Modern Man,* that describes Loman. Pappenheim writes (1967:34),

> Many individuals have found their own lives portrayed in Arthur Miller's *Death of a Salesman*. It shows Willy Loman—the "other directed man" personified—striving all his life to be popular and "liked" but remaining absolutely lonesome and irrelevant, forever dreaming that "personality wins the day" but in reality destined, as his wife fears, "to fall into his grave like an old dog."

People who see this play often have a powerful response to it, in part because Miller deals with the myths about success in America and with the alienation that is so pervasive in American society—and, Marxists would argue, other societies as well.

We may construct our identities on things we buy, but the products we use keep changing, meaning that our personas, to the extent that they are intimately connected to the products we use, keep changing also. And our sense of ourselves—whether we are "successes or failures"—is tied, we are taught by advertising, to what we can afford. Of course, there are people who are frauds—who drive cars and wear clothes that really are too expensive for them; they are putting on a front. And there is the reverse—wealthy people who drive and dress poor (at least in public, that is). Our personas, then, are to a considerable degree products based on the material culture—our clothes, our smart phones, and our automobiles—that we make part of our lives. And so we are doomed to constant change because fashion is based on constant change. This is part of our postmodern world, in which we sample different styles and identities to suit our whims. The problem is that identity suggests some kind of coherence, and a constantly changing identity is a contradiction in terms.

SELLING ONE'S BODY FOR BRANDS

Dan Bilefsky, in the *New York Times* (March 16, 2010, 8), reviews a fictional Polish film *Galerianki* or *Mall Girls*, which deals with a group of young women who sleep with men so they can afford to dine in expensive restaurants and purchase mobile phones, designer handbags, and other brand-name clothing to "support their clothing addiction." The director of the film, Katarzyna Roslaniec, based the film on young women she noticed loitering in malls in Poland. Many of these "mall girls," who tend to be from fourteen to sixteen years old, are from middle-class families. The film caused a sensation when it was shown in Poland and prompted debates on materialism and "moral decadence" in contemporary Poland. These girls do not identify themselves as prostitutes, and they maintain some kind of an illusion that they are turning tricks in shopping mall restrooms and in the backs of automobiles with their "boyfriends." A Polish social worker in Krakow, Marcin Drewniak, who counsels young girls suggests that the behavior of these "mall girls" represents an attempt to obtain self-esteem.

This matter of young girls prostituting themselves to purchase brand-name purses and other things also exists in Japan and other countries as well. In Japan, many young schoolgirls sleep with middle-aged businessmen in order to have money to buy things they want. They describe their behavior as "compensated dating," and this behavior is spreading to other countries as well. What this "mall girl" and "compensated dating" phenomenon represents is the power of brands to shape the behavior of impressionable young women who feel that prostituting themselves is a small price to pay for being able to purchase the brands of handbags and cell phones they desire.

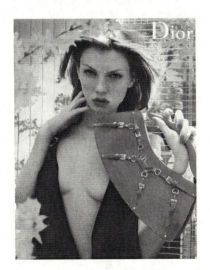

Figure 4.6. The semi-exposed breasts of the model, clutching her handbag, suggest, from a psychoanalytic perspective, that there is an unconscious connection between women's handbags and their sexuality.

THE PROBLEM OF SELF-ALIENATION

What happens, ultimately, is that we become alienated from ourselves; we learn to see ourselves as infinitely malleable "material" that we can mold whenever we have the whim to do so to suit our purposes. But the cost of all of this is a kind of estrangement from any true self that we might have been able to fashion. We become so absorbed in manipulating others that we don't recognize that we have also manipulated our own sense of self and our own identity—or is it identities? In modern capitalist societies, there is—to give the Devil his due—a kind of dynamism and excitement that is not found in some traditional societies, where people have worn the same costume, handed down by tradition, for hundreds of years if not longer. These traditional societies are, let me suggest, a polar opposite of the postmodern societies of modern industrialized nations. There is a kind of stagnation on one extreme and a kind of restless, mind-numbing change at the other. What we must do is find some kind of middle ground that allows for change but does not lead to alienation and estrangement.

I see advertising as one of the central institutions in modern societies, and thus it is important we learn to understand better how advertisements and radio and television commercials work and how they help shape our consciousness. We have to realize that fashion, style, and lifestyle—all of these concerns—are forms of collective behavior. An individual— Lisa Greatgal—reaches out her hand at a supermarket and chooses this or that item. But behind this seemingly free choice, there are all kinds of forces at work that have led to that choice. Lisa, I argue (and all those like Lisa), has been manipulated by the advertising industry but is unaware that this has happened. All she knows is that this skirt or pair of

shoes or jeans or hairstyle that was "hot" last year suddenly looks dull and isn't fashionable anymore.

And Lisa's sense of style and fashion, her desire to be "with it," to have the "hot" things, profoundly affects her choices of friends, mates, restaurants, pets, cars, homes, jobs, clothes, foods, colleges, vacations and tourism destinations, and almost everything else one can think of. The term "affects" is crucial here, for there are often other factors involved in the choices we make in life.

The question of how much autonomy we have and how free we are to make choices leads to a step back in history and the ideas of one of America's most powerful thinkers, Jonathan Edwards.

WE CAN CHOOSE AS WE PLEASE, BUT CAN WE PLEASE AS WE PLEASE?

In the 1740s, the Puritan minister Jonathan Edwards, one of the greatest minds America has produced, tried to reconcile his belief in man's free will with God's omnipotence. He asked, How can man be free if God is all-powerful? His answer was ingenious and quite relevant to our interest in advertising. Edwards argued that there were two realms to be considered: the realm of action and the realm of choice. Men and women are free to act as they wish, suggesting that we have free will. That is, we can act as we please. But in the realm of choice, God is all-powerful and all-determining. Although we can act as we please, we can't please as we please; God determines what will please us. This means, in effect, that we have only the illusion of freedom. For though we can do anything we want to do, God has already determined what it is that we will want to do.

In an introduction to Edwards's *Freedom of Will* (1754), Norman Foerster explains Edwards's ideas as follows (1957:86–87):

> Edwards argues that all acts of will, like events in physical nature, are subject to the law of causation. Since an act of will has its cause in a previous act of will, and this in turn in an earlier one, we must eventually arrive at a first act, which was necessarily caused by the agent's inborn disposition. Having traced the whole series backward to the start, we come to realize that the will has no independent activity but is merely passive and mechanical. Man does have freedom, to be sure, in the sense that he feels no compulsion or restraint but can "do as he pleases." Yet his will cannot determine what he pleases to do. He is free to act as he chooses, but has no freedom of choice.

Thus, because our choices are determined for us, though we can act as we wish, we have only the illusion of freedom. For Edwards, it was an all-powerful God who determined what our choices would be; in contemporary mass-mediated societies, God has been replaced, let me suggest, by advertising agencies and marketing consultants. We can make an argument similar to Edwards's about the role of advertising and our free choice, except that advertising is not all-powerful, just very powerful, and part of its power stems from the fact that we don't recognize how advertising shapes our consciousness and helps determine how we act. Table 4.1 shows these relationships more graphically.

Table 4.1. Freedom and Determinism Compared

Freedom	*Determinism*
Individuals	God (now advertising agencies)
Realm of action	Realm of choice
We act as we please	God (now advertising agencies) determines what pleases us
John buys Colgate	Advertising agencies have helped make John want to buy
Total toothpaste	Colgate Total toothpaste

There is a fascinating image that brings this matter of freedom and determinism into sharp relief. We find it on the cover of Wolfgang Haug's book *Critique of Commodity Aesthetics* (figure 4.7). It is a photograph of pigeons in St. Mark's Square in Venice that have been lured there to eat corn and that form the word "Coca-Cola." Workers scattered birdseed that spelled out "Coca-Cola," and the pigeons gathered to eat the birdseed. The pigeons were free to do whatever they wanted to do, in theory, but we know that when pigeons find birdseed available, they will fly to wherever it is and eat it. As Haug explains (1986:118),

> The pigeons did not gather with the intention of forming the trademark but to satisfy their hunger. But equally the seed was not scattered to feed the pigeons but to employ them on its tracks as extras. The arrangement is totally alien and external to pigeons. While they are consuming their feed, capital is subsuming, and consuming, them. This picture, a triumph of capitalist advertising technique, symbolizes a fundamental aspect of capitalism.

The moral we can take away from this photo is that while we are pursuing our private interests, without our being aware of it, we are often being mo-

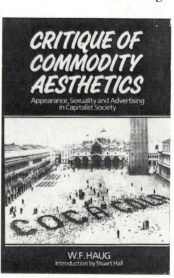

Figure 4.7. The photograph on the cover of this book shows birds forming the word Coca-Cola. The author, Wolfgang Fritz Haug, tied this image to the way people are influenced by advertising and other aspects of consumer culture.

tivated and manipulated by forces of which we are unaware, in their interest. Of course, people are not pigeons and are much more complicated, but we can, in certain situations, be motivated to do things that are not always based on rational thought about what's in our best interest. I am exaggerating and simplifying things, of course. But this little scenario—and ones like it—is acted out countless times in a given day by millions of people who "choose" this brand or that brand of some product and who don't recognize the extent to which their actions have been shaped or, to use a stronger term, manipulated by the numerous print advertisements and commercials they've seen. Many of these advertisements and commercials are brilliant works that involve glamour, sex, drama, humor, and various aesthetic and rhetorical devices to attract our attention and stimulate our desire.

Advertisements and commercials obviously aren't 100 percent effective. If they were, we'd probably buy whichever product we saw advertised last. But companies don't spend hundreds of millions of dollars advertising their products and services for the fun of it. They expect that when they run their product or service "up the flagpole," that is, when they advertise it, people will salute—by purchasing the product. And if people (not just anyone, of course, but the right people) don't salute or don't salute enough, the companies get a different advertising agency—one that promises that it can achieve the desired results, that is, that it can make people salute.

THE AGONY OF CHOICE

A psychologist, Barry Schwartz, discussed what might be described as "the agony of choice" in his book *The Paradox of Choice*. He had an experience of going into a store and asking for a pair of jeans that led him to think about the problems consumers face when they decide to purchase certain products. In his article "When It's All Too Much," he writes about what happened when he went into a Gap store to buy a pair of jeans. He writes (Schwartz 2004:4),

> One day I went into the Gap to buy a pair of jeans. A salesperson asked if she could help. "I want a pair of jeans—32-28," I said. "Do you want them slim fit, relaxed fit, baggy or extra baggy?" she replied. "Do you want them stone-washed, acid-washed, or distressed? Do you want them button fly or zipper-fly? Do you want them faded or regular?"

This experience alerted him to how many different decisions must be made to purchase certain products since there are so many different versions that are available. These increased choices have not made us happier but, it turns out, have decreased our sense of well-being.

He concluded that there are two kinds of consumers, what he called "maximizers" and "satisfizers." The basic characteristics of these two groups are shown below:

Maximizers	**Satisfizers**
Must have the best	Good enough is acceptable
Very high expectations	Modest or low expectations
Anxiety	Ease

The problem the maximizers have is that no matter how good a deal they got on some purchase, they always are troubled by the notion that they could have done better if they looked around more. Searching for the "best deal" led to the maximizers becoming very stressed and anxiety ridden. He suggests that people would do well to avoid trying to maximize and settle for good enough. What his theory suggests is that advertising may lead a person to desire a certain product or service but that, due to personality characteristics of certain people, the implementation of that desire by purchasing that product or service can be very stressful. Implicit in Schwartz's theory is the notion that most people are maximizers.

His ideas may explain why our fantasies about our purchases tend to fade very quickly when we face the reality of buying them and even faster once we have bought them—especially in those cases in which people suffer "buyer's remorse." In such cases, we decide that we made a mistake in purchasing whatever it is we bought, but we blame ourselves and not the advertisements and commercials that persuaded us to buy the product.

NONADVERTISING FORMS OF ADVERTISING

As a result of the development of new technologies such as TiVo (which enables people to record television programs on a hard disk and eliminate all commercials), advertisers have had to find new ways to get television viewers to purchase products and services. One of the most insidious developments has been the spread of "product placements." Advertising agencies pay film companies to have scriptwriters include products they want to push in films and in other media. Thus, the product is integrated into the action of a film, and advertisers get the "halo" effect of having a famous actor or actress actually use a product. For example, advertisers put Pepto-Bismol into *Law and Order* and Bud Light into *Survivor*. There are many other examples that could be given. One added benefit of product placements is that they serve as the equivalent of a testimonial for the product or service by the performer.

One of the most notorious cases of product placement involves what was called a "literatisement." Bulgari, a maker of very expensive jewelry, hired well-known novelist Fay Weldon to write a story featuring Bulgari jewels in it. She came up with a thriller called *The Bulgari Connection*. Ellen Goodman wrote a column on this book, lamenting the development of what she called "literatisement" or "litads." Weldon, Goodman notes, was attacked for being the first well-known author to "erase the line between literature and advertising." By this, she meant serious literature; advertising can be seen, I would suggest, as a form of literature and can be analyzed by the same methods used to interpret higher forms of literature.

There is yet another form of advertising that is not recognized as such—reviews of films, television shows, plays, restaurants, vacation resorts, and anything else that involves people paying for goods and services. These reviews, whether they are positive or not, call the reader's attention to whatever is being reviewed. Over the course of time, many people come to regard certain reviewers as being accurate and having "good taste," so their reviews function, for these readers, as the equivalent of a word-of-mouth endorsement.

Google and other search engines have made billions of dollars when they recognized that people who were searching for information could be looked on as target audiences. These search engines scan messages and provide sites where people using the search engine can find products related to their interests, as reflected in the topic they are investigating. This kind of advertising is very effective since it zeroes in, very directly, on the interests of the person doing the searching.

Another important change from traditional mass-mediated advertising involves the development of what is described as "in-store" advertising. An article by Emily Nelson and Sarah Ellison on the first page of the September 21, 2005, *Wall Street Journal* describes the phenomenon under the title "In a Shift, Marketers Beef Up Ad Spending inside Store." As the reporters note,

> Procter & Gamble Co. believes shoppers make up their mind about a product in about the time it takes to read this paragraph. The "first moment of truth," as P&G calls it, is the three to seven seconds when someone notices an item on a store shelf. Despite spending billions on traditional advertising, the consumer products giant thinks this instant is one of its most important marketing opportunities. It created a position 18 months ago, Director of First Moment of Truth, or Director of FMOT (pronounced "EFF-mott"), to produce sharper, flashier in-store displays. . . . P&G's insight is helping to power a shift in the advertising business: the grown and increasing sophistication of in-store marketing. . . . Now, in response to the fragmentation of television and print ads, it wants to tout its brands directly to consumers where they're most likely to be influenced: the store.

This phenomenon was described by the German media scholar Wolfgang Fritz Haug some twenty years ago in his book *Critique of Commodity Aesthetics*, in which he discussed what might be described as the "aesthetization," beautification, and sexualization of stores and the buying experience. He discusses the idea of the director of Globus, a German department store, named Kaufmann, whose name means "salesman" or "trader." Kaufmann's ideas are found in his book *The Key to the Consumer*. Haug discusses Kaufmann's ideas and the notion of making buying an aesthetic experience (1986:68, 69):

> The commodities are no longer arranged to be displayed in their traditional categories "but should be arranged thematically to fulfill the needs and dreams of the buyers." One must not confront the buyer brusquely with a commodity but "guide them into the entertainment.". . . The exhibition of commodities, their inspection, the act of purchase, and all the associated moments, are integrated into the concept of one theatrical total work of art which plays upon the public's willingness to buy. Thus the salesroom is designed as a stage, purpose-built to convey entertainment to its audience that will stimulate a heightened desire to spend. "On this stage the sale is initiated. This stage is the most important element in sales promotion."

This aesthetic innovation of the salesroom into a "stage for entertainment" on which a variety of commodities are arranged to reflect the audience's dreams, to overcome their reservations, and to provoke a purchase was a pioneering exercise at a time marked by a general change in the selling trend. Haug adds that the Globus department store became a "Mecca" for retailers all over the world who wanted to find out how to transform their stores the way Kauffman had transformed Globus.

We can see, then, that as print media, radio, and television—traditional venues for advertising—decline, advertising agencies and the corporations they work for have been finding new ways of getting their messages across, using devices such as product placement, Internet advertising (including studying blogs to see how people feel about certain products and services), making stores like theaters so that purchasing becomes an aesthetically satisfying experience, and developing in-store advertising.

STUDY QUESTIONS, APPLICATIONS, AND ASSIGNMENTS

1. Update the brands that Lisa uses.
2. What were the most interesting statistics in the eMarketer "Average Time Spent with Media" tables?

3. What is a haul? View some on YouTube and describe what was purchased and your reactions to them.

4. What did Freud say about the unconscious? Did the drawing of the iceberg help you understand the relationship between consciousness and the unconscious? If so, why?

5. What did Freud say about the id, ego, and superego? Do you think buying things is an id or an ego function? Explain your answer.

6. What did Wilson Bryan Key say about the power of advertising and the role of the unconscious in advertising?

7. What is Ivan Pavlov's theory? How does it relate to advertising? How does it differ from Freud's in explaining behavior?

8. What is branding? What role do brands play in our lives?

9. Are there certain brands of products you use? Why? What made you decide to select one brand over the others?

10. What did Martin Solow say about people's relation to brands?

11. How does the "suspension of disbelief" shape our purchasing behavior?

12. What did Anthony J. Cortese say about branding?

13. What was said about "mall girls" and selling oneself for brands?

14. How does branding lead to self-alienation?

15. What did Jonathan Edwards say about the relation between choice and action? How does it relate to our purchasing behavior? What does it mean to say that "we can choose as we please, but we cannot please as we please"?

16. What is the difference between maximizers and satisfizers? Which are you?

17. Do a research study of nonadvertising advertising, such as "product placements." How do product placements work?

18. What was Kaufmann's contribution to our understanding of consumer behavior?

Item: **daring campaign:** models wearing only body paint with strategically placed oranges are part of a new campaign from Campari, an Italian aperitif. The brand import by Diageo's UDV of Fort Lee, N.J., has an initial bitter taste. The pitch suggests drinking Campari with orange juice, in hopes of accelerating sales growth in the U.S., as happened in international markets. The ads were created by Mullen Advertising.

—*Wall Street Journal*

Advertisers have an enormous financial stake in a narrow ideal of femininity that they promote, especially in beauty product ads. . . . The image of the beautiful woman . . . may perhaps be captured with the concept of the perfect provocateur (an ideal image that arouses a feeling or reaction). The exemplary female prototype in advertising, regardless of product or service, displays youth (no lines or wrinkles), good looks, sexual seductiveness . . . and perfection (no scars, blemishes, or even pores). . . . The perfect provocateur is not human; rather, she is a form or hollow shell representing a female figure. Accepted attractiveness is her only attribute. She is slender, typically tall and long-legged. Women are constantly held to this unrealistic standard of beauty. If they fail to attain it, they are led to feel guilty and ashamed. Cultural ideology tells women that they will not be desirable to, or loved by, men unless they are physically perfect.

—Anthony J. Cortese, *Provocateur:*
Images of Women and Minorities in Advertising

5

SEXUALITY AND GENDER
IN ADVERTISING

The exploitation of the female body (figure 5.1)—and more recently the male body (figure 5.2)—for advertising is a common critique of the advertising industry. Women—and now men—are made into sex objects, used to sell everything from automobiles to toothpaste, though women are exploited much more than men in advertising. As Tina Pieraccini and Robert Schell point out in their article "You're Not Getting Older—You're Getting Better," (in C. M. Lont, ed., *Women and Media: Content/Careers/Criticism* [2014:121–29]),

> Women have traditionally been exploited by some advertisers to sell products. And in the process, myths about women have been reinforced. Advertisers have sold us myths that all women must be thin. Advertisers have sold American women the myth that the ideal woman is blond. Media campaigns have reinforced the myth that women must remain youthful to be desirable. The myth communicated is that product use makes a woman sexy. The reality is that sex sells.

This exploitation of woman is commonly recognized, but it still dominates our advertising because, as the authors point out, sex sells.

One problem with advertising is that it has the uncanny ability to resist being affected by critiques of it. Attacking advertising is like throwing thumb-

Figure 5.1. The Ungaro advertisement is highly suggestive and far-fetched at the same time.

Figure 5.2. This advertisement uses the body of the model to stimulate male and female lust. Note the bent knee in the ad. What is the significance of the bent knee in ads?

tacks in the path of a herd of stampeding elephants. As Judith Williamson points out in *Decoding Advertisements: Ideology and Meaning in Advertising* (1978:167),

> Advertisements [ideologies] can incorporate anything, even re-absorb criticisms of themselves, because they refer to it, devoid of content. The whole system of advertising is a great recuperator: it will work on any material at all, it will bounce back uninjured from both advertising restriction laws and criticisms of its basic functions.

It is helpful, nevertheless, to examine one of the most important and most often criticized aspects of advertising—its sexism and its "sexploitation" of the female body to sell products and services.

SEX AND GENDER IN ADVERTISING

In his book *The Signs of Our Time: The Secret Meanings of Everyday Life*, Jack Solomon discusses the difference between sex and gender from a semiotic perspective and writes (1990:194–95),

> When examining the codes that govern our sexual behavior, semioticians distinguish between the biological category of sex and the cultural category of gender. Your sex is determined by nature, and the physiological and anatomical characteristics that accompany it are (barring surgery) largely beyond cultural control. Culture can't change the fact that women are born with a

biological capacity for bearing children which men lack, or that men generally have larger and thus stronger muscles that do women. But culture does define the roles that men and women play in political and sexual society, and to this extent divides the two sexes into opposing genders whose behavioral codes reflect the mythological beliefs of the societies in which they appear.

We have to keep the difference between sex and gender in mind and the cultural codes of various societies tied to gender as we examine the way advertising uses sexuality to attract our attention and look for the codes and myths advertisers use to convince us to buy whatever it is they are trying to sell us. Generally speaking, there's much more to advertisements and commercials than we imagine, and they work in ways that we often cannot explain.

In the article "Primping or Pimping" (*San Francisco Chronicle*, September 26, 2000), Valli Herman-Cohen discusses some "raunchy" sexually explicit fashion ads:

> Fashion's plunge into soft porn didn't happen overnight. In the 1960s, the late French photographer Guy Bourdin brought sex and violence to French fashion magazines, while his American counterpart, photographer Helmut Newton, added a fetishistic element beginning in the 1970s. Now lesbian sex and sadomasochism have been added to the lineup.
>
> Tongues wagged over this year's taboo-touting campaigns for French designers Emmanuel Ungaro and Christian Dior. For Ungaro's spring ads, a model offered suggestive interpretations of "petting" as she caressed her male pooch. This fall, Ungaro used the same model, who intimately embraced a nude classical statue. For Dior's spring 2000 and new fall ads, two women tumbled in designers togs like lovers experimenting in a clothes dryer.

These ads seem to have struck a responsive chord, for when asked about his advertisements, Ungaro said that his "sales have gone through the roof." A look at any high-fashion magazine shows any number of fashion ads that are best described as soft porn. Many of the models have their blouses wide open, revealing most of their breasts, and there is an atmosphere of sexual obsession and decadence that pervades the advertising. Notice in figure 5.1 how the pointed white area leads the eye directly to the model's breasts, which are lighted to give them maximum impact.

SEX IN ADVERTISING

John Berger's *Ways of Seeing* explores human sexuality as one of the most potent tools of advertising. Berger points out that advertising makes greater and greater use of sexuality to sell products and services. As he explains (1972:144),

Figure 5.3. In this Bulgari advertisement, notice how the snake's head directs our attention to the model's breasts and her cleavage.

> This sexuality is never free in itself, it is a symbol for something presumed to be larger than it: the good life in which you can buy whatever you want. To be able to buy is the same thing as being sexually desirable.

The implicit message in advertising is, Berger adds, that if you can buy a given product, you'll be lovable, and if you can't, you'll be less lovable. This means that purchasing products and services is always charged with fantasies and dreams of sexual desirability and power, even though we may not be conscious that such is the case.

Berger's theory explains, for example, why we often see beautiful young women in ads for automobiles, beer, fashions, and so on, ad infinitum. Although this process works in our unconscious, we make a connection between buying a product and becoming desirable to (or emulating) these women. For other products, handsome men are used in the same way. The subtext of many advertisements, then, involves the matter of sexuality and desirability, which explains why the act of buying things is so important to people and yields such great anticipated pleasures. The foundation of modern consumer societies, then, is human sexuality.

It is generally assumed in the advertising industry that there is some kind of a transfer of desire from male lust for sexually attractive women to the products that are being sold. Since it is women who are generally exploited for their sexuality, I will focus on them, but let me point out that there is also a growing use of male sexuality and homoerotic images and scenarios in selling products.

In theory, seeing a beautiful woman in a print advertisement or commercial with a certain amount of cleavage showing and revealing other parts

Figure 5.4. This section of an ad, part of a two-page spread, is unusual in that it shows a nude woman. Her bent knee hides her pubic hair. Which is more erotic: this ad or the Bulgari snake necklace ad?

of her body "excites" men and women who are exposed to the image. In television commercials, the woman can gaze at and directly address viewers, adding the power of the voice to the desired seduction of the viewer. In many commercials, the sexuality of the women is enhanced by lighting, by camera angles, by cutting, and by all the other techniques available to editors. Some advertising agencies have been attacking the stereotypes of women in commercials by using women who are not tall and slender but more normal—in some cases even "pleasingly plump" or heavy.

In his book *Visual Persuasion: The Role of Images in Advertising*, Paul Messaris offers an interesting insight into the use of very slender models in fashion advertising. He discusses studies of male preferences of physical attractiveness in women that give higher ratings to heavy women with narrow waists than slender women with narrow hips. He writes (1997:49),

> Superficially, this preference for thin models among fashion executives may seem to be a perverse, and persistent, miscalculation. But of course, that is not the case. The fashion industry's predilection for thinness does not stem from a misreading of real-world sex cues; rather, it represents a deliberate suppression of those sex cues to heighten the sense of the human body as pure status display. In other words, this situation could be described as a conflict between sexual and social status cues, with the latter coming out on top.

What Messaris reveals is that there is often a sociological and class aspect to the images of women found in advertisements and that the sexual characteristics of the women found in advertisements is not the whole story.

Figure 5.5

This advertisement was a full page one in the April 17th edition of the *New York Times*. It features the name of the fragrance, BONBON, in large letters across the top of the page. Underneath we see a woman, seated with her legs crossed, with her hair combed back and her hand on her face, as in a gesture of surprise. She is naked and ribbons with bows are found across her torso, covering the nipple on her left breast. Her right arm covers her right breast and leads our eyes down past her right breast to a very large pink bottle of the fragrance. The caption underneath the model reads,

> Untie the bow with an exclusive personal appearance
> Of fashion designers Viktor & Rolf
> Today at Saks Fifth Avenue
> Fifth Avenue and 49th Street
> 5:30 PM—6:30 PM
> The New Feminine Fragrance
> VIKTOR & ROLF
> Exclusively at Saks Fifth Avenue and Saks.com

I found this advertisement interesting and puzzling. Advertising seeks to gain our attention and this advertisement certainly gained my attention, in part because it exploits feminine sexuality and in part because it seems to have contradictory messages. Let me suggest some notions about it that are worth considering. The woman is Edita Vilkeviciute, a supermodel from Lithuania.

1. Nakedness suggests innocence. Adam and Eve were naked in the Garden of Eden but didn't realize they were until they ate the

forbidden apple. The pink color of the product also suggests innocence and perhaps childhood, when little girls are often dressed in pink. The color could trigger regressive fantasies in women, enabling them to return, in their imagination, to their childhoods and happy days. She is also wearing pink lipstick and does not have earrings or any jewelry.

2. BONBON literally means "good, good" in French. It is a kind of candy—usually with a soft center and a chocolate cover—and has strong oral associations. It strikes me as curious that a fancy fragrance would be named after a candy, but it may be the Frenchness of the term that was basic in naming the product. The French are associated, in the public mind, with perfumes and with "sophistication." The product has been described as having "caramel notes" along with mandarin, orange, and peach. The *Urban Dictionary* defines "bon bons" as "small and nicely shaped titties."

3. The typography is very simple and incorporates axial balance, suggesting formality. Axial balance has a rather static quality. We often find axial balance and a great deal of white or "empty" space in advertisements for upscale products. The typeface is very simple also suggesting upscale elegance.

4. The model is both feminine and hyperphallic. Her hair, tied (or perhaps "bound" is a better word) tightly behind her head, suggests a man's hairstyling, and she has a huge bottle that vaguely resembles a penis close to her crotch. The position of the bottle and its design strike me as phallic. The bottle is very large and vaguely resembles a bow but could be testicles, and it has a very large cap that gives it a phallic quality. It hides her pubic hair. Her right arm covers her right breast and also leads our eyes directly to the bottle of BONBON. Freud asked, "What do women want?," and BONBON seems to suggest the answer—a fragrant penis.

5. The nipple on her left breast is covered by a bow that we are invited to untie. If we untie all the bows, she will be completely naked. The lighting of the model, with shadows, emphasizes and calls our attention to her breast. If you look carefully at the ribbon around her left breast, you see that it must have been glued to her stomach and that many of the other ribbons with bows were also glued to her stomach.

6. The fact that she is tied up with bows represents a feminization of bondage and thus has sadomasochistic overtones or, perhaps, suggestions about some kind of kinky sex.

7. The copy in the *New York Times* ad uses the terms "exclusive" and "exclusively" that suggest its upscale quality—reserved for those

elements in society that can afford it. Marxists would suggest this ad, with it bondage and exclusivity, reflects the decadence of the upper classes, who maintain social distance from the masses.
8. The product is called a feminine fragrance rather than a perfume. Perfumes are for women, but the term "fragrance" has a unisex quality about it, though it is not very likely that men would use a product that has been described as looking like wrapped candy in a large pink bottle.
9. SAKS appeal and sex appeal. The address of SAKS, on Fifth Avenue and 49th Street, is one for upscale establishments.

This advertisement, I suggest, is loaded with sexual symbols of all kinds, which it uses to attract our attention and sell the product. The typical reader of a newspaper or magazine, where the ads are placed, glances at an ad for a second or two, but in that short period of time, the visual aspects in the advertisement do their work.

A semiotician friend of mine from England, Greg Rowland, offers the following analysis of the advertisement:

Well, it's damn sexy isn't it? And of course I should feel bad about thinking that. But I'm fighting 2 million years of evolutionary urges here. So what can I do? Politically and semiotically it's a stunning representation of how Ironic Post-Feminist tropes enable a literal objectification of women's sexuality in a way that would have been completely unacceptable even in the 1960s. Because the commodification and objectification of the body is so very explicit (she is a confection wrapped up, ready for consumption, commodified by girlish S&M straps) the image invites us both to decry the obscene patriarchal excess behind the idea, and to simultaneously celebrate the sheer creative bravado of this massively un-PC statement. The image is so powerful precisely because we (and I speak as heterosexual men here) can vacillate between hormonal titillation and a political ironic distance. The ironic aspect, brought by the excess of counter-feminist cues, is empowering for the male viewer. Not only can he own the woman as object, but he can own the woman as an ironic statement about breaking the taboos of feminist culture. SO the male viewer is doubly empowered, doubly enticed here. And it goes without saying that the product placement shot represents a phallic state of arousal, carefully angled (perhaps after extensive geometric research) to express masculine arousal in a far more palpable way than if the bottle were to be placed standing upright. There's no biology in perfect angles. Of course those spiky things attached to the bottle (which I can't decode rationally) may be the woman's revenge for the subjugation of the male gaze. She actually has a large purple penis that has metal spikes on it. Perhaps that's the real surprise when you unwrap the gift. Perhaps that's why the model gives us this curious stare. On the one hand it's a pretty conventional image of sexual arousal for the male viewer (and indeed female gaze). On the other hand her slightly shocked, slightly perturbed hand to her face may be questioning her own compliance with her commodification. If so, then that's an even more finely tuned ironic get out of feminist jail free card for the male viewer. She knows it's wrong, you know it's wrong, but it's in an unforgettable present, extending our subsumed guilt about sex, and testifying to the power of the guilty pleasure, of ownership and consummation of a moment/body without consequence, is a powerfully attractive sin. And who are we, as men, to say that a woman can't commodify herself this way, given appropriate material, emotional and erotic reward, as a freethinking erotic entity. To own the process of one's own commodification may be liberating. I'm not sure that this is the case with this ad, but it's certainly explicitly illustrative of the idea and possibility of gifting oneself. Of course this ad could not be made with a black model. The subjugation would connote slavery in a literal rather than erotic and playful sense. So the power to subjugate oneself depends, perhaps on level of social power in the first place. It's a really good ad.

These aspects in fashion advertising—and other kinds of advertising as well—are shown by other things than body shape and involve such matters as the context where the woman is shown, her props, the kind of clothes she is wearing (or almost wearing in some cases), her hairstyle, and her facial characteristics. It could be argued, in fact, that many of the models in fashion advertisements are reflecting their unavailability and sense of separateness and alienation from ordinary concerns and everyday life. Fashion advertising, more than any other kind, I would suggest, generates stereotypes of what women are supposed to look like—and act like. The effects of these stereotypes, which involve being beautiful and yet, as you can see from many of the poses, submissive, are very pernicious. The mixture of sex and sociological and cultural matters means that there is often a great deal more to sexually exciting and erotically stimulating advertising than we might imagine.

SEXPLOITATION AND ANXIETY

Sexuality, sexual desire, sexual lust, and even intimations of sexual intercourse are ubiquitous in contemporary advertising. As Germaine Greer points out in *The Female Eunuch* (1971:51–52),

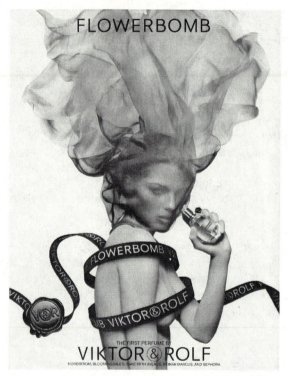

Figure 5.6. This advertisement exploits female sexuality and fantastic imagery to sell a fragrance.

Because she is the emblem of spending ability and the chief spender, she is also the most effective seller of this world's goods. Every survey has shown that the image of an attractive woman is the most effective advertising gimmick. She may sit astride the mudguard of a new car, or step into it ablaze with jewels; she may lie at a man's feet stroking his new socks; she may hold the petrol pump in a challenging pose, or dance through the woodland glades in slow motion in all the glory of a new shampoo; whatever she does her image sells.

Figure 5.7. This advertisement is one of a series for Cabana Cachaca that exudes sexuality. The campaign, which features beautiful photographs of women in suggestive poses, had been criticized by some groups for exploiting the female body.

Figure 5.8

We use beautiful women, in various stages of dress and undress, to sell everything from automobiles to new technological gizmos, as the Palm Pilot advertisement (figure 5.8) demonstrates.

One of the problems that this sexploitation of the female body causes is a sense of inadequacy on the part of many women, who don't have the lean and boyish or, in some cases, anorexic bodies that so many supermodels do—who aren't twenty years old, who aren't six feet tall, who don't weigh ninety-five pounds, who don't wear size three dresses, who aren't made up to kill, and who aren't dressed in expensive fashions. These supermodels, "it" girls, and movie stars also cause problems for many men who see these women and become dissatisfied with their sexual partners. Raphael Patai discusses this in *Myth and Modern Man* (1972:286):

> The movies, television, magazine and newspaper ads, posters, store-window mannequins, life-size, smaller than life, bigger than life, in colors or in black-and-white, in partial or total undress, in all kinds of alluring and enticing positions with the most express indications of availability, willingness, readiness to welcome you into their arms . . . have the combined and cumulative effect of making many men dissatisfied with whatever sexual activity is available to them.

What Patai suggests, then, is that not only women but also men are affected—and to a considerable degree disturbed—by the endless number of sexually provocative advertisements and commercials to which they are exposed (figures 5.9 and 5.10). Men can satisfy their sexual hunger with their wives and girlfriends but not their erotic fantasies. (The same applies to women as well, no doubt—since they are continually exposed to virile, rugged, handsome men in advertisements and commercials.)

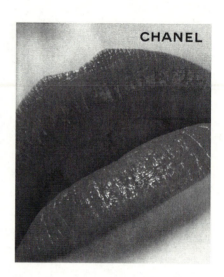

Figure 5.9. This Chanel ad, which features an extreme close-up of a woman's lips, is typical of many ads now that only show parts of woman's bodies. What is the "sell" in this ad?

I am, of course, stating things in a rather extreme way. But the models used in a significant number of commercials and fashion advertisements—for expensive, upscale products, that is—are frequently unusual physical specimens. Advertisements for cosmetics often play on the anxiety women feel as they start getting older about no longer being young and no longer being beautiful. It may even be more extreme than that: no longer young, therefore no longer beautiful.

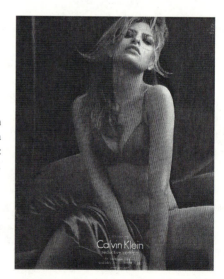

Figure 5.10. The pose of this woman, with her legs spread apart and a sensual look on her face, uses sexuality in a rather overt manner to sell the product.

THE PEACH THAT BECAME A PRUNE:
A CAUTIONARY FABLE

In this respect, consider the copy for a moisturizer that follows. There is a large headline followed by copy that reads,

**There is
a fountain of youth.
It's called water**.

Nature has been telling us this forever. Water keeps a rose fresh and beautiful. A peach juicy. All living things, living. Including your skin. The millions of cells in your skin contain water. This water pillows and cushions your skin, making it soft and young-looking. But, for a lot of reasons, cells become unable to hold water. And the water escapes your skin. (If you'll forgive us, think of a prune drying up and you'll know the whole story.)

This copy was in an advertisement for Living Proof Cream Hydracel by Geminesse, a moisturizer that promises to do two things. First, it promises to help women develop younger-looking skin, and, second, it promises to help women avoid drying up and looking, if you'll forgive the harsh analogy, like prunes.

There is a question that now must be considered. What is this overwhelming need women have to be "moist"? At first glance, and I use the phrase purposefully, it seems to involve looking younger by having soft, peachlike skin. And it also has something to do with being roselike (see Jergens's recent ad in figure 5.12), whatever that might mean. But underneath it all, I think the fear of losing moisture really has to do with anxieties women have—generated by the advertisement or, at least, exploited by the advertisement—about their loss of fertility, about changing from being a "garden" (where things can grow) to being a "desert" (barren, lifeless, and sterile).

This is symbolized in the ad by the two fruits mentioned—the juicy (young) peach and the dried-up (old) prune. And if you aren't one, the bipolar logic of the advertisement suggests, you must be the other. It is this drying up that women must avoid at all costs, this loss of youth and fertility symbolized by having soft, moist skin. And that is where moisturizers come in—especially moisturizers like Hydracel (and Jergens's "Radiance" in figure 5.12). They preserve the illusion women have that they are still young, the illusion of generativity by merging pseudoscience and magic. These products succeed by terrorizing women—who live in constant fear of water gushing out of their cells and flooding out of their bodies, until the magic no longer works or is no longer needed.

Let me cite a number of passages relating to gender in advertising found in Erving Goffman's "Gender Advertisements." The general thrust of his argument is that by various means, such as bent knees, smiles, and being shown smaller than men, women are placed in positions of subordination and weakness. See figure 5.11, in which the woman in the Nautica advertisement is in a subservient position to the man.

1. One way in which social weight—power, authority, rank, office, renown—is echoed expressively in social situations is through relative size, especially height.
2. Women, more than men, are pictured using their fingers and hands to trace the outlines of an object or to cradle it or caress its surface.
3. In our society when a man and a woman collaborate face-to-face in an undertaking, the man—it would seem—is likely to perform the executive role.
4. Smiles . . . often function as ritualistic modifiers, signaling that nothing antagonistic is intended or invited, meaning that the other's act has been understood and found acceptable. (1976)

Figure 5.11

Figure 5.12. This ad for Radiance moisturizer uses a beautiful black woman to sell its product. People of color are used more and more in advertising but are still underrepresented.

As the Living Proof Cream Hydracel by Geminesse advertisement adds, discussing "the truth about moisturizers,"

> Most people think a moisturizer literally puts moisture into your skin. Not true. (Your skin has all the water it needs. Holding it there is the problem.) An average moisturizer holds the water in by blocking its escape. But, unfortunately, this does not affect your cell's ability to retain water. This is where we come in. . . . The name Hydracel tells you what we're all about: water and cell. Cream Hydracel actually helps the cellular tissues retain water. We let nature do the work, not heavy creams. And this can make all the difference. Your skin will breathe and start to recover its water-holding power. And your face will feel softer and look younger, naturally. . . . Nature gave you a fountain of youth. Cream Hydracel keeps it flowing.

This is only one example of the campaign of terror waged by cosmetic companies and all the industries involved with feminine sexuality through such matters as hair, clothes, eyeglasses, jewelry, watches, shoes, stockings—you name it.

Figure 5.13. This advertisement is a graphic representation of sexual passion.

Women are put in a no-win situation. Beauty is associated with youth, and women are made to feel that when they lose their youth, they will lose their beauty. The passage from ripe, juicy "peach" to dried-up old "prune" whose fountain of youth no longer flows is inevitable—though one can, through the magic of cosmetics, so the advertisements and commercials imply, hold off the ravages of getting older. Advertising creates the problem and then provides the solution—some product or service that will help women become beautiful and stay beautiful, which means keeping them looking young and juicy, like a peach.

THE PSEUDOPOETIC APPEAL TO THE ILLITERATI

A good deal of the writing found in advertisements for perfumes and other cosmetics has what might be described as a pseudopoetic character to it. One of the best descriptions of this phenomenon was written by the anthropologist Jules Henry in his book *Culture against Man*. He writes (1963:59),

> Consider the advertisement for Pango Peach, a new color introduced by Revlon in 1960. A young woman leans against the upper rungs of a ladder leading to a palm-thatched bamboo tree-house. Pango Peach are her sari, her blouse, her toe and finger nails, and the cape she holds. A sky of South Pacific blue is behind her, and the cape, as it flutters in the winds, stains the heavens Pango Peach. "From east of the sun—west of the moon where each tomorrow dawns . . ." beckons the ad, in corny pecuniary lingo. But when you are trying to sell nail polish to a filing clerk with two years of high school you don't quote Dylan Thomas! The idea of this ad is to make a woman think she is reading real poetry when she is not, and at the same time to evoke in her the specific fantasy that will sell the product. Millions will respond to poetry as a value and feel good when they think they are responding to it, and this process of getting people to respond to

pseudo-values as if they were responding to real ones is called here pecuni-ary distortion of values.

Henry quotes some other phrases from the advertisement—Pango Peach is described as "a many splendoured coral . . . pink with pleasure . . . a volcano of color," and it adds, "It's full ripe peach with a world of difference . . . born to be worn in big juicy slices. Succulent on your lips. Sizzling on your fingertips. . . . Go Pango Peach . . . your adventure in paradise."

Wise Up to Teens: Insights into Marketing and Advertising to Teenagers

By Peter Zollo

Here at last is the expert analysis that will help you capture your share of the nearly $100 billion that teenagers spend. This book explains where teens get their money, how and why they spend it, and what they think about themselves and the world around them. It presents five rules that will make your advertising appealing to teens. Learn about brands teens think are cool, words to use in advertising to teens, which media and pro-motions teens prefer, and how much influence teens have over what their parents buy. This is a fascinating look into the world of teens—a market whose income is almost all discretionary.

—Advertisement for a book on marketing to teens in the November 1995 *Marketing Power: The Marketer's Reference Library*

He then discusses the significance of the language used in the Pango Peach advertisement. He writes (1963:59),

Each word in the advertisement is carefully chosen to tap a particular yearning and hunger in the American woman. "Many splendoured," for example, is a reference to the novel and movie *Love Is a Many Splendoured Thing*, a tale of passion in an Oriental setting. "Volcano" is meant to arouse the latent wish to be a volcanic lover and be loved by one. The mouthful of oral stimuli—"ripe," "succulent," "juicy"—puts sales resistance in double jeopardy because mouths are even more for kissing than eating. "Sizzling" can refer only to l'amour à la folie.

We can see then that what seems to be a simple advertisement for a new color contains any number of oral stimuli and references to a culture that will, it is hoped, persuade the readers of the advertisement to purchase Pango Peach lipstick and other products and put themselves, like the model, in the South Pacific, where "volcanic" love awaits. Notice, also, that this advertisement—like the Hydracel moisturizer advertisement—makes use of peaches as symbols of youth, beauty, and sexual allure. I return to this subject in chapter 8 in my analysis of an advertisement for Fidji perfume. The ad in figure 5.13 suggests that teenagers are an important marketing category and that certain kinds of appeals can be made to them and can be effective.

SEX APPEAL AND GENDER APPEAL

We have to make a distinction between advertising that is directed toward a particular gender (male or female) and advertising that exploits sexuality to arouse people of either gender (figures 5.14 and 5.15). In her book *Why She Buys: The New Strategy for Reaching the World's Most Powerful Consumers*, Bridget Brennan writes (2009:184–85),

> *Gender appeal* is the type of marketing that resonates strongly with the culture of a particular sex. Its messages and images tap into a gender's collective consciousness—its rites of passage, milestones, communication styles, body issues, desires and motivations. . . . *Sex appeal* is different—it defines words, images, or people that others find arousing. And when it comes to being aroused, most of us have lived long enough to know that women and men have different ideas about what's sexy and what's not.

Figure 5.14. This Tom Ford ad reflects a conscious attempt to confuse viewers. Is the person with the glasses a woman? If so, the ad should appeal to lesbians and members of the LGBT community.

Figure 5.15. What was the thinking behind this unusual ad? Is the foot that of a male or female? Does it make any difference?

Brennan's book argues that marketers and advertisers don't pay enough attention to the difference between genders and don't understand what motivates women. This often leads to advertising campaigns that are ineffective and don't work. In the past few decades, the male body has also been exploited as an object of lust—for women, metrosexuals, and groups with other sexual orientations (figure 5.16). This marks a major transformation in the sexual consciousness of people in contemporary societies.

Figure 5.16. The male body is now seen as an object of lust for females and males. Notice the six-pack abs. What do they signify?

SEX AND THE PROBLEM OF CLUTTER

One reason for using sexuality to sell products is explained by Jack Solomon in his book *The Signs of Our Time*. His thesis is that sexuality enables advertising agencies to avoid the clutter of competing ads and commercials. As he writes (1990:69),

> The sexual explicitness of contemporary advertising is a sign not so much of American sexual fantasies as of the lengths to which advertisers will go to get attention. Sex never fails as an attention-getter, and in a particularly competitive and expansive era for American marketing, advertisers like to bet on a sure thing. Ad people refer to the proliferation of TV, radio, newspaper, magazine, and billboard ads as "clutter," and nothing cuts through clutter like sex.
>
> By showing the flesh, advertisers work on the deepest, most coercive human emotions of all. Much sexual coercion in advertising, however, is a sign of a desperate need to make certain that clients are getting their money's worth.

Figure 5.17. This ad is typical of many ads that only feature parts of a woman's body.

Figure 5.18. Notice the pose of the model. How does this ad sell Gottet?

On the other hand, if advertising agencies compete with one another by using sexuality to sell, they just raise clutter to a different or higher level, creating what might be described as an all-pervasive kind of "sexual clutter." And I think this is, to a considerable degree, what has happened. Sexuality is all-pervasive in American media, and as it becomes more and more common, advertisers have to develop new and more daring and, in some cases, more explicit ways of having their sexual commercials and print advertisements stand out or attain some degree of differentiation. As the Pierre Cardin advertisement (figure 5.19) shows, companies do whatever they can to differentiate themselves from their competitors and catch a reader's attention.

Figure 5.19

There is also the law of diminishing returns to consider. For as the American media becomes oversaturated with sexual images, in programming as well as in advertising, the law of diminishing returns starts operating, and the power of any particular sexual image to attract attention and stimulate demand weakens. This leads to the crisis that advertising now faces as companies and their agencies engage in what has been called "sign wars" to attract the attention of the American public. Sexual imagery is so all-pervasive that the commercials of one company may be neutralizing the commercials of its competitors and leading, ultimately, to a kind of "turning off" by the general public as it becomes overwhelmed by sexuality in advertisements and commercials.

Insights from Advertising Agencies

The sentimentality and warmth appeal is being dropped for a campy sex-and-youth appeal, and they aren't trying to sell people on the idea of cognac but on their particular brand. There was much talk about the Smirnoff Vodka campaign, which was a great success and which was based on sexploitation and the double entendre. The problem they faced involved thinking up an advertisement that would command attention, that was original, and that worked. There was some talk about thinking up some kind of a catchy phrase that would become part of public currency, that comedians might repeat, and that might strike the public's fancy.

In her "Primping or Pimping" article, Valli Herman-Cohen quotes an editor who makes this kind of an argument (2000):

> "Everybody is reaching, and I no longer know what they are reaching for," said Edie Locke, former editor-in-chief of Mademoiselle. "If every image now is centered around sex, or almost-rape, or lesbian chic, the difference between the ads is no longer perceptible."

As I've argued, sex is used to sell everything from video games to milk (figure 5.20) to shoes (figure 5.21). So there is a problem fashion and other advertisers face—their advertisements get lost in the sexual advertising clutter, and no matter how far they are willing to go, it seems that some other advertiser is willing to go further.

Figure 5.20

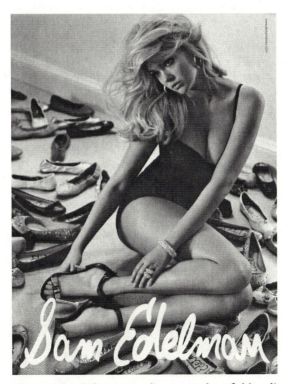

Figure 5.21. What sense do you make of this ad? Why have a woman with lots of cleavage showing surrounded by shoes?

We must never underestimate the power of sexual images to affect us in mysterious and profound ways. But the incessant clutter of sexual images may weaken the power of any one advertisement or commercial to sell us some product or service and may even be having an impact on our sexual lives. There is so much vicarious sex in our lives, found in films, television shows, and now in "sexting" text and image messaging on cell phones, that the "real thing" may be losing its appeal for a goodly number of people.

STUDY QUESTIONS, APPLICATIONS, AND ASSIGNMENTS

1. What did Judith Williamson say about advertising? What does it mean to say it is the "great recuperator"?
2. How does Jack Solomon differentiate sex from gender? Do a research project on this topic as it relates to advertising.
3. What does Valli Herman–Cohen say about advertising and soft porn?
4. What does John Berger say about the way advertising uses sexuality to sell products to people?
5. What insights does Paul Messaris provide about advertising's preference for slim models? Is this still the case?
6. Find a campaign that doesn't use ultrathin models. Was it successful? Explain your conclusions.
7. What is the connection between sexploitation and anxiety?
8. What did Raphael Patai say about advertising and our dissatisfaction with our sexual partners? Do you think he was correct? Explain your answer.
9. How does the Hydracel moisturizer terrify women? Why are peaches and prunes such compelling images?
10. What did Bridget Brennan say about the difference between sex appeal and gender appeal?
11. How do advertisers use sex appeal to counter the problem of clutter?
12. What points does Erving Goffman make about gender, power, and advertising? Are his insights still valid?

13. Using Jules Henry's analysis of the language in the Pango Peach advertisement as a model, make an analysis of two fragrance advertisements: one for women and one for men. Choose ads with lots of text for your analysis.
14. How do you explain the fact that the male body now is used as an object of lust?

The effect of advertiser-driven campaigning has been felt in more than just the professionalization of electoral propaganda, though the slickly produced political advertisement is certainly its most visible product. Promotion has been drawn into the heart of the process. Through the 1970s and 1980s it has become normal practice for the managers of campaign advertising to be recruited directly from the highest ranks of the advertising industry. Their role, moreover, sometimes in collusion with the official party machine, has been not just to supervise the specifics of advertising, but to map out entire campaigns. The scope for involvement is endless. Every public statement or gesture by campaigners, whether intentional or not, can be considered part of the campaign, and is therefore susceptible to promotional orchestration.

—Andrew Wernick, *Promotional Culture:*
Advertising, Ideology and Symbolic Expression

Under the heading of deceptive editing of "documentary" material, we might also want to consider a notorious political ad used in Richard Nixon's 1968 presidential campaign. Aired only once, the ad juxtaposed images of Nixon's democratic opponent, Hubert Humphrey, with scenes of warfare in Vietnam, protests in the streets of Chicago, and poverty in Appalachia. Because Humphrey was smiling in some of the shots, these juxtapositions created the impression that he was indifferent to the suffering and disturbances in the other images.

—Paul Messaris, *Visual Persuasion: The Role of Images in Advertising*

6

POLITICAL ADVERTISING

In recent decades, political advertising has assumed greater and greater importance in campaigns for offices at all levels. There is a reason for this. As political scientists Stephen Ansolabehere and Shanto Iyengar write in their book *Going Negative: How Political Advertisements Shrink and Polarize the Electorate* (1995:52),

> Unlike most channels of communication, advertising allows candidates to reach uninterested and unmotivated citizens—those who ordinarily pay little attention to news reports, debates, and other campaign events. After all, the "audience" for political advertising is primarily inadvertent—people who happen to be watching their preferred television programs. Of course, viewers can choose to tune out or channel-surf during advertising breaks, but the fact remains that the reach of advertising extends beyond relatively attentive and engaged voters.

Thus, advertising is a tool that enables politicians to send their messages to a large number of people who tend to be apolitical, who are not particularly interested in political campaigns. What is important to recognize is that these people are often profoundly affected by the political advertisements to which they are exposed.

What follows is an introduction to an important and very controversial subject—how advertising has become a major instrument of campaigning for and winning political office. I have chosen to discuss political advertising because, although many people do not think about it, our decisions about who we vote for play a crucial role in determining what laws will be passed and how we will lead our lives. From my perspective, political advertising can be seen as the most important genre of advertising. I would hope the information presented in this book will help readers learn to "read" or "decode" political advertisements better by offering insights into the methods used by political advertisers and thus make more informed and more intelligent decisions when they vote.

There are some theorists, I should point out, who consider all advertising to be political in that advertising suggests a political order that produces all the products and services being advertised. Hans Magnus Enzensberger ties advertising to the need that political orders have for acceptance by the public. He writes in his essay "The Industrialization of the Mind" (*The Consciousness Industry*, 1974:8),

> Consciousness, both individual and social, has become a political issue only from the moment when the conviction arose in people's minds that everyone should have a say in his own destiny as well as in that of society at large. From the same moment any authority had to justify itself in the eyes of those it would govern; coercion alone would no longer do the trick; he who ruled must persuade, must lay claim to the people's minds and change them, in an industrial age, by every industrial means at hand.

This leads to the development of what Enzensberger calls the "mind industry," whose basic concern is to convince people that the existing order should be perpetuated. The mind industry's main task—and advertising is a major element of the mind industry—is "to perpetuate the prevailing pattern of man's domination by man, no matter who runs the society and by what means. Its main task is to expand and train our consciousness—in order to exploit it" (1974:10).

We must recognize that all political advertisements are not the same. In her book *30-Second Politics: Political Advertising in the Eighties*, Montague Kern, a social scientist, suggests there are four kinds of political advertisements. We tend to lump all political advertising together, but if you examine political ads over the course of a typical campaign, you discover there really are a number of different kinds of political advertisements, which are used at different times in a typical campaign. With this insight in mind, it is worth examining in some detail Kern's insights into the kinds of political advertisements and how political advertising works.

Kern discusses political advertisements and points out some changes that have taken place in them in recent years (1989:6):

> If recent research indicates that contemporary political advertising has an impact that includes but is much broader than that of informing the public about candidate positions on the issues, content research based on ads sup-

Figure 6.1. This frame was found in a Republican commercial, using the last four letters of the word "Democrats" to—some critics suggest—subliminally influence voters. The image lasted only a fraction of a second.

plied by campaigns also suggests that the purpose of advertising has changed since 1972. It is concerned as much with conveying impressions about candidate character as with providing information about issues. Richard Joselyn has argued that there are four types of ads, with issue statements that are largely sloganistic relating to only two of them: prospective and retrospective policy satisfaction appeals, as opposed to election as ritual and his largest category, benevolent leader appeals.

The most significant development in political advertising in recent decades, of course, is just the opposite of the benevolent leader appeal. Much political advertising is now negative (figure 6.1), and it attacks political figures for their policies and often for their character and behavior as well. This leads to counterattacks so that negative advertising becomes a dominant method in many campaigns. These attack ads are used, as Kern explains, generally only at certain times in campaigns.

She discusses different kinds of commercials one finds at different stages in a typical campaign for political office. It isn't just a matter of developing name awareness in voters anymore. As she explains (1989:6),

> Further, now-classic theory of media use argues that there are four types of ads associated with four stages in a campaign: first, name identification spots, which are shown early in the campaign; second, argument spots, which present candidate positions on issues; third, attack spots, which focus on the opponent; and fourth, positive visionary appeals, which are used at the end of a campaign to give voters a reason to vote for the candidate.

We see then that political advertising has developed over the years and that television spots have different purposes at different times in a typical campaign. Political advertising in electoral campaigns is, ultimately, aimed at persuading voters to do what the person paying for the advertisements wants them to do—that is, to vote for a particular candidate, which means not voting for any other candidates, or, in the case of political propositions, to vote the way the advertiser wants them to vote.

We must remember that when advertisers pay to have something "run up a flagpole," they always expect large numbers of people to "salute." Or to use a different metaphor, it may always be the case that "he who pays the piper calls the tune," but it doesn't always work out that the tune is one that people like or one that convinces them to sing along. In the case of political advertising, "saluting" or "singing along" means voting for a particular candidate or in a certain way on propositions.

Table 6.1 lists the four stages in a typical political campaign and describes the kinds of political advertisements found at each stage in the campaign. I've also suggested what the specific function of each kind of advertisement is, using words beginning with "I" as a mnemonic device to facilitate remembering them. Early in the campaign, the politician wants to gain name recognition or persuade voters to associate him or her with the position he or she is running for. Then the campaign moves into issues the politicians believe in or don't believe in. Later, the politicians use attack ads, or what we commonly call "negative ads," to put opponents on the defensive. Finally, politicians offer "visionary" ads to give voters reasons to vote for them on the basis of their character.

John Sides and Lynn Vavreck discuss the 2012 presidential election in their book *The Gamble: Choice and Chance in the 2012 Presidential Election*. A description of the book on Amazon.com discusses the book (2013, Princeton University Press):

> Which mattered more—Barack Obama's midsummer ad blitz or the election year's economic growth? How many voters actually changed their minds—and was it ever enough to sway the outcome? *The Gamble* answers important questions like these by looking at the interplay between the

Table 6.1. Stages and Kinds of Advertisements in Political Campaigns

Time in Campaign	Kind of Advertisement	Function
Early	Name identification ads	Identity
Later	Argument ads	Ideology
Later still	Attack ads (negative ads)	Insult
End of campaign	Positive visionary ads	Image

candidates' strategic choices—the ads, speeches, rallies, and debates—and the chance circumstances of the election, especially the economy. In the Republican primary, the book shows, the electioneering and the media's restless attention did matter, producing a string of frontrunners. But when Obama and Mitt Romney finally squared off in the general election, there were few real game-changers. The candidates' billion-dollar campaigns were important but largely cancelled each other out, opening the way for Obama to do what incumbents usually do when running amid even modest economic growth: win.

Sides and Vavreck argue that it was gains in the economy that was basic to Obama's success, though there are many other theories about why Obama won, from his turnaround in the Romney–Obama debates to gaffes made by Romney in his campaign and his off-putting personality. Although many Americans didn't know who would win the election, Obama's winning had been forecast by a columnist in the *New York Times*, Nate Silver, in his FiveThirtyEight (for the number of congressmen and -women and senators) with remarkable precision.

THE COST OF PRESIDENTIAL CAMPAIGNS

The 2008 election, in which Barack Obama defeated John McCain, was the costliest race in history. Politico.com offers cost estimates for the last three presidential races:

Year	Cost of Advertising
2004	$528.9 million by all candidates
2008	$880 million by all candidates
2012	$1 billion by all candidates

It is estimated that for the 2008 presidential election, Obama raised around $650 million, a great deal more than McCain's $200 million. This was one of the few times in recent years in which the Democratic candidate for president raised more money than the Republican one. The amount of money spent by all candidates, political parties, and interest groups in congressional and presidential races in 2008 was $5.3 billion, approximately a billion dollars more than was spent in 2004. We can see, then, that presidential campaigns are growing increasingly expensive. Obama raised much of his money through contributions made on the Internet and didn't take any government money. His celebrity status, to a considerable degree, helped him raise the money.

THE COST OF THE 2012 PRESIDENTIAL ELECTION

An article by Stephen Breun and Jack Gillum in the HuffPost Politics edition of November 23, 2013, offers us statistics on the cost of the 2012 presidential election. They write,

> The 2012 presidential election broke the $2 billion milestone in its final weeks, becoming the most expensive in American political history, according to final federal finance reports released Thursday. The reports detailed a last-minute cascade of money from mega-donors and an onslaught of spending by the Obama and Romney campaigns and "super" political action committees.

The final campaign finance tallies filed with the Federal Election Commission included nearly $86 million in fund-raising for the losing presidential candidate, Republican Mitt Romney, in the election's last weeks. That final burst brought the Romney campaign's total for the election to above $1 billion. Final fund-raising and spending totals for President Barack Obama's victorious drive also topped $1 billion.

This means the 2012 presidential election cost twice as much as the 2008 election. We have figures for all the money spent on all the elections in 2012, and they are quite large. An article by Nicholas Confessore in the *New York Times*, "Total Cost of Election Could Be $6 Billion," calls our attention to the amount of money spent on the 2012 presidential and other campaigns. As he explains,

> The total cost of the 2012 election could reach $6 billion, according to estimates from a leading research organization, which would obliterate the previous record by more than $700 million.

The increase has been driven largely by rapidly increased spending among "super PACs" and outside groups that can raise unlimited amounts of money from donors. Spending by outside groups could reach to more than $970 million for the 2012 cycle, although precise estimates are difficult because the rate of spending by outside groups has been rising so quickly since Labor Day.

And this figure underestimates the amount of money spent after the Citizens United ruling by the Supreme Court, which opened the floodgates to spending on political campaigns by entities that operate "under the radar" and define themselves as "educational" rather than political organizations.

QUESTIONS RAISED BY THE ELECTION CAMPAIGNS

The 2012 elections raise some interesting questions about the relationship between political advertising and voting.

1. *Are people no longer affected by negative campaigns?*

People always say, in polls, they don't like negative campaigns, but voting records seem to indicate that they are affected or influenced by them. Numerous case studies of elections show that negative campaigns, full of attack commercials, are effective. One theory is that negative campaigns turn many viewers off (dissuade them from voting at all) and thus play into the hands of politicians, generally conservative Republican ones, who rely on the minority of conservative Republicans who do vote (in contrast to the majority of generally liberal Democrats, who don't vote).

2. *Is it the number or the quality of the advertisements that counts?*

The tendency, nowadays, is to saturate the airwaves with advertisements as early as possible in an effort to "define" the opposition candidate. Thus, the Democratic commercials portrayed Romney as a wealthy businessman out of touch with America. Romney didn't help his cause when he made a disparaging comment about the "47 percent" of Americas who would never vote for him:

> There are 47 percent of the people who will vote for the president no matter what. All right, there are 47 percent who are with him, who are dependent upon government, who believe that they are victims, who believe the government has a responsibility to care for them, who believe that they are entitled to health care, to food, to housing, to you-name-it. That that's an entitlement. And the government should give it to them. And they will vote for this president no matter what. . . . These are people who pay no income tax.

Someone in the audience videotaped Romney when he was speaking to a group of his supporters, and the video was then broadcast and caused Romney many problems. Romney's team relied on statistics that were flawed; they suggested that he would win the election, and he was so confident about the election that he did not write a concession speech. But statisticians who studied state polls predicted, correctly, that Romney would lose by a large margin.

3. *Is it the advertising or the record of the candidate that is crucial?*

This matter is particularly significant. Do people vote for someone because of advertising per se or because the advertising points to a person's record or stand on important issues (and attacks opponents' positions)?

It is estimated that by a ratio of something like four to one, Americans get their information about the positions of candidates from advertising rather than the news. Much of the news in political campaigns tends to focus on the horse race aspect of the campaign—who's ahead rather than differences on issues. And, curiously, what the news programs on television decide to cover is often shaped by the candidates' political advertisements. The advertisements set the agenda for the newspapers and radio and television news programs.

Kathleen Hall Jamieson explores the relationship between news and advertising in her book *Dirty Politics: Deception, Distraction, and Democracy*. She writes (1992:124),

> News reporting can provide a frame through which viewers understand ads. Conventional campaign wisdom holds that news sets the context for ads. If the news accounts are inconsistent with the ad, the power of the ad is diminished. When the two are consistent, the power of both is magnified. But news can only reframe ads if reporters question the legitimacy of their claims, point out the false inferences that they invite, and so on. Without such reframing by reporters, campaign ads have the potential to shape the visual and verbal language of news, and in recent campaigns they have become increasingly successful.

This failure of news reporters to deal with misleading statements by and about candidates and matters of that nature is due, in part, to the obsession news people have with who is winning a campaign rather than the truth or falsity of advertisements. In addition, written critiques of political commercials in newspapers generally cannot undo the damage done by them since the impact of television commercials is so great.

Political advertisements about issues can be divided into two categories. There are so-called platform ads, which are full of broad generalities, and slogan ads, which contain some slogan related to an action the candidate promises to take or gives an important insight into the candidate's character. When Dwight David Eisenhower said "I will go to Korea" in 1952, he was offering a slogan ad. And Gray Davis's "Experience money can't buy" in a California race for governor was another slogan ad that took his primary campaign and reduced it to one slogan that people could remember.

A NOTE ON THE CALIFORNIA CAMPAIGN FOR GOVERNOR IN 2010

To show that nothing much changes in life, the 2010 campaign for governor was similar to the campaign in 2002. In the 2010 campaign, Republican Meg Whitman, a billionaire who used to run e-Bay, waged another virtual campaign against Steve Poizner, a multimillionaire, and defeated him. Whitman, as of August 2010, spent around $100 million on "Can't Trust Steve" attack commercials about Steve Poizner and other commercials to introduce her to Californians and attack the Democratic candidate for governor, Jerry Brown.

In an article by Michael Roth Feld and Patrick McGreevy in the March 22, 2010, *Los Angeles Times*, we read,

> Republican Meg Whitman spent $27 million on her campaign for governor in the first 11 weeks of the year, setting a record-shattering pace with a prime-time television ad blitz to introduce herself to voters and attack her GOP opponent, according to a disclosure statement she filed Monday. Whitman, the billionaire ex-chief of EBay, has spent $46 million since joining the race early last year, seven times more than either of her main rivals.

After March, Whitman spent another $50 million or so. In addition, she avoided press conferences in which she would be required to answer questions from reporters. The question many political commentators debated was whether Whitman, who was a Democrat for many years and who didn't vote in a number of elections in California, could "buy" the nomination and win the election and become governor, essentially by spending millions of dollars for political commercials. The answer was "no." Whitman was defeated by Jerry Brown, who ran a very shrewd campaign. Whitman ended up as the head of Hewlett Packard.

THE CODE OF THE COMMERCIAL (AND OTHER POLITICAL ADVERTISING)

The television commercial, because it is the most powerful form of advertising, is the most interesting and most complex kind of political advertisement. In these commercials, a set of emotional values is established around common themes, values, or beliefs. Table 6.2 shows these values by offering a set of opposites and listing the negative notions that most Americans find repellent. Political advertisements use symbols, as best they can, that generate the positive appeals listed in table 6.2. These appeals lead to positive feelings about a candidate, which then translate into votes for the candidate.

Table 6.2. Positive Appeals and Their Negations

Positive	*Negative*
Hope (for the future)	Despair
Compassion (for those in need)	Coldness, aloofness
Ambition (to do what's needed)	Lethargy
Trust	Deviousness
Nostalgia (for the mythic past)	Unconcern for the past
Intimacy	Distance
Reassurance	Gloominess
Local pride	Local shame
National pride	National shame

We want candidates who reassure us, who give us hope, who are compassionate toward the poor and disadvantaged, who make us feel proud about where we live and about America. We like to feel that our candidates are like us and aware of people like us, even though they may be quite far removed—in distance and socioeconomic status—from us. One of the most important things candidates do is to use visual symbols to get their messages across directly and viscerally. Thus, we see them appropriating important American symbols—the flag, the hard hat (identification with the blue-collar worker), a "visionary" look over the horizon, the all-American family, and so on—to generate the emotional responses that lead to instant and powerful identification with the candidate and, it is hoped, as a consequence, votes for the candidate. Not that language is unimportant, but in commercials a great deal of the communication burden is carried by physical symbols.

And that is why politics has become, to such an important degree, dominated by advertising—just like so many other areas of American life. Presidents (and other politicians) are just one more product to be sold to the American public, and while advertising isn't the only determining factor, it does play a major role in political campaigns and, by implication, in the governmental process.

THE EMOTIONAL BASIS OF PARTISAN POLITICS

A psychologist at Emory University, Dr. Drew Westen, did some research using MRI scanners that revealed something very interesting about political choices. What he discovered, by scanning the brains of partisan Democrats and Republicans when they were given information that either attacked their beliefs or reinforced them, was that most of the decisions people make are unconscious. Political scientists have suggested that unconscious emotional forces shape our political decision making, and Westen's research proves it by showing that certain regions of the brain have increased activity when people are shown material that leads to dissonance—that is, material that conflicts with strongly held beliefs.

When material that was unwelcome to the participants in his experiment was shown to them, certain areas of their brains flared with activity due to their unconscious rejection of this material. The experiment also found that people who unconsciously rejected certain information that was contrary to their beliefs had spikes in areas of their brain that are associated with feeling relieved or being rewarded.

What this suggests is that our political decision making is guided primarily by unconscious forces and that the arguments we make to support our positions can be seen as, to a large degree, rationalizations to justify our views. At least this is the case with people with strong commitments to one or another political party. What these findings imply is that political commercials are most effective when they strike hidden chords in our psyches that resonate with our beliefs, when they "touch" us in ways whose importance we cannot, generally speaking, fathom. In essence, we believe what we want to believe for reasons we cannot fathom. The notion that our political decision making is shaped by unconscious forces should not surprise us. If we consider a vote for a candidate similar in nature to buying something, as I explained earlier, most of our decisions to purchase something take place in our unconscious.

Westen said that it is possible, in theory, to overcome our unconscious beliefs and biases but that it is very difficult to do so. As Freud pointed out, the unconscious is not accessible to people under ordinary circumstances, so to the degree that our political behavior is shaped by unconscious forces, generally speaking we are unable to recognize the extent to which this has occurred and do anything about it. Freud said that where there is id (that is, unconscious emotional desires that shape our behavior), there should be ego (by which he meant logical and rational behavior), but in life and in politics, it isn't very easy to do this.

We should also keep in mind how grid-group theory relates to political decision making. Political scientist Aaron Wildavsky argued that the four lifestyles or consumer cultures, discussed earlier, also have relevance to politics and that these cultures affect our politics and voting. He argued that people cannot know what their interests are, so they must have other ways of deciding how to vote, and what guides them is their membership in one of the four political cultures—even though they may not recognize that they belong to one of these political cultures. What voters do recognize is that they don't accept the ideas and beliefs of members of the other political cultures, so they vote accordingly. What Westen's research shows is that this process of determining how to vote, based on one's membership in a political culture, is largely an emotional one, shaped by unconscious imperatives.

STUDY QUESTIONS, APPLICATIONS, AND ASSIGNMENTS

1. What was said in *Going Native* about political advertising?
2. What does Hans Magnus Enzensberger say about the "industrialization of the mind"? What does he say is the mind industry's main task? Do you think he is correct? Explain your answer.
3. What are the four basic kinds of political advertisements, and when are they used in a typical campaign?
4. What did John Sides and Lynn Vavreck say about the role of advertising in the 2012 presidential election?
5. How much money was spent in the 2012 presidential election? On all elections in 2012?
6. What questions are raised by election campaigns relative to political advertising and voting?
7. What did Kathleen Hall Jamieson say about the relation between news programs and voting?
8. What's the difference between platform advertisements and slogan advertisements? Apply this distinction to a political campaign of interest to you.
9. What was said about the California campaign for governor in 2010?
10. What does the failure of Meg Whitman to become governor of California in 2010 teach us about politics and advertising? What problems did she face in her run for governor?
11. What are the basic appeals found in political advertising in America? Which ones do you think are most important?

12. Drew Westen's research suggests emotion is what shapes our political behavior. Investigate recent scholarly work on the relation between emotion and political decision making and write a paper on your findings.

13. Why do you belong to the party (or faction in the party) to which you belong? Explain your decision making regarding your party affiliation (or nonaffiliation, if that is the case).

In Japan, firms suffering severe competition have devised a course of instruction which aims to instill the fanaticism of selling for its own sake. The pressure of competition faced by these companies is heightened by the structure of each sector: they specialize too little, and thus too many firms crowd into the market. In particular, the virtual absence of specialization makes additional demands on the sellers. The programme developed under these conditions is called moretsu (or "feverishly active"). It involves "breeding," the goal of which is the fanatical seller whose drives and energy are subordinated to their selling activity. "The aim is to breed a sales genius, with an elbow of cast-iron, brain like a computer and the constitution of a horse." In short, "they want to breed the sales robot." The breeding programme starts its day with an hour of strenuous exercise. After breakfast it is time to practice "self-forgetting." "They achieve this by hitting the furniture with clubs and yelling war-cries." This is succeeded by detailed discussion of the company's sales figures. Whoever is criticized by the instructor must literally wallow in the dust while accusing themselves of worthlessness. "After a time the conviction grows inside the participants on the course that the sales plan must be fulfilled at any cost."

—W. F. Haug, *Critique of Commodity Aesthetics:*
Appearance, Sexuality, and Advertising in Capitalist Society

If we were to sum up the total number of product advertisements we are exposed to on TV, radio, newspapers and magazines, the number could be as high as 400 per day. . . . If we were to add up all promotional messages—including logos on products, program promos and ads on billboards (two media that carry nothing but advertisements)—this number could reach 16,000. . . . Jacobson and Mazur . . . argue that typical Americans will spend almost 3 whole years of their lives just watching commercials on television. The United States, in fact, is ad burdened. This country accounts for 57% of the world's advertising spending, yet the U.S. population makes up less than 10% of the world's population.

—Matthew P. McAllister, *The Commercialization of American Culture:*
New Advertising, Control, and Democracy

7

THE MARKETING SOCIETY

It is fair, I would suggest, to describe America as a "marketing society." As I will show, every day we are exposed to many more advertisements and commercials than people in other countries. Let me start with some statistics that reflect the extent to which American society is saturated with advertisements and commercials.

STATISTICS ON ADVERTISING

An article on advertising written a couple decades ago calculated that "the average U.S. adult is bombarded by 255 advertisements every day—100 on TV, 70 in magazines, 60 on the radio and 45 in newspapers" (Jamie Beckett, "Ad Pitches Popping Up in Unusual Places," *San Francisco Chronicle*, July 17, 1989). By 2008, the figures were much higher. In his book *Shoptimism*, Lee Eisenberg writes (2009:108),

> There's just too damn much advertising? Ad agencies and their clients are quick to concede that their greatest challenge is bulldozing through the clutter of their own making. Studies show that on average each of us is exposed to between three thousand and five thousand advertising impressions a day. Most ads whip by so fast we don't register them as impressions.

If you add up all the television commercials you see in a typical day (around sixty minutes worth if you watch four hours of television a day, the national average), ads on the Internet, and ads in magazines and newspapers and on billboards, you can understand why Eisenberg argues that we are "bombarded by advertising"—the title of his chapter on advertising. Some media critics suggest that we are exposed not to 5,000 but to 15,000 advertisements of one kind or another in a typical day. Whether it is 5,000 or 15,000, it is obvious that we are exposed to an enormous number of advertisements.

In the years since Beckett's article was written, the problem has only grown worse since television commercials are now frequently much shorter—

often only ten seconds long. The thrust of Beckett's article is that advertising is now found in many places, such as videos, shopping carts in supermarkets, luggage carts in airports, walls of sports arenas, sides of buses, and numerous other places. The following information, compiled by the author based on U.S. total media ad spending from eMarketer, shows total advertising spending in the United States from 2011 projected to 2017:

	2011	**2012**	**2013**	**2014**	**2015**	**2016**	**2017**
Billions	165.03	177.76	171.01	183.35	190.86	196.95	158.26

We have statistics for world media advertising spending, also supplied by eMarketer:

	2011	**2012**	**2013**	**2014**	**2015**	**2016**	**2017**
Billions	503.0	517.0	542.5	566.4	592.5	616.7	481.06

According to eMarketer, total advertising spending for 2014 in the United States will be $177.76 billion, and the total for all advertising spending in 2014 will be $566.4 billion:

United States	**The World**
$177 billion	$542 billion ($365 billion if you subtract American advertising)
330 million people	6 billion people

Based on these numbers, we spend around $536 per person on advertising here in the United States. The average in the whole world is $90. The average in the world, if you subtract advertising expenditures in the United States, is $64. So Americans are exposed to approximately ten times as much advertising as people in other countries.

The world average is a bit misleading because people living in many First World countries also are subjected to a great deal of advertising, while people in some Third World countries, where advertising isn't as ubiquitous as it is in the First World, see relatively fewer commercials and print advertisements.

MORE COMMENTS ON THE ILLUSION OF FREEDOM

Hans Magnus Enzensberger, a Marxist poet and cultural critic, argues in his book *The Consciousness Industry* that we have illusions about our freedom and the power of our wills. He writes (1974:3),

All of us, no matter how irresolute we are, like to think that we reign supreme in our own consciousness, that we are masters of what our minds accept or reject. Since the Soul is not much mentioned anymore, except by priests, poets, and pop musicians, the last refuge a man can take from the catastrophic world at large seems to be his own mind. Where else can he expect to withstand the daily siege, if not within himself? Even under the conditions of totalitarian rule, where no one can fancy anymore that his home is his castle, the mind of the individual is considered a kind of last citadel and hotly defended, though this imaginary fortress may have been long since taken over by an ingenious enemy.

No illusion is more stubbornly upheld than the sovereignty of the mind. It is a good example of the impact of philosophy on people who ignore it; for the idea that men can "make up their minds" individually and by themselves is essentially derived from the tenets of bourgeois philosophy.

Enzensberger then quotes Karl Marx, who wrote, "What is going on in our minds has always been, and will always be, a product of society" (1974:3). You don't have to be a Marxist philosopher railing against bourgeois society to recognize that Enzensberger and Marx make a valid point. We are, after all, social animals. The idea of "individualism" is something we learn from growing up in an advanced society, where philosophers and others talk about the idea.

Ernest Dichter, one of the founding fathers of motivation research, makes a similar point in his book *The Strategy of Desire* (1960:12):

> Whatever your attitude toward modern psychology or psychoanalysis, it has been proved beyond any doubt that many of our daily decisions are governed by motivations over which we have no control and of which we are often quite unaware.

We are all, then, under the illusion that all our decisions are based on logic, rationality, need, and our own notions of what is best for us. Gerald Zaltman offers an important insight into this matter. He writes, in *How Customers Think* (2003:50), "At least 95 percent of all cognition occurs below awareness in the shadows of the mind while, at most, only 5 percent occurs in higher order consciousness." He then quotes Daniel Wegner, a psychologist at Harvard University, who writes (2003:52), "The illusion of will is so compelling that it can prompt the belief that acts were intended when they could not have been. It is as though people aspire to be ideal agents who know all their actions in advance." Zaltman points out that (2003:52) "our experience of consciously willing an action does not mean that we consciously produced it. Far from it." Zaltman argues that it is our unconscious that shapes most of our behavior, not our consciousness.

It is the power of unconscious desires working on us that explains why it is, as Paco Underhill writes in *Why We Buy* (2009:47), that when we go into a store "more than 60 percent of what we buy wasn't on our list" of things to buy. In his discussion of supermarket shopping, he adds (2009:105) that "supermarkets are places of high-impulse buying for both sexes—fully 60 to 70 percent of purchases there were unplanned, grocery industry studies have shown us."

THE MARKETING VIEW

It may be true, as I've pointed out a number of times, that exposure to an advertisement or commercial for a particular brand of blue jeans or beer may not lead to a purchasing decision by a given individual, but when we take a broader look at American society, we discover that large numbers of people do purchase that brand of blue jeans or beer. You might object that many people buy things on the basis of price. The question, then, is, when two products cost the same price, why does someone purchase one product and not another? Conventionally, a distinction is made between marketing, which deals with selling goods and services in general, and advertising, which involves selling products and services by creating texts (such as print advertisements and commercials) that are paid for by a sponsor of some kind. Most advertising agencies have marketing experts who supply the copywriters and artists with information about what the target audience for an advertising campaign is like and how to appeal to this audience.

Insights from Advertising Agencies

People in advertising agencies are practical individuals who have a mission—selling both themselves and the products they are engaged to advertise—and who must have a grasp of their publics and audiences. It is fascinating on the theoretical level and often tedious on the practical level, and since it attracts people who are frequently highly intelligent, articulate, and sophisticated, it is a trying job.

Marketers have broken American society down into various segments—what we might think of as target audiences—on the basis of *demographic* factors (such as age, race, religion, income, marital status, gender, sexual preferences, geographical region, and ZIP code) and *psychographic* factors (values and beliefs). And they've developed typologies—essentially classification systems—to deal with the various types of consumers in America. A valid or useful typology or classification system should have several features. First, it must cover the entire population—in this case, Americans who have money to purchase products and services. Second, its categories must be (to the extent possible) mutually exclusive. That is, the type of person who fits into one category shouldn't fit into any others. There are many different ways we can classify any group of people—according to race, religion, ethnicity, age, income, educational level, socioeconomic class, gender, or occupation. The important thing, as far as marketers are concerned, is to find some typology that will help get people to buy a given product or service.

We all see ourselves as special and unique individuals—and we are—but marketers see us in broadly demographic terms, for example, as senior citizens or members of Generation X or Generation Y, members of the Asian American market, or members of the thirty-five to fifty-nine age-group. Marketers have created numerous marketing typologies—categories of consumers—that they use to reach their target audiences.

All the following typologies or classification systems are attempts to put people into categories that will be useful to advertising agencies. The psychographic classifications that Eisenberg suggests (in *Shoptimism*) draw on the work of psychologist Abraham Maslow. Eisenberg describes Maslow's work as follows (2009:82):

> In 1943, when he was in his midthirties, Abraham Maslow outlined how our behavior is driven by the quest to satisfy a series of needs. Once we address what Maslow called . . . "lower-order needs" we move on to ascending "higher order needs." Some of these needs can be more material than others, meaning that the Buy comes into play as a means to satisfy them. Our need for safety and security is first, followed by our need to belong—our need for love and friendship and all that. Then there's our need for self-respect and dignity. And finally there's our need to "self-actualize," to realize our full, individual potential.

I list these needs below so you can see how we evolve as we move up the needs ladder from lower-order ones at the bottom to higher-order ones at the top:

Self-actualization needs:	realize one's potential
Psychological needs:	self-esteem, recognition
Social needs:	community, belonging
Physical needs:	food, health, material goods, safety

Maslow saw the American Dream as basically involving lower-order needs, such as the desire for material things. His theory of different levels of needs, Eisenberg believes, is central to all the classification schemes developed by psychographic marketers, whose work I will now explore. I begin with the VALS typology.

THE VALS 1 TYPOLOGY

VALS is an acronym for "Values and Life Styles," a typology developed by SRI International, a think tank in Menlo Park, California. This typology focuses on people's lifestyles rather than on demographic statistics. The VALS 1 typology is based on theories of psychological development and argues that there are nine different and distinctive kinds of consumers. This is important, SRI suggests, because advertisers can target their appeals to the specific values of each kind of consumer. My description of the VALS 1 typology uses material from articles by Niles Howard (*Dun's Review*, August 1981) and Laurie Itow (*San Francisco Sunday Examiner and Chronicle*, June 27, 1982).

In her article, Itow explains the VALS system as follows:

> The system, called Value and Lifestyles Program (VALS), draws on behavioral science to categorize consumers, not only by demographics such

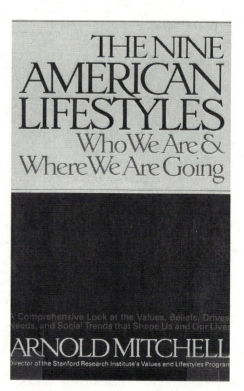

Figure 7.1. This book explains how the VALS typology was developed.

as age, sex, and the products they use, but according to their state of mind. Marie Spengler, VALS director at SRI, says the program is based on an analysis of cultural trends that can be used to develop products and target markets as well as match employees with jobs and make long-range business decisions such as where to build plants. . . . VALS, Spengler says, captures "a deep, underlying sense of what motivates the consumer," using data from a 30-question survey. Consumers are questioned about demographics, such as age and sex. But more importantly, they're also asked about their attitudes and values.

This provides SRI with the data needed to create the various categories of consumers found in VALS. The nine categories of consumers in the VALS typology are as follows:

Need Driven

These consumers are "money restricted" and have a hard time just affording their basic needs. They are divided into two subcategories:

1. *Survivors:* These people are old, poor, and out of the cultural mainstream.
2. *Sustainers:* They are young, crafty, and on the edge of poverty but want to get ahead in the world.

Need-driven consumers make up approximately 11 percent of the adult population in the United States.

Outer Directed

These consumers, who often live in middle America, want others to feel positive about them. There are three subcategories of outer-directed consumers:

3. *Belongers:* They are conservative and conventional in their tastes, nostalgic, sentimental, and not experimental.
4. *Emulators:* These people are upwardly mobile, status conscious, competitive, and distrustful of the establishment. They want to make it big.

5. *Achievers:* They are the leaders of society, who have been successful in the professions, in business, and in the government. They have status, comfort, fame, and materialistic values.

Outer-directed consumers make up about two-thirds of the adult population in America.

Inner Directed

These consumers tend to purchase products to meet their inner needs rather than thinking about the opinions of other people. There are three subcategories of inner-directed consumers:

6. *I-Am-Me's:* They are young, narcissistic, exhibitionist, inventive, impulsive, and strongly individualistic.
7. *Experientials:* This group is in essence an older version of the I-am-me's and is concerned with inner growth and naturalism.
8. *Societally Conscious Individuals:* They believe in simple living and smallness of scale and support causes such as environmentalism, consumerism (not the same thing as consumption), and conservation. This group made up around 28 percent of the adult population in the United States in 1990 and has, perhaps, grown considerably since then.

Integrateds

9. *Integrateds:* This is the last subcategory, one that is characterized by psychological maturity, tolerance, assuredness, and a self-actualizing philosophy. These people tend to ignore advertising, and relatively few advertisements are made to appeal to them. Integrateds make up only around 2 percent of the adult American population, but they are very influential and are disproportionately found among corporate and national leaders. While integrateds may not be as susceptible to advertising as other groups, their taste in lifestyle products may be highly influential, and they may function as what might be described as "taste opinion leaders."

USING THE VALS 1 TYPOLOGY: A CASE STUDY

As an example of the usefulness of the VALS typology, Itow explains why Merrill Lynch switched its ad campaign from "Bullish on America" (illustrated with a herd of bulls) to "A Breed Apart" (illustrated with a lone bull). The "Bullish on America" appealed to belongers—the essentially middle-class conservative members of the mass market who want to fit in. Belongers were not as good a market for Merrill Lynch as achievers—who liked the "Breed Apart" advertisements much better than the "Bullish on America" ads and who had more money to invest. Itow discusses the developmental structure of the VALS typology (1982):

> It's based on the theory that as people grow they fill certain needs for survival and security and then seek a sense of belonging. Next, they strive for self-esteem and then move upward to "self-actualization," developing their inner self and realizing their full potential.

Thus, using the VALS 1 typology, advertisers are able to make appeals that will resonate most directly with the deep-seated beliefs, values, and lifestyles of different segments of the American population. The VALS 1 typology is a logical one—but it has certain problems. So, in 1989, SRI revised the VALS typology.

VALS 2: A REVISION OF THE VALS 1 TYPOLOGY

The VALS typology was revised because it was thought that it did not adequately connect consumer motivations with economic status and the ability to purchase goods and services being advertised. VALS 2 was an attempt to remedy this deficiency by doing a better job of matching consumers with products they could afford. Wanting to buy something is only one step; consumers have to be able to afford what they want. So VALS 2 came up with a set of categories that took into account such matters as income, education (the two are often correlated), health, and the strength of a consumer's desire to purchase something. This led to a modification of the original VALS typology—one that focused on matters involved in consumer decision making. The VALS 2 categories are described below.

1. *Actualizers:* They are successful individuals with a great deal of money. They are concerned with their image as a reflection of their taste and their character, not as a reflection of their power or socioeconomic status. They are interested in social issues and amenable to change.

2. *Fulfilleds:* They are practical and value functionality and durability in products they purchase. They tend to be mature, financially comfortable, and satisfied with their lives and situations but also open to social change.
3. *Achievers:* Achievers are career oriented and value stability and structure, self-discovery, and intimacy. They purchase products to gain an image reflecting their success.
4. *Experiencers:* They love to spend money and tend to be young, impulsive, and enthusiastic. They are willing to try the offbeat and the new and are risk takers.
5. *Believers:* They are highly principled conservative consumers who purchase well-known brands. They are similar to fulfilleds but have less money.
6. *Strivers:* They are like achievers, except they aren't as well off. They are concerned about the opinions of others and greatly desire their approval.
7. *Makers:* People in this category are like experiencers and are active, with much of their energy going into various forms of self-sufficiency, such as fixing a car or canning vegetables.
8. *Strugglers:* These people are at the bottom of the economic totem pole and have to struggle to make ends meet.

It's interesting to compare the two VALS typologies—VALS 1 and VALS 2. In table 7.1, I, to the extent that it is possible, line up the various categories according to similarities, starting with the wealthiest groups and working my way down to the poorest ones. The two systems are different in that VALS 2 is concerned with income level and the ability of consumers to purchase goods and services they desire. But there are some similarities.

Table 7.1. Comparison of VALS 1 and VALS 2

VALS 1	VALS 2
Integrateds	Actualizers
Societally conscious	
Experientials	
I-am-me's	Experiencers
Achievers	Achievers
Emulators	Strivers
Belongers	Believers
Sustainers	
Survivors	Strugglers

One problem with this system is that it assumes rationality. That is, it assumes, on the one hand, that people won't purchase things they can't afford and, on the other hand, that people won't purchase things that are "beneath" them. Thus, it assumes that rich people won't "dress poor" and poor people won't "dress rich" or "drive rich" or be willing to become "house poor" (that is, spend most of their income on a mortgage and the upkeep for a house). But many a person driving an expensive car has leased it and doesn't have much money in the bank. There are numerous other ways of understanding consumers and what makes them tick (and buy or not buy), a number of which I will discuss in the material that follows.

ZIP CODES AND KINDS OF CONSUMERS

Market researchers can tell (so they claim) what you eat for breakfast, what newspapers and magazines you read, what you watch on television, what kind of car you drive, and so on—all on the basis of your ZIP code. According to Michael Weiss, author of *The Clustering of America* (1988), people who have the same ZIP codes tend to be remarkably similar. Weiss has developed a typology of forty different lifestyles—each of which is quite different from all the others—with relatively little overlap. His ideas are described in an article by Sam Whiting in the *San Francisco Chronicle* (November 23, 1988, B3).

Weiss gives each ZIP code a nickname. Some typical nicknames are as follows:

Nickname	ZIP Code	Location
"Blue-Blood Estates"	94025	Atherton, California
"Money and Brains"	94301	Palo Alto (Stanford University)
"Single City Blues"	94704	Berkeley (University of California)
"Hard Scrabble"	94103	Inner Mission (San Francisco)

As Weiss explains things, "We're no longer a country of 50 states but of 40 lifestyle clusters. . . . You can go to sleep in Palo Alto and wake up in Princeton, NJ, and nothing has changed except the trees. The lifestyles are the same. Perrier is in the fridge, and people are playing tennis at three times the national average." This material is dated, but I'm using it to show how marketers have classified people. We find that some of Weiss's categories are found in the Claritas typology, which is still in use.

Weiss offers an interesting comparison between two neighborhoods—what he calls the Urban Gold Coast and the Bohemian Mix (table 7.2). We must keep in mind that Weiss's statistics are from 1988, and there have been considerable changes in America since then. Still, his information is quite interesting. You can see from this comparison that there are considerable differences between Urban Gold Coasters and Bohemians. Both, of course, are relatively small percentages of the U.S. population.

Table 7.2. Urban Gold Coast and Bohemian Mix Compared

Urban Gold Coast	*Bohemian Mix*
94111 Embarcadero (San Francisco)	94117 Haight-Ashbury (San Francisco)
10021 Upper East Side (New York)	20036 Dupont Circle (Washington, DC)
10024 Upper West Side (New York)	02139 Cambridge, MA
20037 West End (Washington, DC)	60614 Lincoln Park (Chicago)
60611 Fort Dearborn (Chicago)	15232 Shadyside (Pittsburgh, PA)
0.5 percent of U.S. households	1.1 percent of U.S. households
Age-group: 18–24 and 65+	Age-group: 18–34
Median household income: $36,838	Median household income: $21,916 Liberal/
	moderate politics

High Usage	
Aperitifs, specialty wines	Environmental organizations
Champagne	Irish whiskey
Tennis	Downhill skiing
Pregnancy tests	Country clubs
Passports	Classical records

Magazines and Newspapers	
New York	*Atlantic Monthly*
New York Times	*Harper's*
Metropolitan Home	*Gentlemen's Quarterly*
Atlantic Monthly	*The New Yorker*

Food Preferences	
Rye/pumpernickel bread	Whole-wheat bread
Tomato/vegetable juice	Frozen waffles
Butter	Fruit juices and drinks
Fresh chicken	TV dinners

Some of Weiss's other clusters are as follows:

Young Influentials	Black Enterprise
Two More Rungs	Dixie-Style
Pools and Patios	Heavy Industry
New Beginnings	Levittown, USA
Gray Power	Hispanic Mix
Public Assistance	Furs and Station Wagons
New Melting Pot	Small-town

We can guess, just from the descriptive names, what people living in such ZIP codes might be like.

Weiss explains that eventually marketers may move beyond ZIP codes to specific mailing addresses. As he points out,

> Right now, Americans are bombarded with 15,000 messages a day. Marketers keep trying to match that little clustering niche that's your lifestyle with whatever they're trying to sell you. People leave a paper trail of warranties and subscriptions. Pretty soon Big Brother will know what's going on in your household. It's only a matter of time until businesses get into the black box of what's in a consumer's head.

Weiss's fears have long been realized. Now shoppers who use Safeway or other supermarket cards or purchase products with credit cards feed computer databases that keep track of their purchases and know what they eat and drink, where they travel, and all kinds of other things about them. Weiss's book is, to some degree, a popularization of the typology developed by the Claritas Corporation, which uses ZIP codes to classify 250,000 neighborhoods in the United States into the consumer clusters that Weiss writes about.

THE CLARITAS TYPOLOGY

The Claritas Corporation, which was acquired by Nielsen recently, argues that "birds of a feather flock together," which suggests that people who live in a given ZIP code tend to have similar socioeconomic levels. Claritas argues that there are, in fact, some sixty-six different categories of consumers in the United States, and it has come up with jazzy names for each of them. The complete list of these groups (some of whom were described by Weiss earlier) follows.

01. Upper Crust
02. Blue Blood Estates
03. Movers & Shakers
04. Young Digerati
05. Country Squires
06. Winner's Circle
07. Money & Brains
08. Executive Suites
09. Big Fish, Small Pond
10. Second City Elite
11. God's Country
12. Brite Lites, Li'l City
13. Upward Bound
14. New Empty Nests
15. Pools & Patios
16. Bohemian Mix
17. Beltway Boomers
18. Kids & Cul-de-Sacs
19. Home Sweet Home
20. Fast-Track Families
21. Gray Power
22. Young Influentials
23. Greenbelt Sports
24. Up-and-Comers
25. Country Casuals
26. The Cosmopolitans
27. Middleburg Managers
28. Traditional Times
29. American Dreams
30. Suburban Sprawl
31. Urban Achievers
32. New Homesteaders
33. Big Sky Families
34. White Picket Fences
35. Boomtown Singles
36. Blue-Chip Blues
37. Mayberry-ville
38. Simple Pleasures
39. Domestic Duos
40. Close-in Couples
41. Sunset City Blues
42. Red, White, & Blues
43. Heartlanders
44. New Beginnings
45. Blue Highways
46. Old Glories
47. City Startups
48. Young & Rustic
49. American Classics
50. Kid Country, USA
51. Shotguns & Pickups
52. Suburban Pioneers
53. Mobility Blues
54. Multi-Culti Mosaic
55. Golden Ponds
56. Crossroads Villagers
57. Old Milltowns
58. Back Country
59. Urban Elders
60. Park Bench Set
61. City Roots
62. Hometown Retired
63. Family Thrifts
64. Bedrock America
65. Big City Blues
66. Low-Rise Living

If you go to the Claritas website and go to its My Best Segments in its Prism NE Segmentation System, you can check for the clusters in your ZIP code.

In my ZIP code, 94941, which is in Marin County, one of the wealthiest counties in the United States, you find a number of clusters at the top of the list: 01, Upper Crust; 02, Blue Blood Estates; 03, Movers & Shakers; 10, Second City Elite; and 12, Bright Lites, Li'l City. Cluster 03 offers the following information:

03: Movers & Shakers (for 2013)
U.S. Households: 1,845,997 (1.55%)
Median Household Income: $100,170
Lifestyle Traits:
Shop at Nordstroms
Play tennis
Read *Yoga Journal*
Watch NHL games
Drive a Land Rover
Demographic Traits:
Urbana city: Suburban
Income: Wealthy
Producing Assets: Elite
Age: 45–64

This description of Movers & Shakers varies considerably from the description I used in the fourth edition of this book, in 2011, when members of this category drove Porsches, read *PC Magazine*, listened to adult contemporary radio, and liked to go scuba diving and snorkeling. Claritas provides similar descriptions of each of its sixty-six clusters. It argues that by knowing who you are targeting for your advertising and what they are like, you can do a better job of reaching them. There are, I should point out, other marketing research organizations that don't believe that "demographics is destiny" but rather rely on psychological characteristics of targeted consumers and other kinds of information as well.

Another typology that claims to be more accurate than demographic factors or ZIP codes, based essentially on magazine choice, is also available to marketers.

MAGAZINE CHOICE AS AN
INDICATOR OF CONSUMER TASTE

Yankelovich Partners, a well-known marketing and research company located in Westport, Connecticut, conducted a survey in 1992 that led to a very interesting discovery. According to Yankelovich, the publications that consumers read, especially the magazines they like, are a better indicator of consumer behavior than demographic factors, such as age, marital status, gender, and residence. This is because people, so the argument goes, choose magazines based on their editorial content, and this content is generally congruent with (or a reflection of) their interests, beliefs, and values.

The Yankelovich survey divided the American public into five groups, or media communities, based on their media tastes. These groups and the basic magazines read by members of each group are described below. Like many marketing typologies, the names of the groups are jazzy and meant to characterize each group in a clever and memorable manner.

1. *Home Engineers:* Women who read magazines such as *Family Circle, Woman's Day,* and *Good Housekeeping* that contain instructions and are didactic in nature.
2. *Real Guys:* Men who choose magazines based on their hobbies. They read magazines such as *Hot Rod, Popular Mechanics, Mechanix Illustrated,* and *Guns and Ammo.*
3. *Ethnic Pewneps (People Who Need People):* Readers of magazines such as *Entertainment Weekly, Sporting News,* and *Ebony,* who are interested in celebrities and identify with them, treating these celebrities as if they were involved in their lives. Both men and women can be members of this category.
4. *Information Grazers:* People who think of themselves as intellectuals and read magazines such as *Time, Bon Appetit,* and *People* to obtain opinions and gain information they can discuss with others. Information grazers are generally male.
5. *Armchair Adventurers:* Older, conservative, more traditional people who experience the world vicariously through magazines such as *Reader's Digest* and *Modern Maturity.* Both men and women are members of this group, and they tend to vote Republican.

The theory behind this typology is that the media choices consumers make are key indicators of their behavior as consumers. This notion suggests that there is a logic to people's behavior as consumers and that certain basic interests and beliefs, reflected in magazine choice, shape consumer behavior in general. This discussion draws on an article by Stuart Elliott in the January 7, 1993, issue of the *New York Times.* Elliott points out that the Yankelovich survey didn't cover people in their twenties and people with annual household incomes of more than $150,000. The question we must ask about this typology—and all typologies, for that matter—is whether it is the best way of doing justice to the information discovered in a survey or whether, somehow, it is reductionist.

Marketers are basically interested in consumer behavior, so they always reduce groups of people to various consumer categories. Does the Yankelovich classification system do justice to the survey results? Are there more than five categories that could be elicited from the data? And, most important, is it describing a correlation (for our purposes, something that's associated with something else) or discovering causation (the "real" reason why people buy this or that product)? It may be, of course, that all we can get from marketing research are correlations between some factor or factors and consumer behavior.

TYPES OF TEENAGE CONSUMERS

In 1998, there were around 30 million teenagers living in America, and these teenagers spent around $4 billion on clothing, cosmetics, and various other kinds of fashion items. Most teenage spending is discretionary and not based on purchasing essentials, such as food or housing. Teen-Age Research Unlimited, a Northbrook, Illinois, market research company that specializes in teenagers—known as "Generation Y" or more recently the "Internet Generation"—has come up with a typology that argues that all teens can be placed in one of four categories: Influencers, Edge Group members, Conformers, and Passives. The characteristics of each group are as follows:

1. *Influencers:* They are quick to embrace fashion trends, spend a good deal of money on fashion trends, and influence spending habits of other teenagers.
2. *The Edge Group:* Members of this group continually change their looks in an attempt to be antifashion and drop their fashion looks when influencers adopt them.
3. *Conformers:* Most teenagers fall into this category. Conformers use popular brands to strengthen their self-esteem.
4. *Passives:* Teenagers in this category aren't particularly interested in using fashion as a statement or a means of fitting in. They buy clothes based on what is available rather than being concerned about being fashionable.

The thing we must remember about these consumers is that they not only spend billions on fashions but also have a significant influence on purchases made by their parents.

An article by Derek Thompson that appeared in the April 12, 2013, issue of the *Atlantic*, "How Teenagers Spend Money," published a chart by Piper Jaffrey that shows typical teenager consumption patterns. The table below is based on the Piper Jaffrey chart.

21%	Clothing
18%	Food
10%	Accessories and personal care
9%	Shoes
8%	Car
8%	Electronics
7%	Music and movies
6%	Concerts and events
3%	Other
2%	Books
2%	Furniture

We see that teenagers, who have mostly discretionary income, spend it on clothes, food, accessories, shoes, cars, and electronics, with other items, such as books, having less importance. What follows is a chart based on one from Statistic Brain showing the amount of income teenagers have and their role in American consumer culture in 2012.

Number of teenagers in the United States	25.6 million
Products bought by and for teens	$208.7 billion
Total teen income in United States	$91.1 billion
Average annual income of 12- to 14-year-olds	$2,167
Average annual income of 15- to 17-year-olds	$4,023

Teenagers spend a lot of time shopping, in part because it is the only "adult" role they are offered in American society and because they have been raised in American culture to be consumers. What does it mean to be an adult in American society—one characterized by some critics as based on "consumer lust"? An adult, so it seems to many teenagers, is someone who buys things, and thus, in their effort to be adults, they become consumers.

An article, "The Young Are Getting and Spending, Too," by Trish Hall (*New York Times*, August 23, 1990, B7), quotes Selina Guber, a psychologist (and president of Children's Market Research Inc. in New York), about the similarity between children and adults as far as consuming is concerned:

> Throughout the country there is a tremendous emphasis on possessions. [Children] reflect that. Like adults, they face pressure to possess the right brands and the right objects. Their wishes are of increasing interest to marketers because American children 6 to 14 years old are believed to have about $6 billion in discretionary income.

Thus, children, as well as adults, are of "consuming" interest to marketers, especially since children have so much discretionary income. This figure, $6 billion, is for 1990; in 2007, it is, no doubt, considerably higher.

As a blurb for *Kids as Customers* (in the November 1995 catalog *Marketing Power: The Marketer's Reference Library*) explains,

> This indispensable handbook describes 4-to-12 year olds as having the greatest sales potential of any age or demographic group. Each year, children spend over $9 billion of their own money; they influence $130 billion of adults' spending; and as future adult customers, they will control even more purchasing dollars tomorrow.

The various citations of billions of dollars differ in various studies because of differences in age-groups being dealt with and in when the studies were made. Whatever the case, the amount of money young children and teenagers have to spend—and do spend—is simply astonishing.

A more recent report by John Stossel (on the television show *20/20*) on teen spending offers an insight into the teen mind and its concern with brands and logos:

> Adolescents have always had a thing for fashion, but now they're spending serious cash on clothing, jewelry and handbags from the "right" designers. These young ladies are interested in products from Tiffany, Coach, and Armani Exchange. "Logos are everything," said Suzanne Zarilli, owner of Wishlist in Westport, Conn. "I get phone calls [asking] what came in this week." The teens say designer labels contribute to their social ranking. "There's almost like this . . . boundary that you don't want to cross . . . because then you'll just be like, weird," Melanie Burg, a 13-year-old from suburban New York, said during a panel discussion *20/20* held with several teens and their moms. One teen, Cheryse Pickens, explained the merits of a $200 bag which she called a "magic bag" for its mix of style and convenience. "You have everything you need in there," said the 17-year-old from New Jersey. "I mean you don't need a huge bag. You just need the cute little . . . you know, don't overstuff it." When asked why a less expensive bag, of the same size, would not do the job, she replied, "No, it's not the same."

According to Stossel, young shoppers spent $170 billion, which is twice the amount they spent ten years earlier. They get their money mostly by working or from allowances from their parents (http://abcnews.go.com/2020/story?id=124346&page=1).

BLOGS AND MARKETING

The Web logs that people write are now being mined as a source of valuable information about consumer preferences. An article in the June 23, 2005, *Wall Street Journal*, "Marketers Scan Blogs for Brand Insights," points out that marketing organizations are gaining valuable insights into people's attitudes toward various products by searching through chat rooms, message boards, electronic forums, and the millions of Web logs that are on the Internet. The opinions of the bloggers, which are unsolicited and honest, can be seen as a kind of gigantic focus group. Rick Murray, executive vice president of Edelman, a Chicago public relations firm, says, "We look at the blogosphere as a focus group with 15 million people going on 24/7 that you can tap into without going behind a one-way mirror."

Tastes have, no doubt, changed since this article was published, but the point of the article, that advertisers use blogs—and now we would add Facebook, Twitter, and other social media—to get information on people's taste, remains valid. Advertising agencies are also using blogs to get their message across. They do this by purchasing space on popular blogs, some of which are read by thousands—even hundreds of thousands—of people. But blog ads have to be done carefully lest the blog reader be turned off, so most blog ads are not conventional. An article, "Bloggers' New Brand Starts to Click with Advertisers," in the March 28, 2005, *Financial Times*, mentions an advertising campaign by the United Church of Christ, which spent $15,000 on a blog campaign. Some 74,000 people clicked on the advertisement, meaning that the cost per viewing of their ad was around twenty cents.

A company in Boulder, Colorado—Umbria Communications—has software called "Buzz Report" that data mines millions of blogs to find out what bloggers are saying about various products and trends. As the article by Bridget Finn in the September 2005 issue of *Business 2.0* reports, "Umbria uses language-processing algorithms that track positive and negative mentions of a brand and predict the age range and gender of every opiner" (36). Now, market research firms are deeply involved in studying blogs where people offer private thoughts and opinions in a very public forum that is accessible to everyone. An article by Jeff Gibbard, on June 27, 2012, "Using Social Media to Determine Consumer Preferences," reads,

The smart business determines where relevant conversations take place online. If you are a restaurant, you need to know about Yelp and Foursquare, and you should probably take notice of Twitter and Facebook. If you are a software company, you'll want to find forums or blogs and certainly monitor Twitter. If you are a company that sells a retail product, you'll want to find the online channels that sell your widget, and consult the reviews. The key is to actively seek out places where people share their ideas and opinions about your product or service. The information there is incredibly valuable and requires far less effort to gather than through other means. (http://www.socialmediaphilanthropy.com/2012/06/27/use-social-media-to-determine-customer-preferences)

Gibbard's point is that social media offers companies a great deal of information that they can use in making advertisements that will be of interest to members of target audiences.

A TYPOLOGY FOR EVERYONE IN THE WORLD

All the typologies I've been discussing to this point have been for people in the United States—the country where marketing has reached its highest level of development. People who live in America and are considered "normal" in terms of the amount of television they watch are exposed to many more advertisements and commercials than people in other countries, all things considered.

On the basis of 35,000 interviews with consumers in thirty-five different countries, Roper Starch Worldwide claims that it has identified basic values that are universal in nature, values shared by people in all countries (or at least values that cross national borders). People were studied in North America, South America, Europe, and Asia in terms of their bedrock values and the basic motivations that shape their behavior. Roper Starch released a study, "Global Consumer Hot Buttons," that claims there are six basic categories of consumers in all countries. They are listed below, with the traditional catchy names that market researchers use.

1. *Strivers:* This is the largest group, with 23 percent of the world's adult population. They tend to be middle-aged and materialistic and value status, wealth, and power. They tend to be found in developing and developed countries.
2. *Devouts:* They are almost as large as strivers, with 22 percent of the world's adult population. As the term "devout" suggests, they believe in more traditional values, such as faith, obedience, duty, and respect for elders. Devouts tend to be found in the Middle East, Africa, and Asia.

3. *Altruists:* Some 18 percent of the world's adult population are altruists. They are, as a rule, well educated, older (median age forty-
   four), and interested in social causes and political issues. They tend
   to be found in Latin America and Russia.
4. *Intimates:* Only 15 percent of the world's adult population are
   intimates. They are very similar to a different typology called
   Pewneps—people who need people. That is, intimates are concerned primarily with relationships with spouses, family, friends,
   colleagues, and significant others. Intimates are primarily found
   in the United Kingdom, the United States, the Netherlands, and
   Hungary. They have in common a heavy use of media.
5. *Fun Seekers:* About 12 percent of the adult population falls in this
   category. They are the youngest group in the typology and are
   interested primarily in excitement, pleasure, and adventure. They
   value looking good and spend a good deal of time in restaurants,
   bars, and clubs. Fun seekers are an MTV generation.
6. *Creatives:* At 10 percent, creatives are the smallest category in the
   worldwide typology. Their focus is on technology and knowledge, and they are trendsetters who own and use computers,
   surf the Web, and consume the greatest amount of media—especially print media, such as newspapers, magazines, and books,
   of any category.

Table 7.3 shows the basic characteristics of the six groups so that you can
see how they compare with one another.

The question we must ask about these categories is whether they miss any
important groups of people—that is, does this typology cover all the adults,
and are the categories mutually exclusive? Can every adult in the world be
put into one and only one of these six categories? In some cases, as table 7.3

Table 7.3. International Consumer Values and Beliefs

Strivers	*Devouts*	*Altruists*	*Intimates*	*Fun Seekers*	*Creatives*
23%	22%	18%	15%	12%	10%
Wealth	Obedience	Social issues	Relationships	Adventure	Knowledge
Newspapers	Least media use	Like media	Music	MTV	Highest media use
Developed nations	Middle East, Asia, Africa	Latin America, Russia	United Kingdom, United States, Netherlands		

shows, there was no information (or, more precisely, no information in the article that discussed the report) for some categories. That explains the gaps. What I wonder is, are some of the fun seekers also altruists? And are some of the devouts also creatives? We must remember, of course, that this typology, like all of the typologies I've described, focuses on consumer behavior and thus is, by definition, reductionist. The Roper Starch typology is about consumers and their values and is concerned primarily with the belief systems or "hot buttons" that can be used to understand the minds of consumers.

In 1951, Marshall McLuhan explained in *The Mechanical Bride* what advertising agencies were doing. He compared advertising agencies with Hollywood and wrote, in his chapter "Love-Goddess Assembly Line" (1951:97),

> The ad agencies and Hollywood, in their different ways, are always trying to get inside the public mind in order to impose their collective dreams on that inner stage. And in the pursuit of this goal both Hollywood and the advertising agencies themselves give major exhibitions of unconscious behavior. One dream opens into another until reality and fantasy are made interchangeable. The ad agencies flood the daytime world of conscious purpose and control with erotic imagery from the night world in order to drown, by suggestion, all sales resistance. Hollywood floods the night world with daytime imagery in which synthetic gods and goddesses [stars] appear to assume the roles of our wakeaday existence in order to console us for the failures of our daily lives. The ad agencies hold out for each of us the dream of a spot on Olympus where we can quaff and loll forever amid the well-known brands. The movies reverse this procedure by showing us the stars—who, we are assured, dwell on "beds of amaranth and holly"—descending to our level.

The advertising agencies and marketing experts, with their various typologies, do offer some very interesting information about the human psyche and about what it is that makes us tick. They are continually probing us, trying to get at the G-spot of consumer behavior and decision making, doing everything they can to understand us so that they can—in starkest terms—manipulate us.

A COMPARISON OF THE DIFFERENT TYPOLOGIES

Now that I've offered a number of different marketing typologies, it's worth looking at them all together to see what they reflect about the way marketing research sees human beings. In table 7.4, I list the various typologies—though, in

Table 7.4. Marketing Typologies Compared

VALS1	VALS 2	ZIP Codes	Yankelovich	Teenagers	Roper Starch
Survivors	Actualizers	Blue Blood Estates	Home engineers	Influencers	Strivers
Sustainers	Fulfilleds	Money & Brains	Real guys	Edge group	Devouts
Belongers	Achievers	Big City Blues	Ethnic Pewneps	Conformers	Altruists
Emulators	Experiencers	Urban Gold Coast	Information grazers	Passives	Intimates
Achievers	Believers	Bohemian	Armchair adventurers		Fun seekers
I-am-me's	Strivers	Young Influentials		Creatives	
Experientials	Makers	Two More Rungs			
Societally conscious	Strugglers	Gray Power Pools & Patios			
Integrateds		Hispanics Mix			

some cases, not all the subcategories. Table 7.4 does not compare types and categories horizontally. That is, there is no similarity between survivors, actualizers, and so on. What is interesting is how more than 100 million adult Americans can be classified in the first four typologies, how 30 million teenagers are characterized in the teenager typology, and how around 3 billion adult human beings are characterized in the last typology, the Roper Starch system.

One generalization that emerges from the chart is that certain people are trendsetters or opinion leaders, and others, who form the majorities, imitate and follow the trendsetters. And there are various other subcategories, depending on the typology, of those who fit on various rungs of the ladder below that of the trendsetters, opinion leaders, and creatives. There are some who have opted out of the system and are very hard for marketers to reach, such as the integrateds and others who follow the trendsetters and purchase things to generate an image of success. Some of the typologies, such as the Yankelovich one, don't seem to be directly involved with fashion and such, but the magazines people in the various categories read suggest that these people are motivated by the same things as are those people in categories more directly related to marketing.

We can also see various oppositions in these typologies:

Actives	Passives
Leaders	Followers
Creatives	Imitators
Achievers	Strugglers
Influencers	Conformists
Experience seekers	Safety seekers

These polarities reflect the way the human mind functions. According to the Swiss linguist Ferdinand de Saussure, concepts are by nature differential—and our minds find meaning by setting up paired oppositions.

A CONCLUSION TO THIS DISCUSSION IN THE FORM OF A QUESTION

The primary goal of advertising and marketing, of course, is to shape our behavior; advertising agencies can be looked at as hired guns whose main job is to destroy consumer resistance and shape consumer desire and action—whether it be to sell cigarettes, beer, politicians, or, lately, prescription medicines. And in some cases, it is to sell socially positive messages. There is little question that the information that marketers have about consumer motivation and the minds of consumers is a source of power. Is this power used ethically and for socially constructive purposes? That is the question.

STUDY QUESTIONS, APPLICATIONS, AND ASSIGNMENTS

1. How much advertising is the typical American exposed to each day? How many television commercials and how many print advertisements?
2. What do the statistics on total media advertising worldwide reveal?
3. How much money, per person, is it estimated that we will spend on advertising in 2015 in the United States?
4. What effects does our exposure to advertising have on us—as a society and as individuals?

5. What does Hans Magnus Enzensberger say about our being masters of what our minds accept or reject? What do you think of his argument?

6. Marxists argue that our ideas come from society and are not based on our individual personalities and experiences. What do they say to justify this position? What do you think of this argument?

7. What does Gerald Zaltman say about cognition and our "consciously willing an action"?

8. What role does our unconscious play in our behavior? How do we know what role it plays?

9. What was said about the relationship between marketing and advertising? Do some research in recent scholarly journals about this matter and write a short paper on your findings.

10. Contrast demographics and psychographics. Do you think one or the other plays the most important role in our purchasing behavior? If so, which one? Explain your answer.

11. What are the attributes of a valid classification system/typology?

12. Abraham Maslow constructed a theory of human needs. What are its components? Investigate how his theory has been used by marketers and advertisers.

13. What are the different categories in the VALS 1 typology? How does it differ from the VALS 2 typology?

14. How did the VALS 1 typology shape a Merrill Lynch advertising campaign?

15. How have ZIP codes been used by marketers? Do some research in scholarly journals and books on the relationship between ZIP codes and purchasing behavior.

16. What is the Claritas typology? Are there really that many different kinds of consumers, or is Claritas inventing them? Explain your answer. Go to the Claritas website Prism NE and check your ZIP code. Look at the different groups in that ZIP code and see what Claritas says about their possessions. Do you think Claritas is accurate?

17. What is the relationship that exists between magazine choice and consumer taste according to Yankelovich? Do some scholarly research on this subject and see what is said about this matter.

18. What are the four kinds of teenage consumers? Which one are/were you?
19. What insights does John Stassel provide about teen spending?
20. How do marketers and advertising agencies use social media to find out about consumer preferences?

To manufacture a product without at the same time manufacturing a demand has become unthinkable. Today the manufacture of demand means, for most large companies, television—its commercials as well as other program elements. The growing scale of mass production has inevitably made advertising more crucial, but this understates the situation. As society becomes more product-glutted, the pressure on the consumer to consume—to live up to higher and higher norms of consumption—has become unrelenting.

The pressure, as various observers have noted, centers on selling the unnecessary. The merchandising of necessities—which, to some extent, will be bought anyway—can seldom sustain the budgets applied to the unnecessary, unless the necessary is cloaked with mythical supplemental values. The focus is on the creation of emotion-charged values to make the unneeded necessary.

All this is now so taken for granted that it is seldom discussed. The young writer entering advertising assumes that hope and fear are the springs he must touch—hope of success and fear of failure in sex, business, community status. As a dramatic medium that can draw on the resources of every art, and has as its stage the privacy of the home, television has unparalleled opportunity for this psychic pressure.

—Erik Barnouw, *The Sponsor: Notes on a Modern Potentate*

Beyond attracting the viewer's attention, the image(s) in an ad are typically meant to give rise to some emotional disposition toward the product, politician, social cause, or whatever else the ad is about. The iconicity of visual images serves this process by making it possible for images to draw upon the rich variety of visual stimuli and associated emotions to which we are already attuned through our interactions with our social and natural environments: facial expressions, gestures, postures, personal appearance, physical surroundings, and so on. Moreover . . . visual images are capable of simulating certain aspects of these interactions by means of the variables that control the viewer's perspective: degree of proximity, angle of view, presence or absence of subjective shots, and so on.

—Paul Messaris, *Visual Persuasion: The Role of Images in Advertising*

8

ANALYZING PRINT ADVERTISEMENTS

or: Six Ways of Looking at a Fidji Perfume Advertisement

The thing we have to realize about radio and television commercials and print advertisements (and all other forms of advertising as well) is that they are, aside from their commercial functions, works of popular art. Or maybe "commercial" art is a more fitting term. In this chapter and the next, I focus on print advertisements and television commercials, the two most interesting—from my point of view—kinds of texts. I will use the term "text" here for both; it is a term conventionally used in criticism nowadays to cover all forms of artworks.

LOTMAN'S CONTRIBUTIONS
TO UNDERSTANDING TEXTS

One important thing to remember about these texts is that every aspect of them is significant. This point is made by the Russian semiotician Yuri Lotman in *The Structure of the Artistic Text*. Lotman writes, "The tendency to interpret *everything* in an artistic text as meaningful is so great that we rightfully consider nothing accidental in a work of art" (1977:17). Lotman also explains why texts yield to so many different interpretations (1977:23):

> Since it can concentrate a tremendous amount of information into the "area" of a very small text . . . an artistic text manifests yet another feature: it transmits different information to different readers in proportion to each one's comprehension; it provides the reader with a language in which each successive portion of information may be assimilated with repeated reading. It behaves as a kind of living organism which has a feedback channel to the reader and thereby instructs him.

Lotman's two points are very important for us to keep in mind:

1. *Everything* in a text such as a commercial is important.
2. *The more you know, the more you can see* in a text.

This is because texts store a tremendous amount of information in themselves and are a great deal more complicated than we might imagine. This notion that texts are storehouses of information explains, for example, why we can read novels several times and see films a number of times and still enjoy the experience. That's because we see new things in the novel each time we read it, and we see new things in the film each time we see it. And the same, of course, applies to many other kinds of artworks—paintings, music, sculpture, poems, and so on.

WHAT'S THERE TO ANALYZE IN AN ADVERTISEMENT?

Let me start with an imaginary print advertisement in which we find a photograph of a man and a woman and some textual material. Here's a list of possible topics to consider in analyzing the advertisement:

1. How would you describe the design of the advertisement? Do we find axial balance or an asymmetrical relationship among the elements in the advertisement?
2. How much copy is there relative to the amount of pictorial matter? Is this relationship significant in any respect?
3. Is there a great deal of blank (white) space in the advertisement, or is it full of graphic and textual material?
4. What angle is the photograph shot at? Do we look up at the people in the advertisement? Do we look down at them from a height? Or do we look at them from a shoulder-level position? What significance does the angle of the shot have?
5. How is the photograph lit? Is there a great deal of light, or is there a little light and very dark shadows (chiaroscuro lighting)? What is the mood found in the advertisement?
6. If the photograph is in color, what colors dominate? What significance do these colors have?
7. How would you describe the two figures in the advertisement? Consider such matters as facial expression, hair color, hair length,

hairstyling, fashions (clothes, shoes, eyeglasses design, and jewelry), various props (a cane or an umbrella), body shape, body language, age, gender, race, ethnicity, signs of occupation, signs of educational level, relationships suggested between the male and female, objects in the background, and so on.

8. What is happening in the advertisement? What does the "action" in the photo suggest? Assume that we are seeing one moment in an ongoing narrative. What is this narrative, and what does it reveal about the two figures?

9. Are there any signs or symbols in the photograph? If so, what role do they play?

10. In the textual material, how is language used? What arguments are made or implied about the people in the photograph and about the product being advertised? That is, what rhetorical devices are used to attract readers and stimulate desire in them for the product or service? Does the advertisement use associations or analogies or something else to make its point?

11. What typefaces are used in the textual parts of the advertisement? What importance do the various typefaces have? (Why these typefaces and not other ones?)

12. What are the basic "themes" in the advertisement? How do these themes relate to the story implied by the advertisement?

13. What product or service is being advertised? Who is the target audience for this product or service? What role does this product or service play in American culture and society?

14. What values and beliefs are reflected in the advertisement? Sexual jealousy? Patriotism? Motherly love? Brotherhood of man? Success? Power? Good taste?

15. Is there any background information you need to make sense of the advertisement? How does context shape our understanding of the advertisement?

This list of questions will direct your attention to various matters that might be considered when interpreting a typical print advertisement found in a newspaper or magazine.

ANALYZING THE FIDJI AD

The more critics know, the more they can find in commercials or any kind of artistic or literary text. There are a number of standard approaches to interpreting commercial texts—such as semiotic analysis, psychoanalytic

Figure 8.1

Fidji: le parfum
des paradis retrouvés.

Available at Bloomingdale's

Fidji de Guy Laroche.
De la Haute Couture à la Haute Parfumerie

criticism, Marxist analysis, and sociological analysis—which I briefly exemplify in my interpretation of one of the most interesting print advertisements in recent decades—the Fidji "Woman with the Snake" perfume ad. This ad is reproduced in figure 8.1.

The methods of analysis I will use on the Fidji ad are the following:

1. *Semiotic Analysis:* What signs, symbols, and codes are found in the text? How does the advertisement or commercial generate meaning in people?
2. *Psychoanalytic Theory:* How does the text make use of the basic elements of the human psyche to sell goods and services? What appeals to unconscious elements, id/ego/superego aspects of the psyche, sexuality, anxiety, and so on are found in the text?

3. *Sociological Analysis:* What does the text contain that is relevant to such matters as socioeconomic class, gender, race, status, and role? What is the product, and what does it reflect about social concerns and the problems of people in their everyday lives?
4. *Historical Analysis:* How have advertising and its methods evolved over the years? If the advertisement or commercial is part of a campaign, what is the campaign like? Where does this text fit into the campaign? How do advertising texts relate to historical events?
5. *Political Analysis:* What role does the advertisement or commercial have in the political process? What techniques were used? What appeals are made? What effects does it have on an election or some aspect of political decision making?
6. *Myth/Ritual Analysis:* What mythical or ritualistic aspects of the text are of interest? How does the advertisement or commercial relate to ancient myths?

I will use many of these techniques in the interpretations of the Fidji advertisement that follows. Since I quoted from Yuri Lotman, a semiotician, at the beginning of this chapter, let me start by discussing the Fidji ad from a semiotic viewpoint.

A SEMIOTIC INTERPRETATION OF THE FIDJI ADVERTISEMENT

Semiotics, as I explained earlier, is defined as the science of signs—a sign being anything that can be used to stand for something else, to deliver some kind of a message, to generate some kind of meaning. There are two dominant systems for analyzing signs—one created by the Swiss linguist Ferdinand de Saussure and the other by the American philosopher C. S. Peirce.

Saussure said that signs are made up of *signifiers* (sounds or images) and *signifieds* (concepts or ideas). Our facial expressions, our hair color, our body language, our clothes, our voices—just about everything we do functions as a signifier of something (our moods, feelings, beliefs, religion, and so on). The important thing about the relationship that exists between signifiers and signifieds is that it is arbitrary. That is, it is based on convention and has to be learned; it is not natural and universal.

The other system, Peirce's, includes three kinds of signs: signs that signify by resemblance—what he calls *icons*; signs that signify by some kind of cause-and-effect relationship—what he calls *indexes*; and signs that signify by convention—what he calls *symbols*. A photograph is an icon, smoke coming out of a house is an indexical sign, and a flag, the Star of David, a cross, and so on are symbolic signs. Each of these systems is rather complex, but just using the fundamental notions of Saussure and Peirce, we can make a decent semiotic analysis of the Fidji advertisement.

Note that the design of the advertisement is formal and has a good deal of empty or white space. This kind of design is typical of expensive, upscale products. We see only the bottom of the woman's face. This enables women looking at the advertisement to put themselves into the advertisement. The woman's lips are full and partially open, suggesting, perhaps, sexual passion or excitement.

We can't be certain, but she seems to be a Polynesian woman—the kind of woman found on Fiji, the kind of woman painted by Paul Gauguin who "escaped" from France to Polynesia. The lighting is rather extreme, with strong darks and lights; the lighting emphasizes the woman's long neck. She has long, dark hair and is wearing a yellow orchid in it. Dark hair is connected in the American mind (so D. H. Lawrence suggested) with notions of sexual passion—in contrast to blond hair, which is connected with innocence and sexual coldness and unresponsiveness. And long hair has, for the popular mind, a sexual dimension to it; in many cosmetic advertisements (for hair color and so on), we often see women striding across fields with their long hair blowing wildly and voluptuously in the wind.

The name of the perfume, Fidji, and the photograph of the Polynesian woman generate a sense that we are in the tropics, where there is heat and sexual passion is natural and pervasive. We associate the tropics with earthy, almost primitive passions and with sexual freedom, for in Fiji and other tropical islands, we have, we believe, escaped from the prohibitions of civilization.

There is also the use of French—a form of snob appeal that relies on the stereotype of the French as sexy and not as burdened by Puritanical repression as Americans. French is also a language for sophisticated people, people who—in America—are cultivated or educated enough to be able to read the copy, which is all in French.

Saussure explained that we understand what concepts mean only differentially. As he put it, "Concepts are purely differential and defined not by their positive content but negatively with the other terms of the system. . . . The most precise characteristic of concepts is in being what the others are not" (1966:117). Thus, it is relations that determine meaning, not content per se. Nothing, strictly speaking, has meaning in itself; it is the relationships of concepts to one another that generate meaning, especially negation. That explains why we find it so easy to make paired oppositions: rich and poor, happy and sad, dark and light, and so on.

We can use Saussure's insight about the role of oppositions to help make sense of the Fidji advertisement. It posits two worlds, which are described in table 8.1.

Table 8.1. Polar Oppositions (Implied) in Fidji Advertisement

Fidji	Civilized World
Polynesian woman	White woman
Paradise	Hell
Escape	Imprisonment
Dark hair	Light hair
Free sexuality	Repressed sexuality
Magic	Rationality
Fidji perfume	Other perfumes

These are some of the more important signs and meanings generated by these signs found in the Fidji advertisement. There are many others, of course, but my aim here is to give you an idea of what semiotic analysis can do when it is applied to an advertisement, not to do a complete semiotic analysis.

A PSYCHOANALYTIC INTERPRETATION OF THE FIDJI ADVERTISEMENT

Serge Lutens, who makes perfumes, explains the effects of perfumes as follows (www.mimifroufrout.com): "Perfume, in and of itself, is not just an aroma. It is potentially a carrier for the imagination. Perfume is thick; it is poison and pure desire. It is Eros in prison."

With this insight into the power of perfume in mind, I would like to consider one of the most interesting perfume advertisements of recent years—the Fidji "snake" ad. One of the most striking elements of the Fidji advertisement is the presence of the snake wound around the woman's neck. In Freudian psychoanalytic theory, snakes are phallic symbols—that is, they represent the penis by nature of their shape—an iconic resemblance, semioticians would say. (In some countries, I should point out, this advertisement appeared without the snake; see figure 8.2.)

Snakes and women are part of the Adam and Eve story and are thus known to millions of people. There is, then, a mythological significance to images of snakes and women—one that I explore in more detail later. For those who have not read the passages in the Bible that deal with this all-important story, I offer them below (King James version of the Bible, the book of Genesis):

> And the Lord God called unto Adam, and said unto him, "Where art thou?"
>   And he said, "I heard thy voice in the garden, and I was afraid, because I was naked and hid myself.
>   "Who told thee that thou wast naked? Hast thou eaten of the tree, whereof I commanded thee that thou should not eat?"

Figure 8.2

Fidji de Guy Laroche, Paris.

And the man said, "The woman whom thou gavest to be with me, she gave me of the tree, and I did eat."

And the Lord God said unto the woman, "What is this that thou hast done?"

And the woman said, "The serpent beguiled me, and I did eat."

And the Lord God said to the serpent, "Because thou hast done this, Thou art cursed above all cattle. And above every beast of the field; Upon thy belly shalt thou go, And dust shalt thou eat all the days of thy life; And I will put emnity between thee and the woman, And between thy seed and her seed.

Unto the woman he said, I will greatly multiply thy sorrow and thy conception; In sorrow thou shall bring forth children; And thy desire shall be to thy husband, And he shall rule over thee.

So the snake tempted Eve, and she convinced Adam that he should eat from the Tree of the Knowledge of Good and Evil. The results of this act were calamitous for men and women and snakes as well.

There is also anxiety related to snakes and to fears deep in the psyches of some women of being penetrated by men's genitals. Ironically, it could be ar-

Insights from Advertising Agencies

Advertising agencies search for universal metaphors that people everywhere will be able to understand easily. Account executives are involved, among other things, with developing a creative brief—it tells what the advertisement should accomplish. We ask ourselves, If we could say one thing about the client, what would it be?

gued that perfume is in certain ways seen by women as analogous to venom—a magical substance that has incredible effects. The most important of these effects is to make women irresistible to men. This would be an example of magical thinking—a feeling of being powerful and able to get what you want.

If you think of the snake forming an "S," the top of the cover of the Fidji bottle, its two sides and the thin black cording that is used on the bottle forming an "E," and the woman's intertwined fingers as forming an "X," you have the word "sex" hidden in the advertisement. Even though we may not consciously be aware that we are reading this word, in psychoanalytic theory, seeing it would have some kind of subliminal impact on our psyches and make us feel more inclined toward sexual activity.

The orchid is also a sexual symbol—flowers being the sexual apparatus of plants. We humans use these flowers to make products that use their smells to excite one another sexually—or so the argument goes. Animals, we know, use smell to determine when females are sexually receptive and fertile. We use the same notions when we use perfumes and aftershave lotions. We try to bring out the animal in those we hope will become our sexual partners, except that the smells we use are not natural, based on our reproductive cycles, but artificial. (Recent scientific studies suggest that subtle and hard-to-detect body smells may in fact have a sexual arousal function.)

We can also look at this advertisement (and most advertising) using Freud's structural hypothesis—his suggestion that the psyche has three components: the id, the ego, and the superego. These phenomena are shown in table 8.2.

According to Freud, the id can be described as a "cauldron of seething excitement." It is disorganized and seeks, essentially, to satisfy instinctual needs. The superego is the element of the psyche that is always approving or disapproving of acts the id is planning, and it also provides critical self-observation and the need for reparation in cases of wrongdoing. In between these two forces is the ego, trying to keep the psyche in balance. Too much id, and a person's life is chaotic; too much superego, and a person lacks energy and becomes obsessed with guilt.

Table 8.2

Id	Ego	Superego
Drives	Reason	Conscience
"Do it now"	Wait	"Don't do it"
Lust	Balance	Moral precepts
Energy	Survival	Guilt
Desire	Wallet	Fear of debt
Buy it	Limited funds	Do without
Advertising	Budget	Bank account

In terms of advertising, the factors shown in table 8.2 are the most important. Advertising appeals to the id and tries to evade the strictures of the superego. And the ego tries to control the id's desire to buy everything by suggesting that it might be a good idea to reconsider the desired purchase, by appealing to the superego of limited funds (one's budget) or reminding people that they are maxed out on their credit cards.

In the Fidji advertisement, we are in the tropics, away from civilization, which seeks to curtail our id impulses. That is the point Freud made in *Civilization and Its Discontents*: the price we pay for civilization and culture is repression.

A SOCIOLOGICAL INTERPRETATION
OF THE FIDJI ADVERTISEMENT

One thing we might consider when we apply sociological concepts to the Fidji advertisement is its target audience. Who is the advertisement designed to reach, and why do the appeals in the Fidji ad sell it to its target audience? On the basis of the woman in the advertisement, one would say it is young women who feel frustrated by the constraints of their everyday lives in contemporary urban societies and who seek, in fantasy, an escape.

This escape involves nature, which is where the Polynesian fantasy takes place, and romantic love, which is why the product is utilized. The target audience is also, we can infer, somewhat sophisticated, in that it knows French, or is pseudosophisticated, in that members think buying a French perfume shows one has class. That is, users of Fidji think of themselves as elites—if not economically, then in terms of their lifestyles or what might be called their taste culture. Maybe wearing Fidji, a refined perfume (it's French, isn't it?), also indicates one's socioeconomic class. You have to be able to afford it, after all.

Fidji is functional in two ways. First, it is designed either to attract a new sexual partner or to stimulate a sexual partner one already has—the main reason for wearing perfume. Second, Fidji consolidates the wearer's sense of herself as sophisticated and desirable. That is, it confers status—or so those who purchase Fidji think. Thus, perfumes in general and Fidji in particular reaffirm the value and importance of romantic love, and wearers of Fidji signify that they are interested in making love.

The fact that the model in the advertisement is a woman of color may signify our sense, common in American culture, that women of color are more passionate and less inhibited than white women. In America, we tend to see blonds as innocent, cold, and frigid, and women of color as just the opposite. We assume, of course, that the woman in the advertisement is Polynesian because of the name of the perfume and from what we can see of her face.

A MARXIST INTERPRETATION
OF THE FIDJI ADVERTISEMENT

One point a typical Marxist would make about this advertisement is that it reflects, in graphic manner, the exploitation of people of the Third World, the world of people of color, by people in the First World and, in particular, by bourgeois capitalist societies—the kind that encourage capitalist corporations like Fidji's maker, Guy Laroche. According to Marxist theory, capitalism has survived by exporting its problems, and thus the woman in the Fidji advertisement is really an advertisement for capitalist imperialism, not for perfume.

The Fidji advertisement is also a classic example of the excesses of bourgeois consumer culture, which has come to dominate every aspect of our lives, especially our sexuality. Our sexuality can be used against us, so to speak, to encourage us to make ever greater wasteful expenditures in the name of a spurious value—glamour. Advertising is, then, one of the central institutions of contemporary bourgeois cultures and is not to be thought of as merely a form of product entertainment. It has a political mission—to distract us from the breakdown of our civic cultures and focus our attention on private expenditures. We revel in our personal luxuries as our society disintegrates into chaos and take refuge in gated communities to escape from the dangers of the social disorganization we have generated.

What advertisements like the one for Fidji perfume demonstrate is that alienation is very functional for those who own the means of production. We attempt to assuage our alienation by creating consumer cultures and by continually purchasing things, which creates greater and greater profits for those who own the instruments of production and distribution. That is, alienation leads to consumption and higher profits. And since in recent years bourgeois capitalist societies have sexualized the act of consumption, as W. H. Haug points out, there are even stronger inducements for people to participate in consumer cultures.

One problem with the Marxist analysis of this advertisement and of advertising and consumer cultures is that it is doctrinaire. The party line, so to speak, covers all advertising and just about every other aspect of capitalist societies. In addition, Marxism, politically speaking, has imploded, and former Soviet societies are now feverishly consuming, trying, it would seem, to make up for lost time. And while the Marxist critique of bourgeois societies may be logical and even correct, it lacks resonance. Studies have shown that Communist Party members and members of political elites in previously communist societies exploited people terribly and consumed enormous amounts of food and goods in proportion to their numbers.

The bottle of Fidji perfume that the maiden holds so lovingly in her hands might be construed to represent, finally, the domination of bourgeois capitalist cultures over Second and Third World cultures. That is, this advertisement might be seen as a reflection of the cultural imperialism that we find in contemporary society. Because the cost of making media texts is so high, Third World countries import most of the programs they show on their television stations and most of the films they see. The cultural imperialism argument made by Marxists and others is that First World media are destroying the native cultures found in the Third World, leading to an eventual homogenization of culture, dominated by capitalist bourgeois values.

THE MYTH MODEL AND THE FIDJI ADVERTISEMENT

We can apply the myth model, explained earlier in my discussion of marketing and myth, to the Fidji advertisement. I would argue that one myth that informs this advertisement is that of Medusa, the mythical creature—a Gorgon—whose hair was made of snakes. If you looked at Medusa, you would turn to stone. Medusa was killed by Perseus, a hero who escaped death by looking at her reflection in his bronze shield and beheading her. What is important is that we have here a woman and a snake intimately connected.

With her hair of snakes, she was, in psychoanalytic terms, a hyperphallic female, since snakes, for Freudians, are phallic symbols. There may also be an element of ambivalence about Medusa in many men: a beautiful female who killed all who looked on her. (This ambivalence is best reflected in an early churchman's definition of women: *templus supra cloaca*, which means "a temple over a sewer.") A contemporary aspect of the Medusa story is found in the belief some women have that their hair has life and is powerful. Hair color and hairstyle now play an important role in many women's lives. Finally, it might be possible that the fear many men have of snakes is connected, somehow (as this mythic story suggests), to an unconscious unification of snakes and women that leads to seeing women as snakelike. This, in turn, enables us to identify perfume as being like venom.

I interpret myths in conventional terms: they are sacred stories, often dealing with the creation of the world and the activities of various gods, demigods, heroes, and heroines that provide people with core values and a comprehensive belief system. These beliefs are passed down, according to some anthropological thinkers, in a coded manner and are hidden in various stories and other narratives we learn.

With Medusa as our myth, we can see in table 8.3 the way the rest of the myth model might be filled in.

Table 8.3

Myth	Medusa
Historical act	Cleopatra kills herself with an asp
Elite culture text	Shakespeare: *Antony and Cleopatra*
Popular culture text	Fidji "Woman with Snake" advertisement
Everyday life	Woman dabs on Fidji perfume

The point, then, is that many of our everyday activities and rituals are intimately connected to ancient myths, though we may not recognize that what we are doing has any connection to myths or to the past. We may think we have escaped from the past and that it is irrelevant, but in more ways than we might imagine, ancient myths inform (though in disguised form) our arts, our media, and our everyday lives. Women and snakes go back, of course, to the story of Adam and Eve in the Garden of Eden. The connection between women and snakes—the beguilers—is ancient and is part of the consciousness of all who have read the Old Testament or heard about it.

A FEMINIST INTERPRETATION
OF THE FIDJI ADVERTISEMENT

One of the basic contentions of most contemporary feminist thinkers is that we live in a phallocentric society—one dominated by males and what might be called the invisible power of the phallus. We may not be aware of the power of the phallus, but the institutions of society and social relations are shaped, so the argument goes, by the power of males, by male sexuality, and ultimately by the phallus. Males, of course, are blind to their power and to the role of the phallus in the scheme of things; they assume that the power relationships found in any society are logical and natural.

What could be a better expression, then, of the power of the phallus than the image of the woman in the Fidji advertisement with the snake—a phallic symbol—draped around her neck (figure 8.3)? The woman stands there, accessible to the male gaze (the look men give women that reduces them to sexual objects). She is holding a bottle of perfume that will make her (and all women

Figure 8.3

who use Fidji, so they think) irresistible to men and thus, without recognizing it, is participating in her own domination and subjugation. In Paradise, we must recall, Adam was given dominion over Eve, whom he named.

God then casts Adam and Eve out of the Garden. Thus, the return to Paradise is in effect a return to being dominated by men. So, not only the image of the maiden with the snake but also the text of the Fidji advertisement are connected with male sexuality and male domination. These images may also be connected in interesting ways with the unconscious fear that some men have of female sexuality and the female genitalia. This advertisement, then, is one that lends itself to feminist analysis.

CONCLUSION

These interpretations are only a few examples of the many different kinds of analyses that could be made of the Fidji advertisement. Critics and analysts with different areas of knowledge and expertise could find numerous other things to talk about in this advertisement—and in most advertisements and commercials. They are often rich in symbolism and interesting material for those who have the keys—that is, the theories and the conceptual framework—to unlock their meaning. Advertisements and commercials are richer in meaning than we might think, and it takes a good deal of work to understand how they communicate ideas and meanings and, to the extent that they are successful, shape our behavior.

STUDY QUESTIONS, APPLICATIONS, AND ASSIGNMENTS

1. What did Yuri Lotman say about why texts yield many different interpretations?
2. What two points did Lotman make about analyzing texts?
3. Review the list of topics to consider when analyzing print advertisements and select the ones that interest you most. Why did you choose those techniques? Explain your answer.
4. Using these techniques and the methods discussed in this chapter, find an interesting and symbolically rich print advertisement and write a paper analyzing it. Attach the advertisement to your paper.
5. What are the six methodologies used in analyzing advertisements in this chapter?

6. What was Ferdinand de Saussure's approach to semiotics? What was Charles S. Peirce's approach? How do they differ?

7. What did D. H. Lawrence say about hair color and sexual passion in America?

8. What does it mean to say that we understand what concepts mean differentially?

9. What are the polar oppositions in the Fidji advertisement?

10. What insights into the Fidji advertisement does psychoanalytic theory provide?

11. In the analysis in the book, the letters "S," "E," and "X" were found. Do you think they are actually in the advertisement, or are they in the imagination of the analyst of this text? If they are in the text, were they put in consciously by the art director, or are they messages from the art director's unconscious? Explain your answer.

12. How does Freud's theory about the id, ego, and superego relate to this advertisement and advertising in general?

13. Investigate psychoanalytic approaches to advertising and write a paper on what you found. It would be best if your research found analyses that dealt with specific advertisements.

14. What points were made in the sociological analysis of the Fidji advertisement?

15. How do Marxists analyze advertising? What would Marxists say about the Fidji advertisement? What does it mean to say that Marxism is often doctrinaire?

16. How was the myth model applied to the Fidji advertisement? Can you find a different mythic heroine who would help explain the advertisement better?

17. What do feminists say about the Fidji advertisement? Do a research paper on feminist interpretations of advertising and find analyses that deal with specific advertisements for your paper. Attach duplicated copies of any advertisements dealt with in the articles.

[Dan] Nichols' McDonald's spots possess the most accelerated time sense of any on television. "Quick Cuts" contains more cuts than can be counted: after repeated views the author had to slow down the tape to count 65 different scenes in 60 seconds. A seven-second segment of this spot contains fourteen separate scenes, or two per second. Incredible as it may seem, it *is* possible for the viewer to perceive these different scenes even though they go by faster than they can be counted.

The effect on the viewer is a sense of extreme urgency and of the present tense: the action is thrust into the immediate present because it is rendered as more alive and exciting than even the most engaging real-life experience. Nichols taps the "live" associations of television in this way more insistently than any other director. Because of the sense of urgency and of presentness which the spots communicate, the viewer actually experiences the exciting life style which Nichols depicts rather than passively observing events which occur to someone else.

The excitement communicated by way of life the viewer thus experiences is associated with the product even though the product is not the primary subject of the spots. More than promoting a particular product, these spots advertise an appealing way of life associated with the restaurant, causing the viewer to turn to the product for gratification.

—Bruce Kurtz, *Spots: The Popular Art of American Television Commercials*

Postmodern advertising—characterized by a rapid succession of visually appealing images (the speed-up effect), repetition, and high-volume, mood-setting music . . . is much more symbolic and persuasive than informative. Advertising is an arena in which conspicuous role display and reversal, preening, and symbolically enticing situations are evident. . . . While modern advertising presented itself as an unquestionable authority figure—a high priest of sorts—postmodern advertising presents itself as an insider, an ally of the common person. Modern advertising uses a paternalistic model; like your physician, it knows what is best for you. Now advertising is trading in the semblance of godlike knowledge for the role of a funny, self-deprecatory chum.

—Anthony J. Cortese, *Provocateur:*
Images of Women and Minorities in Advertising

ANALYZING TELEVISION COMMERCIALS

THE MACINTOSH "1984" COMMERCIAL

Television commercials are much more complex than print advertisements because they can have many more elements in them: a narrative structure, dialogue, music, various kinds of shots, various editing practices, and so on. From Yuri Lotman's perspective, they store a great deal more information than print advertisements with photographs do; that is because they are in essence minivideo or film dramas, and each frame or image in a commercial is, in a sense, similar to a print advertisement with a photograph in it.

In this chapter, I offer a list of topics to consider when analyzing commercials and then offer an analysis of the famous "1984" Macintosh commercial, a sixty-second commercial that was recently selected by people in the industry as the second-best television commercial made in the 1980s. What follows is a list of things to consider in a "complex" television commercial—not a simple one in which someone is shown talking about a product and there's relatively little in the way of production values or narrative line.

1. What is the plot of the narrative in the commercial? That is, what happens to the characters? Are there narrative tricks used—flash-forwards or flashbacks? What dramatic techniques are used?
2. What characters do we find in the commercial? What are they like? What are their ages, genders, educational levels, occupations, and so on? How do they communicate their personalities? What roles do they play? How do they relate to one another?
3. How would you describe the faces of the characters? Their bodies? Their clothing? What about the color of their hair? The way their hair is styled? Their voices? Their use of body language and facial expressions when they see some product or service?

4. What do the characters say to one another? Consider the words they use and the role the dialogue has in the commercial. What arguments, if any, are made? How does the commercial sell people? What do you think the target audience of the commercial is? What techniques of persuasion are used by the characters? What appeals are made? Does the commercial try to scare you? Appeal to your vanity? Provide valuable information? Plead with you?

5. If there's a narrator, is it a male or female (or child or something else)? What role does the narrator have?

6. Where does the commercial take place? What significance does the setting have?

7. Are there any props (objects) used? If so, what are they? Why do you think they were used?

8. How is color used in the commercial?

9. How would you describe the lighting? Does it vary?

10. How is sound used? Is there music? If so, what kind?

11. What kinds of shots are used? Make a list of all the shots found in the commercial and try to determine what significance they have. Are they mostly close-ups or something else?

12. What kind of editing techniques are used? Are there quick cuts, lingering dissolves, or zooms? Tie these editing decisions to the dialogue and the goal of the commercial.

13. Are there intertextual references found in the text—parodies, use of famous shots, well-known characters, and so on?

14. In what ways does the commercial rely on background knowledge on the part of the viewer/listener? How does it relate to widely held ideas, beliefs, notions, myths, values, archetypes, and so on?

15. What role does the product have in society? Who uses it? Why do they use it? What does it tell us about social, economic, and political matters? For example, does it reflect anomie, alienation, anxiety, stereotyping, generational conflict, or boredom?

These questions are ones we should deal with in analyzing commercials. We may not need to cover every part of every question, but we should submit the commercial to as complete an analysis as we can. The nature of the commercial determines the methods and concepts we use to interpret it.

Consider, for example, a "complex" commercial. It may last only sixty seconds, but it may have as many as sixty or seventy different images in it, as well as music, dialogue, print, and human beings with different attributes who use body language and facial expressions to send some message to us about some product or service. Every image is loaded with information, even though we may not realize how much information there is in the image or recognize how the image is impacting us.

A SYNOPSIS OF THE TEXT

As the commercial begins, the number "1984" appears on the screen (see the storyboard in figure 9.1). The director then cuts to an extreme long shot of vaguely perceived figures marching through a tunnel joining gigantic structures. Next, he cuts to a long shot of figures marching. All of them have shaved heads and are wearing dull uniforms. The figures have no expression on their faces. Then there is an extreme close-up of their heavy boots. A quick cut shows a blond woman with a white jersey and red shorts, running (figure 9.2). We see her for only an instant. The next cut shows the figures again, and then there is a cut to a shot of the woman being pursued by storm troopers. There is cutting back and forth in the commercial between the blond woman and the troopers pursuing her. Then we see another extreme long shot of the inmates of this institution sitting in a huge room. They are staring at a gigantic television set. A figure wearing glasses is addressing the inmates (figure 9.3), who sit gazing at the television image as if in a hypnotic trance. He is talking about the inmates being free, united, and so on. Then suddenly, the blond woman, who is carrying a sledgehammer, enters the room. She hurls her sledgehammer at the television screen, and when it hits it, there is a gigantic explosion. The explosion creates an image that looks somewhat like that generated by an

Figure 9.1

Figure 9.2

Figure 9.3

atomic bomb. The inmates gaze, dazed and openmouthed, at the screen. Then a message from Apple Computers appears on the screen informing viewers that Apple will be introducing a new computer, the Macintosh, shortly.

THE BACKGROUND

This commercial, directed by Ridley Scott, the distinguished British film-maker (*Alien* and *Blade Runner*), was shown nationally in the United States only once—during the 1984 Super Bowl—though it (or parts of it) also has been aired, from time to time, in news features on advertising and the computer industry. The commercial was created by Apple's advertising agency, Chiat/Day of Los Angeles. According to an advertising executive from Chiat/Day, it cost $500,000 to make and another $600,000 for airtime (sixty seconds).

Apple was hesitant to use it and decided to do so only at the very last minute. An executive in the agency revealed that Apple actually called England to stop production of the commercial, but by that time the commercial had already been shot.

Insights from Advertising Agencies

It is imperative not to try too many different ways of solving a problem for a client since this costs the agency a lot of money and confuses our customers. There should be then only one campaign suggested; it must be made to seem to be the only answer to the company's problems, so the company's advertising director is sold before he sees the proposed advertisement.

TESTING THE "1984" MACINTOSH COMMERCIAL

Fred Goldberg, who was involved with the commercial, offers some previously unknown (to the general public) information about the results of testing the "1984" commercial before it was released. As he writes in his book *The Insanity of Advertising: Memoirs of a Mad Man* (2013:107) about pretesting the commercial with the ASI: Advertising Specialty Institute,

> That single Super Bowl commercial generated massive awareness and conviction and went on to help sell vast numbers of Macintoshes. Sales over six hours the next day were $3.5 million and $155 million over the next 100 days. Ultimately it made Apple the multi-billion-dollar company that it is today.
>
> Turns out I never showed anyone the results from an ASI copy test conducted on the "1984" commercial. The agency had paid for it and if I didn't want to share, so what?
>
> You see, according to the ASI in their final report, the "key predictive" measure of commercial effectiveness was what they called the pre/post performance change. The norm for all :30 business commercials at the time was 29, with a range of results between 13 and 43, in all the commercials that they had ever tested.

The Apple Macintosh "1984" commercial scored a 5.

And it was a .60 commercial to boot, not a .30, on which the norms were built. Had Goldberg shown the results to people at the agency, they probably would have made sure to cancel the "1984" commercial since the results of the API testing were so terrible. What this little episode shows is that pretesting commercials and relying on so-called scientific research can lead advertisers and advertising agencies astray.

The "1984" commercial is a remarkable text. The actors in the commercial were English skinheads who were recruited to play the prisoners. (Since 1984, when the commercial was made, skinheads have emerged as a worldwide phenomenon of disaffected youth who are attracted to right-wing neo-Nazi organizations.) The "1984" commercial has a look much different from the average commercial and takes a considerably different approach to the matter of marketing a product than we find with most commercials.

Ridley Scott, the director (auteur), is a distinguished figure in the film world, and the commercial bears his signature—its look, its narrative structure, and its message all suggest an art film rather than a television commercial. I believe many "creative" people in the advertising industry are capable of creating aesthetically interesting and artistically pleasing works (and sometimes they do) when they are not prevented from doing so by the companies whose products they are advertising. Of course, a great deal depends on the nature of the product being sold and the nature (that is, the corporate culture) of the company selling the product.

In the remainder of this chapter, I discuss some of the most important images from the text and speculate about how these images generate meaning, what that meaning is, and how viewers might be affected by these images. I also discuss the narrative itself.

It is often held that there is no minimal unit in a television text to deal with (unlike film, which has the frame). I don't think this is a major issue for our consideration since one can always isolate important images and scenes to analyze, so even though a television text doesn't have frames, it does have shots, which serve the same function.

GEORGE ORWELL'S *1984* AND RIDLEY SCOTT'S "1984"

The title of this commercial brings to mind George Orwell's novel *1984*, and the text of the commercial is based on the idea of totalitarian anti-utopias or dystopias. The ambience of the "1984" commercial is that of a perverted utopian community, a total institution in which every aspect of people's lives is controlled—especially their minds. We see "1984," the commercial, in terms of *1984*, the book. Here we have an example of what is known in semiotic literature as intertextuality. That is, we read or interpret one text in terms of another text or with another text in mind. The events in the commercial would have far less significance if we hadn't read or didn't know about Orwell's classic novel *1984*.

This concept is explained by the Russian literary theorist M. Bakhtin as follows (1981:279–80):

> Every extra-artistic prose discourse—in any of its forms, quotidian, rhetorical, scholarly—cannot fail to be oriented toward the "already uttered," the "already known," the "common opinion" and so forth. The dialogic orientation of discourse is a phenomenon that is, of course, a property of any discourse . . . every word is directed toward an answer and cannot escape the profound influence of the answering world that it anticipates. The word in living conversation is directly, blatantly, oriented toward a future answer-word: it provokes an answer, anticipates it and structures itself in the atmosphere of the already spoken; the word is at the same time determined by that which has not been said but which is needed and in fact anticipated by the answering world. Such is the situation in any dialogue.

When we write or communicate in any manner, we always have an audience in mind, and what we write or say is always connected intimately to thoughts and ideas that have been communicated in the past. Communication of any kind is then always dialogic as opposed to monologic and involves a real or imagined audience and the responses the communicator can expect from it. In some cases, this dialogical aspect of communication is vague and in the realm of the anticipated; in other cases, it is tied directly to something in the past. This is the case with the Macintosh commercial and the citation of the Orwell novel.

The title of the Macintosh commercial is also connected to a great deal of speculation that occurred in America during the year 1984 about Orwell and his dire predictions. Thus, merely seeing the title generated ambivalent feelings. Would it be about the year 1984 or about the novel *1984*? (A number of social commentators have argued that the year 1984 did not by any means bring the kind of society that Orwell imagined.) The title left people in suspense.

THE IMAGE OF THE TOTAL INSTITUTION

The first shot resolved any questions that might have been generated by the title. We see an extreme long shot of gigantic structures connected by a tubular tunnel in which we can dimly perceive figures marching. The scale of the scene is terrifying. The figures are minute and seemingly irrelevant when contrasted with the huge buildings in which they are incarcerated. One almost thinks of blood flowing through veins.

Thus, the spatiality of this scene and the images of control and conformity generated by the columns of figures tell us immediately that the commercial, "1984," is indeed about an Orwellian world. This is reinforced in the next shot, which is a long shot of the prisoners, all with shaved heads and heavy, ill-fitting uniforms, marching sullenly in columns in a long tunnel.

THE PRISONERS' BOOTS

A really important shot occurs shortly after the commercial begins when there is a cut to a close-up of the prisoners' boots (figure 9.4). The heavy, thick-soled boots, shown moving in unison, reflect the degree to which the inmates are under the control of their masters. (This is an example of *metonomy*, which confers meaning by association. And, in particular, it is an example of *synecdoche*, in which a part can stand for a whole.)

Figure 9.4

The shot of the boots is meant to intensify the message. (We may even recall, as another example of intertextuality, the famous shot of the boots in Eisenstein's *The Battleship Potemkin*, though the situation in that film was somewhat different.) Uniforms suggest lack of individuality and deperson-alization and, in the content of the "1984" commercial, dehumanization. Thus, the shot of the boots moving in unison strengthens this message by emphasizing one part of the human being and isolating it from the image of the whole human being.

The rather sullen and lethargic nature of their marching and the unifor-mity of the prisoners' feet as they march suggest that these inmates have been reduced to the status of automatons. It is the same kind of reductionism that occurs when we talk about young people being "college material" or football players as "horses," though it is much more exaggerated and intensified here.

THE BLOND AS A SYMBOL

Into this scene of marching zombies, of dehumanized and radically de-personalized bodies, there appears for just an instant an image of a beautiful blond woman who is running down a corridor. She wears a white shirt and red shorts. We can see her breasts heaving as she runs directly toward us, the viewers, on the Z-axis of the screen. The blond woman appears for perhaps a second or two, and then we return to the marching bodies and various scenes of totalitarian control.

Who is she? We do not know—but the fact that she exists tells us that there must be forces of resistance in this totalitarian society, that not all are enslaved. We see shortly that she is being pursued by a troop of burly po-licemen who look terribly menacing in their helmets with glass face masks. Her color, her animation, her freedom, and even her sexuality serve to make the situation of the inmates even more obvious and pathetic. Her image functions as a polar opposite to the enslaved men, and even though we see her the first time for only a second or two, her existence creates drama and excitement.

THE BRAINWASHING SCENARIO

In this brainwashing scene, we have a long shot of the inmates, sitting in rows, gazing at a gigantic television screen in the front of the auditorium, where a "Big Brother" figure is shown speaking to them. They are mute and expressionless and seem almost hypnotized by the figure on the television screen. The message we get from this image is that mind control is an important element in the operation of this totalitarian society.

By implication, of course, control of the media (the gigantic television screen reflects this) is vital for control of the minds of the inmates—and perhaps, by implication, everyone. We must ask ourselves, is this scene a metaphor for contemporary society, in which we, like the inmates, gaze in a hypnotic stupor at figures who "brainwash" us (or try to at least)? Is the distance between the world of the "1984" commercial and American society less than we might imagine? Questions like these are raised by this dramatic image.

Is it possible that we are like these prisoners and that we are mind controlled the way they are? We may not wear their uniforms, have shaved heads, or be prisoners (or recognize that we are prisoners, that is) in some kind of a total institution. But that may be because the control is more subtle, the indoctrination less apparent. There may be more control over us than we imagine. That is one of the questions raised by this image.

THE BIG BROTHER FIGURE

We don't see a great deal of the Big Brother figure, only several shots in which we see him spouting ideological gobbledygook to the inmates. The choice of the actor to portray this character is very interesting. He looks like a clerk or minor bureaucrat from some organization. He is in his fifties or sixties, wears glasses, and is definitely portrayed as bland, unanimated, and without much in the way of personality. He speaks in a low, rather monotonous voice. Indeed, for all we know, he may be only a minor functionary in whatever vast organization runs this society.

What we learn from considering this figure is that most totalitarian institutions are essentially bureaucratic, held together not by charismatic individuals but by drab, conformist, rule-following bureaucratic types who do their jobs in a routine manner and do whatever they are told to do. They are not that different from the inmates in many respects, although the control exerted over these figures may be less overt. (There may, of course, be charismatic leaders in totalitarian societies, but we don't see them in this commercial.)

THE BRAINWASHER'S MESSAGE

Here is a transcript of the message the Big Brother figure gives to the inmates. He speaks it, but it is also shown in captions running across the bottom of the screen:

Today we celebrate the first glorious anniversary of the information purification repentance. We who created from out of this time in all history a
garden of pure ideology, where each worker may loom secure from the pest
of purveying contradictory thoughts. Our communication is enormous. It
is more powerful than any fleet or army on earth. We are one people with
one will, one resolve, one cause. Our enemies shall talk themselves to death
and we will bury them with their own confusion. We shall prevail. [At this
point, the television screen is shattered.]

Notice the degree to which this rhetoric is garbled and confusing. We have
here a good examination of double-talk or bafflegab: words that don't add up
to anything. He talks about events we know nothing of, though we can imagine what might have transpired. The language has the ring of political indoctrination—there is a "glorious revolution" being "celebrated." The language
contrasts, starkly, with the scenario in which it is being used. There is talk in
this futuristic, oppressive, hyperurban setting of a "garden of pure ideology"
and the "security" that the workers should feel from all this.

It is *communication* that is given the major role here—it is a more powerful force than the military, and it unites the workers/inmates/prisoners
into a collectivity (or is it a mass society?) with "one will, one resolve, one
cause." And then there is that wonderfully comic line about the enemies of
this society "talking themselves to death." It is the rhetoric of persuasion,
and we have the sense that the inmates of this society have been exposed to
this kind of talk almost endlessly. That is, they have all been brainwashed by
this double-talk.

The language, with phrases such as "information purification repentance," is that of mind control and psychic domination, and the commercial
does a wonderful job of imitating it (and perhaps, in a sense, of parodying
it). The goal preached is escape from "contradictory thoughts," which enables the inmates to have "one will." In other words, the essentially human
function of considering options and alternatives is to be obliterated—or has
it been already?

THE BIG EXPLOSION

In the "1984" commercial, there are several scenes in which we see
the blond woman twirling a sledgehammer (as she prepares to throw it at
the screen) and the police racing toward her (figure 9.5). She launches the
sledgehammer, and it smashes into the gigantic television screen. There is
an enormous explosion, and we see, briefly, an image vaguely similar to that
produced by an atomic bomb.

Figure 9.5

The explosion, which destroys the screen image—and, by implication, the domination by the mass media of the inmates—is the most significant act in the commercial. With this act, a great blow is struck for freedom, and we are led to imagine what might follow. We are shown very little. Implicit in this scenario is the notion that once the control of people's minds by a totalitarian regime is broken, the destruction of that regime more or less follows automatically. This does not have to be spelled out. It is like lancing a boil: when the system of pressure is punctured, healing can take place. The exploding screen signifies then the destruction of the totalitarian order that generates mind-controlling images on that screen.

THE INMATES' RESPONSE

After the explosion, the commercial cuts to a scene in which the inmates are shown openmouthed, staring in disbelief at what has happened. They are, relatively speaking, emotionless and display no affect other than bewilderment or shock. They have been so brainwashed, we are led to believe, that they are incapable of any kind of response—at least in the immediate present.

We hear a low hissing sound, as if air is escaping from the gigantic television apparatus in the front of the room. The camera pans the inmates as the announcement from Apple rolls onto the screen.

THE MACINTOSH ANNOUNCEMENT

We see the following announcement:

On January 24th, Apple Computers will introduce Macintosh and you will see why 1984 won't be like "1984."

The brevity and simplicity of this announcement, which takes but a few seconds, contrasts with the excitement and visual richness of the commercial. In this situation, the understatement serves to shout at us and to gain a great deal of interest. Apple is telling us not only that it is introducing a new computer but also that this new computer has enormous political and social implications—for it has the power to save us from ending up like the prisoners, victims of a totalitarian state.

There had been an enormous amount of material about the Macintosh in the press and computer fanzines, so those interested in computers already knew about it. And when the Macintosh computer went on sale, Apple sold something like 17,000 the first day, a figure far beyond what they had anticipated. People from Chiat/Day talk about that as if it were the commercial that sold all those computers—an assumption that is very questionable.

THE HEROINE AS MYTHIC FIGURE

In this microdrama, the blond heroine calls to mind several different heroic or mythic figures from our collective consciousness. First, there is something of David and Goliath in this story—a small, seemingly weak, and, in this case, female character brings down a Goliath figure by hurling a stone (sledgehammer) at it. In the commercial, there are some close-ups of the Big Brother/Goliath figure that simulate the size relationships between David and Goliath.

In both cases—the "1984" commercial and the David and Goliath story—it is a missile to the head that does the job. And with the destruction of the evil Goliath figure, of course, the forces of good can prevail. So it seems reasonable to argue that the blond represents a female version of David, and I would imagine many people might see some kind of a resemblance between the David and Goliath story and the events in this commercial. Here we find how intertextual readings can enrich an event and give an image a great deal of cultural resonance.

The woman can also, let me suggest, be interpreted as an Eve figure. The fact that the Apple corporation's symbol is an apple with a bite out of it tells us that. But the blond heroine also functions like Eve, for ultimately what she does is lead to knowledge of good and evil in a reverse Garden of Eden. Before she shattered the image, the inmates were brainwashed and had but "one will, one resolve, one cause." What information these poor souls had was "purified." Their state is vaguely analogous to that of Adam before he ate of the apple. It is the tasting of the fruit that led to Adam and Eve's "eyes being opened," and that is the beginning of human history, one might argue.

The blond heroine, then, is an Eve figure who brings knowledge of good and evil and, by implication, knowledge of reality to the inmates. We do not see their transformation after the destruction of the Big Brother/Goliath figure—indeed, their immediate reaction is awe and stupefaction—but ultimately we cannot help but assume that something important will happen and that they will be liberated. It is quite possible that this beautiful blond figure may also represent, in our psyches, the Apple corporation. We know that corporations have different images in people's minds—often based on symbolic figures in advertisements and commercials. On the basis of this commercial, one might guess that the corporate image we have of Apple is that of a beautiful blond woman (who liberates men from political and psychological domination and ignorance). Much of this would be at the unconscious level, of course.

It's probably a good image for a computer company to have since one of the biggest problems computer manufacturers have is fighting anxiety about technology and the difficulties of operating computers—Macintosh's very reason for being, as a matter of fact. If people see Apple computers as beautiful blonds, so much the better for the corporation.

PSYCHOANALYTIC ASPECTS OF THE COMMERCIAL

From a psychoanalytic standpoint, the heroine is an ego figure who mediates between a monstrous and perverted superego figure, Big Brother, and the deenergized and devastated ids of the inmates. The id, as it is commonly defined, involves impulses and desires; the superego involves guilt; and the ego mediates between the two, trying to maintain equilibrium. Ids are needed to give us energy, and superegos are needed to prevent us from becoming creatures of impulse. Both can, I suggest, become perverted.

We see how the blond is an ego figure here:

Id	Ego	Superego
inmates	blond	Big Brother
perverted	normal	perverted
no energy	strong	no heart

As an ego figure, the heroine has to mediate between the inmates, whose ids have been weakened and drained of energy, and the brainwasher, whose superego has become monstrous and distorted. One might see vague elements of an Oedipal conflict in which a young female and an older, perhaps even "fatherly" figure have a very difficult relationship, to put it mildly.

THE BLOND AS MEDIATOR

One important function of the mythic hero or heroine is to mediate between opposing forces in an attempt to resolve a basic opposition. The text of this commercial is very binary, and the blond heroine serves to identify and highlight the oppositions found in it. There are in essence three characters in this text. First, there are the inmates who function as one character. Then there is the Big Brother character (and the police who are part of him). And there is the blond heroine. Her function is to resolve the oppositions, one way or another, and she does this.

In the list that follows, I will contrast the inmates and the Big Brother figure. Here we are eliciting the paradigmatic structure of the text, which, according to Claude Lévi Strauss, tells us its real but hidden meaning (as opposed to the surface meaning, which we get with a syntagmatic or linear narrative analysis):

Inmates	Big Brother
obey	commands
uniforms	regular clothes
hairless	hair
listen	speaks
brainwashed	brainwasher
look at	is looked at
mindless	calculating
dehumanized	dehumanizing
alienated	alienating
emotionless	heartless

The blond heroine (figure 9.6), with her gorgeous hair, her vitality, her energy, and her force, resolves the dialectic by destroying Big Brother and making it possible (we imagine) for the inmates eventually to regain their humanity. She also makes us aware of the depths to which the inmates have sunk, for, unlike them, she resists; she has a mind of her own, and she accepts danger.

Thus, she contrasts with both the inmates and Big Brother, whom she destroys. The inmates and Big Brother are reverse images of one another—both drab, depersonalized, and locked into a slave–master relationship that defines each character and on which both may turn out to be dependent.

We can analyze the image of the blond woman with the sledgehammer at a number of different levels:

- *The Literal Level*: The image we see in "1984"
- *The Textual Level*: Where the image fits in the commercial

Figure 9.6. In this image from the Macintosh "1984" commercial, we see the blond woman in the gigantic auditorium where the inmates are being brainwashed.

- *The Intertextual Level*: The way the image calls to mind Orwell's *1984*
- *The Mythic Level*: The story of David and Goliath in the Bible

It is possible, in many print advertisements and commercials, to consider the different levels of meaning an image may have. Even static images in print advertisements always assume some kind of backstory that occurred to bring the characters together, and they often imply a future story generated by the product being advertised.

Images, we can see, are resonant and have many different levels of meaning—some of which are not apparent to us when we first see them. The Macintosh, so Apple suggests, will save us from IBM and MS-DOS, but who, we may ask, will save us from the Macintosh and the Apple corporation if it becomes an instrument of psychological domination?

ALIENATED PROLES

The inmates, workers, or prisoners, whatever you wish to call them, reflect with terrifying clarity the power that modern bureaucratic states have to destroy humanity and lead people into a state of radical alienation. We have here a classic case (even if somewhat oversimplified and parodied) of, in Marxist terms, a mindless proletariat—maybe a classic example of what Marxists call a *Lumpenproletariat*—being manipulated by a heartless bourgeoisie.

This bourgeoisie rules by virtue of its monopoly of power and its control of the media and the manipulation of the consciousness of the proletariat. The situation in the commercial is one in which the horrors of a capitalist society are shown pushed to their logical conclusion, where workers are now enslaved and brainwashed and the society in which they live has become a totalitarian one.

The blond heroine's actions then symbolize revolution. She stands for the role of progressive forces (pushed underground in this society) in leading a stupefied proletariat out of its chains. Since this proletariat has been brainwashed, it is incapable of action and is, perhaps, even reactionary. Hence, it remains passive while the revolution takes place and can only stare in openmouthed wonder at the destruction of the power structure that enslaves it.

In this scenario, the power of the media is shown as central, and when it is put out of action, the rest is almost automatic. Interestingly enough, this message is not too far removed from the overt message of the Apple corporation—that access to user-friendly computers will prevent a totalitarian society from coming into being. Apple thus defines itself as a revolutionary force in the quasi-totalitarian world of hard-to-use computers where power will be held by those who know how to function in the information society.

The Macintosh will prevent society from splitting into two groups—those who have access to computers and are part of the information society and those who know nothing about computers and are condemned to menial jobs and will form a class of workers who will have little economic power or status.

Apple is, in our imaginations, the beautiful blond who will prevent a rigid information-based class system from evolving and, by implication, a totalitarian society. The Macintosh brings knowledge of good and evil to humankind; all it takes is a bite (or is it a byte?).

THE BIG BLUE

It is not too far-fetched, I would argue, to suggest that the totalitarian society shown in this commercial is an indirect representation of IBM, International Business Machines. It was seen, years ago, as a gigantic uptight organization full of uptight people, with countless rules to be followed by people who worked for the company. The IBM image was of conformity and regimentation. Apple positioned itself as a small, humanistic, open corporation battling a gigantic, superpowerful, and highly bureaucratic corporation, IBM. There are two readings to which this insight leads.

> *Scenario 1:* In the first reading, the whole story is about IBM. The Big Brother figure is the corporate leadership, and the inmates are meant to symbolize the IBM workers who are controlled (white shirt and tie and so on) by IBM. IBM has a reputation for being rather strict about the way its workers and salespeople dress, and this commercial may be alluding to the regimentation identified with IBM.
>
> *Scenario 2:* The second reading suggests that IBM is the Big Brother and that the American public is the inmates—who have been duped and controlled by IBM but who are about to be liberated by Apple and its revolutionary Macintosh computer.

The battle resolves itself down to one between the beautiful blond heroine and the monolithic monster—a bureaucratic corporation full of faceless nobodies mindlessly following rules and regulations and enslaving the multitudes. The Macintosh is the sledgehammer that Apple has to throw against IBM—a user-friendly machine that will, democratically, make computing available to all.

A CLEVER MARKETING STRATEGY

Although the "1984" commercial cost a great deal of money to produce (perhaps three or four times as much as a typical high-budget commercial) and air, due to the notoriety it attracted, it ended up being a very good buy. We must remember that it aired only once nationally in the United States—yet it was the subject of a great deal of media attention and it fascinated the huge audience that was watching the Super Bowl when it was shown.

As someone in the creative department at Chiat/Day explained to me, "Good campaigns end up being relatively inexpensive." A good commercial (and campaign) may cost a great deal to produce and air, but if its impact is sufficiently strong, on an attention-per-thousand basis, it might work out to be relatively cheap.

Chiat/Day (and Apple) took an unusual approach with this commercial. It focused its attention not so much on the benefits derived from using a Macintosh as on the dangers inherent in not using one. The commercial wasn't selling a specific product in a direct manner. Instead, it used indirection to build an image for Apple and Macintosh and, at the same time, cast aspersions on its main rival, IBM.

In the course of sixty seconds, it created a memorable microdrama (which is what many commercials are actually) that worked subtly and indirectly. Like many commercials, it was highly compressed, with neither a beginning nor an ending. (Many commercials don't have a beginning but do show a happy ending, with someone using the product or service advertised.)

The ending implied in the "1984" commercial focused on the avoidance of something hateful rather than the gaining of something desirable. In its own way, there is an element of conditioning involved here; we have a condensed form of *aversion therapy*. The argument, like the commercial, is binary. If there are only two possibilities, Apple and IBM, and IBM (and all that it and its imitators stand for) is shown to be horrible, one is led to choose Apple. One acts not so much to gain pleasure (though that beautiful blond attracts us) as to avert pain—Big Brother and the dystopian world (IBM) that he represents.

The "1984" commercial launched the Macintosh brilliantly. Apple continued to attack conformity in the business world in its 1985 commercial, which showed blindfolded businessmen jumping off a cliff like lemmings. But this new commercial lacked the polish and aesthetic complexity found in "1984," and it was followed by a rather meager event, Apple announcing a few minor items in its campaign to get businesses to purchase Macintoshes. The "1984" commercial was a brilliant success, but the new commercial did not translate into great business success for Apple for a variety of reasons.

THE "1984" COMMERCIAL AND A BIT OF SCHOLARLY RESEARCH

In 1991, two communication scholars, Sandra Moriarty and Shay Sayre, presented a paper at the sixteenth annual meeting of the Semiotic Society of America, "A Comparison of Reader Response with Informed Author/Viewer Analysis." The purpose of this research on the Macintosh "1984" commercial was (1991:1) "to find out what meanings an audience can derive from a single showing of a very complex television commercial text, and to test the level of agreement that exists among the author's intention, critic's analysis and reader's response." The sixty-second Macintosh commercial, they point out, had won thirty-four national and international advertising awards and was commonly described as "the commercial that outplayed the game."

The authors say the commercial cost $1.6 million—which differs by a million dollars from what someone in Chiat/Day told me. In any case, they quote Lee Clow, creative director for Chiat/Day, who described the commercial as follows (1991:7):

We placed our audience within the context of Orwell's view of society, a place where the dominant computer technology held consumers captive. The intended message was that Mac would set consumer [*sic*] free from the unfriendly technology of the competition. We gave the message impact with body imagery designed to contrast Apple with the competition. . . . All you have to do is look at IBM's historic approach to computers as something for the few, where they might let you in if you conformed and learned their language, programming. Then look at how Apple makes computers accessible to people.

This, then, is what the advertising agency that was responsible for hiring Ridley Scott wanted to do.

Moriarty and Sayre then describe an earlier version of my "1984" article (on which this chapter is based) as a representative semiotic interpretation of the "1984" commercial. They then describe the methodology used in their research (1991:8):

First, the respondents' analyses of the commercial will be compared with the main message points stated by both the creator of the commercial and the semiotic critic to determine if viewers are getting the point of the message. Then the significant images identified by the respondents will be compared with the images noted and interpreted by the critic to determine if the student readings are the same or similar to the reading of an informed viewer. . . . The respondents' level of interpretation also will be analyzed to determine their sophistication in story analysis. . . . Finally, it is expected that differences in the respondents' readings, if any, will be found more in their level of interpretation than in their story focus.

The respondents in this study were two hundred undergraduate students taking mass communication courses at two state universities.

The conclusions Moriarty and Sayre reached from analyzing the data from the two hundred respondents are quite interesting. As they write (1991:21–23),

In terms of the big question, there is rather high agreement between the student respondents and the critic and creator on the element of the message that focuses on the introduction of the Macintosh computer. This is particularly important since advertising researchers know that the miscomprehension rate of television advertising message points is close to 25 percent. Other elements which the creator and critic thought were important message points were rarely or barely noted, which suggests that a deep reading from a fleeting exposure to a television commercial is probably not realistic. . . . While the 1984 story line was extremely powerful, the Macintosh message was still the focus of their interpretations. While in slightly more than half the cases they were reading and interpreting the stories at a simple level, the number that engaged in a more elaborate decoding with some interpretation beyond simply re-telling was higher than the researchers expected almost reaching 50 percent. This suggests that viewers of a fast paced, complex commercial may be able to engage in sophisticated interpretation even from a brief exposure.

This conclusion is extremely interesting, for it suggests that a relatively high percentage of the students were able to interpret the "1984" commercial—and, by implication, all commercials—in a relatively sophisticated manner. The authors suggest that their research indicates how important images (and the codes we use to interpret them) are for generating commercials whose meaning people can understand.

What this research demonstrates is that large numbers of people don't have to know what semiotics is or know the somewhat arcane jargon that semioticians use to get the message in commercials and other mass-mediated texts. And that is because we learn how to decode commercials and everything else as we grow up in a society. We are all semioticians whether we know it or not. We are always sending messages to others—via the words we use, our facial expressions, our hairstyles, the clothes we wear, our body language, and so on—and interpreting messages others send us. Like the character in one of Moliere's plays who didn't realize he was always speaking prose, we are all semioticians, with varying degrees of understanding of certain basic semiotic principles—whether we recognize it or not.

STUDY QUESTIONS, APPLICATIONS, AND ASSIGNMENTS

1. What techniques are listed for analyzing complex commercials? Which ones are of most interest to you? Why?
2. Pretesting the "1984" television commercial revealed what interesting results? What do the results of the "1984" pretest suggest about the value of testing commercials?
3. Do a research paper on pretesting advertising. What conclusions do you take away from your research?
4. What is the relation that exists between George Orwell's dystopian novel *1984* and Ridley Scott's "1984" Macintosh commercial.
5. How does Mikhail Bakhtin's theory of "intertextuality" help us understand the "1984" Macintosh commercial?

6. What does it mean to say that the boots of the prisoner are an example of synecdoche?
7. What was said about the Big Brother figure? What does he symbolize?
8. What points were made in the analysis of Big Brother's message?
9. What is the symbolic significance of the explosion in the commercial?
10. In what ways is the blond woman a symbolic heroine?
11. What insights are revealed in the psychoanalytic interpretation of the commercial?
12. What are the polar oppositions found in the commercial? Do they reveal the "meaning" of the text? Explain your answer.
13. What are the four levels that can be used in analyzing an image in a commercial?
14. What does a Marxist analysis of the "1984" commercial reveal? Would Marxists make the same kind of arguments about any commercials? Explain your answer.
15. What are the two "readings" of the "1984" commercial relative to IBM? Why is IBM the target?
16. Why can it be said that we are all semioticians whether we realize it or not? How can people be semioticians without realizing it? Explain your answer.
17. Do a research paper on other analyses of the "1984" commercial. What insights do these studies provide into the meaning of the text? Do they support or contradict anything in the analysis of the text in this chapter?

As a society, we are embedded in a culture of consumption. Neil Postman
. . . notes that by the age of forty the average American will have seen well
over one million commercials and have "close to another million to go
before his first social security check." In order to comprehend the impact
of all this advertising on society we must learn how to see through advertisements, for they are not just messages about goods and services but social
and cultural texts about ourselves.

—Katherine Toland Frith, *Undressing the Ad*

If our material needs are not satisfied, we die from hunger or exposure; if
our social needs are not satisfied, we are liable to suffer psychological problems. Now the crucial point is that in our consumption of goods, we satisfy
both material and social needs. Various social groups identify themselves
through shared attitudes, manners, accents, and habits of consumption—for
instance, through the clothes they wear. In this way the objects that we
use and consume cease to be mere objects of use; they become carriers of
information about what kind of people we are, or would like to be.

—Torben Vestergaard and Kim Schrøder, *The Language of Advertising*

10

WHERE NEXT?

We have covered a great deal of ground in this analysis of advertising and its impact on American character and culture. The soft economy of 2008 and 2009 in the United States meant that companies cut back on the amount of money they spent on advertising, causing great problems for the industry. But, as is usually the case, when the economy shows signs of improving, things will look up for advertising. When companies have problems, it seems that the first thing they cut is the amount of money they spend on advertising. A good case could be made that they should do just the opposite and spend more on advertising, for it is when the economy is not doing well that organizations need advertising the most.

Where next? we might ask. Let me suggest, here, a number of areas of considerable importance that are good candidates for further research: drug advertising, advertising to children, advertising on smart phones, and, related to our obsession with smart phones, advertising on social media, such as Facebook and Twitter. They are all quite complicated and the subject of considerable controversy.

DRUG ADVERTISING

Advertising is, as I have suggested all through this book, one of the most interesting, vital, and problematic influences on us as individuals and on American society. Take, for example, direct-to-consumer prescription drug advertising. In recent years, pharmaceutical companies have considerably increased the amount of advertising they do, which has led to a rapid rise in the prices of certain prescription drugs. In addition, patients now demand that their physicians prescribe certain drugs they see advertised, such as Prozac, Allegra, and Viagra. The page spread in figure 10.1, from a many-page advertising insert for a variety of prescription drugs, shows an ad for Breo Ellipta, with one page set up to look like a regular article about COPD. The medical profession considers drug advertising to be a nuisance at best and a potential menace at worst.

Figure 10.1. This ad for Breo Ellipta has a great deal of space devoted to possible negative side effects of the drug.

A front-page article in the November 22, 2002, issue of the *New York Times*, "Madison Ave. Plays Growing Role in the Business of Drug Research," deals with this matter and quotes a scientist, Dr. Arnold S. Reiman, a professor emeritus from Harvard Medical School, who said, "You cannot separate their advertising and marketing from the science, anymore." Advertising agencies have also bought some companies involved in testing drugs and other areas associated with discovering new drugs. We can see the impact that the advertising industry has had on the pharmaceutical industry in a more recent article by Alexander Eichler in *Huff Post Business* on December 5, 2013, with the title "Pharmaceutical Companies Spent 19 Times More on Self-Promotion Than Basic Research." Eichler explains,

> Big Pharma might be working a lot harder to sell you products than to develop new ones. Prescription drug companies aren't putting a lot of resources toward new, groundbreaking medications, according to a recent report in BMJ, a medical journal based in London. Instead, it's more profitable for them to simply create a bunch of products that are only slightly different from drugs already on the market, the report's authors said.
>
> "[P]harmaceutical research and development turns out mostly minor variations on existing drugs," the authors write. "Sales from these drugs generate steady profits throughout the ups and downs of blockbusters coming off patents." The authors go on to say that for every dollar pharmaceutical companies spend on "basic research," $19 goes toward promotion and marketing.

And apparently it's been working. Drug company revenues climbed more than $200 billion in the years between 1995 and 2010, according to the website MinnPost. Meanwhile, in recent years, more than one in five Americans age fifty and up have had to cut down on their dosages or switch to cheaper generic drugs because the cost of medication is so high.

It seems, then, that advertising agencies are now influencing the kind of research that pharmaceutical companies are doing, suggesting, it must be assumed, which areas would be most fruitful (profitable). Advertising now dominates our politics and is in the process of dominating our medicine. It turns out that there is also a relationship between pharmaceutical companies and political advertising. Pharmaceutical companies have formed a lobbying association, the Pharmaceutical Researchers and Manufacturers of America. It gave a great deal of money to an organization with strong Republican leanings, the United Seniors Association, which paid for ads in a number of campaigns, generally supporting Republican candidates whose interests were close to those of the pharmaceutical industry. Major drug companies are also behind Citizens for Better Medicare, which spent $50 million in the 2000 election on television commercials in twenty-six congressional districts. They also gave the U.S. Chamber of Commerce $10 million and spent another $27 million in individual campaign contributions, 70 percent of which went to Republican candidates. This investment paid off handsomely for the pharmaceutical industry, which now has an administration that is very receptive to its wishes. (This material comes from an article by Tom Hamburger, "Drug Industry Ads Aid GOP," *Wall Street Journal*, June 18, 2002.)

In 1970, I appeared before a subcommittee of the U.S. Senate and gave a presentation on drug advertising. My argument was that drug advertising follows what I call a "pain–pill–pleasure" model. Someone has a terrible headache, takes a pill, and in no time flat is better. I also pointed out that a large percentage of advertising in the United States is for drugs of one kind or another—alcohol, nicotine, caffeine, aspirin, and so on, ad infinitum. We are, it can be argued, an over-the-counter and prescription-drug culture, and we learn, from the many advertisements and commercials we are exposed to, that if there is a problem, there is always a drug to solve that problem, as if by magic.

It's not difficult to see how people might move from legal, over-the-counter drugs for minor problems and prescription drugs for health problems to illegal drugs such as heroin, cocaine, and crack for other problems. The pain–pill–pleasure model still works, except that there are side effects to be considered to using illegal drugs, such as addiction or related problems, such as getting AIDS from sharing needles and destroying one's life.

In 2009, an article on National Public Radio offered the figure of $4 billion dollars per year spent on drug advertising to consumers and quotes a Nielsen report to the effect that there are eighty drug commercials on American television every hour of every day. We are bombarded with these commercials. Anyone who watches *60 Minutes* would conclude, from the commercials on that program (which are almost always exclusively drug commercials), that people in America suffer from an incredible number of ailments and illnesses. The audience of *60 Minutes* tends to be elderly, and they are the primary target audience for drug commercials. The pharmaceutical companies now spend much more on advertising than they do on research. An article on a website, FiercePharma, brings advertising spending on drugs up to date (www.fiercepharma.com/special-reports/top-10-drug-advertising-spends-q1-2012):

> While the grand party in direct-to-consumer (DTC) advertising may have peaked about 5 years ago, it remains an important method of marketing drugs. The industry last year spent $2.4 billion on television ads, according to Nielsen. That is a 23% drop from the $3.1 billion spent in 2007.

We should recognize that most countries do not allow direct-to-consumer advertising. There are countless articles by physicians and others on the Internet and in consumer publications about the negative effects of this advertising on the public. But because of the political clout the pharmaceutical companies have—they contribute millions to political campaigns—it is unlikely that drug advertising will be prohibited.

CHILDREN AND ADVERTISING

We're used to subjecting children to advertising here in the United States, but in Sweden and some other countries, advertising directed toward children is forbidden. There is, I would suggest, an ethical problem of subjecting children to advertising. Until the age of seven or eight, they often do not understand what advertising is and can't distinguish between advertising and regular content. Should we subject these children to advertising? Personally speaking, I would say no.

A website that deals with advertising, Commercial Alert, offers these data on young children (www.commercialalert .org/news/archive/1999/12/kids-buying-power):

Commercialism is intrinsic to American culture, but marketing to children has reached an unprecedented intensity. Where there used to be a few TV channels, now the typical home has 78, including 24-hour channels directed at children like Nickelodeon and the Cartoon Network. The Journal of Advertising Research reports that nearly one out of every four children under age 6 has a television set in their bedroom. The average child sees between 20,000 and 40,000 commercials a year.

Young children generally can't tell the difference between a commercial and a program until they are around seven, so young children do not realize that they are being subjected to advertising and have little defense against it. One effect of subjecting children to advertising is to turn them into whiners. People in the advertising industry call the kind of nagging that children do, to get something they see on television and want, "pester power." An article by Martha Irvine in the Associated Press points out that when parents say "no," children nag them an average of nine times before they give in. Some children nag fifty times.

These figures come from children from twelve to seventeen who were interviewed for a survey on children and advertising. The survey, commissioned by the Center for the New American Dream, revealed that 60 percent of the children said that even before they reached the first grade, they knew how to manipulate their parents for small things.

Young children, we must realize, have a great deal of spending power and also influence the spending habits of their parents for everything from new cars to kinds of vacations to take. I've seen figures suggesting that children influence around $700 billion in adult spending. As Underhill notes (2009:142)

> The marketplace wants kids, needs kids, and they're flattered by the invitation and happy to oblige. They idolize licensed TV characters the way children once were taught to worship patron saints, and manage to suss out the connection between brand name and status at a very early age. . . . You no longer need to stay clear of the global marketplace just because you're three-and-a-half-feet tall, have no income to speak of and are not permitted to cross the street without Mom. You're an economic force, now and in the future, and that's what counts.

A survey by the Center for the New American Dream also revealed that children who didn't have the right kind of clothes felt they wouldn't be able to have any friends and would be rejected by other children.

In recent years, as the problem of obesity has exploded in the United States (and other countries as well), consumer groups have been attacking cereal makers and fast-food restaurant companies for contributing to the obesity epidemic in young children. They have accused advertisers of using commercials that sell cereals and other food products to children that are full of sugar and of luring children into eating foods full of fat, such as hamburgers and French fries.

Increasingly larger numbers of young children now are suffering from type 2, so-called adult-onset, diabetes, and the arteries of some adolescents are similar, in terms of the fat blockages in them, to those of middle-age men. In addition, there is a diabetes epidemic in the United States, and various consumer groups have argued that the advertising industry is a major contributor to this and other medical problems. The burden of our unhealthy eating habits on our medical system and the costs of treating people with these diseases are growing to astronomical levels.

It is impossible to pin all the blame for our problems with obesity and diabetes and other medical diseases only on the advertising agencies, but there is little question that the commercials to which young children are exposed and the marketing of hamburgers with toys for children have played a major contributing role in the spread of these diseases.

BATTLING FOR PEOPLE'S ATTENTION

There is a kind of imperialism inherent in the advertising industry; it has a methodology for shaping desire and seeks to use its methods and powers everywhere. So there is good reason to investigate advertising and consider what role it's been playing and may play in the future in America and elsewhere.

There is, ironically, a countervailing force affecting advertising, and that is the work of other agencies that are engaged in an endless battle for people's attention. That is the first step in getting people to buy something—and agencies now seem to be willing to do almost anything to get our attention. Advertising agencies are battling one another, and as this battle intensifies, it creates more and more clutter. This means that ordinary people, deluged by commercials, become victims of information overload, which sometimes leads them to become confused and turned off, so to speak.

So there may be a point of diminishing returns that the advertising industry faces, though, for the moment, as we are subjected to thousands and thousands of print advertisements and television commercials, we have no way of knowing when a particular advertisement will become a tipping point, a straw that will break the advertising camel's back, metaphorically speaking. It is conceivable, on the other hand, that we can be taught to process an almost infinite number of commercial messages, though I tend to doubt that this is possible. Eventually, there will be a turning point, and people will be unable to react the way advertising agencies want them to. New technology may also play a role; with the development of TiVo and other hard disks that store television programs and delete the commercials, many people are finding ways to avoid commercials in their television viewing. So things are in considerable flux, and much research is needed on advertising's role in politics, in the lives of children and teenagers, and in medicine—topics I have discussed in this book. The list of possible subjects goes on and on.

SMART PHONES, SOCIAL MEDIA, AND ADVERTISING

The incredible popularity of smart phones in America (and just about everywhere) offers advertisers a new "screen" to fill with advertisements of one kind or another (figure 10.2). In Japan, people use cell phones to read novels and manga, and now, increasingly, Japanese cell phone users are being exposed to advertising. Mobile phone advertising is common in a number of other countries as well. In his book *Buying In: What We Buy and Who We Are,*

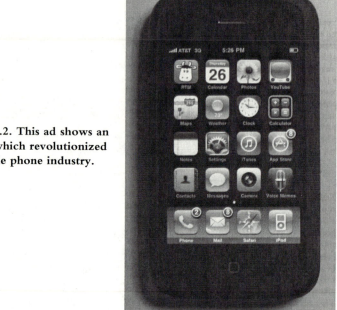

Figure 10.2. This ad shows an iPhone, which revolutionized the mobile phone industry.

Rob Walker, *New York Times Magazine* "Consumed" columnist, discusses cell phone advertising.

He mentions the notion that young people see mobile phones as symbolizing freedom and then points out that marketers are excited about advertising on mobile phones. He writes (2008:128),

> "This is the one medium you carry with you," one marketer says. "Another says that, yes, television spots just don't have the reach the used to, but "The mobile phone is very personal, and it's always with you." A third agrees: "By communicating with consumers through the mobile phone, you can deliver your message right in their hip pocket."

Thus, a symbol of freedom becomes a selling machine in every pocket.

Ironically, then, mobile phones are not instruments of freedom, as many people believe, but carriers of yet another kind of sell, to be exploited by corporations and advertising agencies.

Statistica.com offers data on projected smart phone penetration in America:

2014: 160 million
2015: 178 million

2016: 193 million
2017: 207 million

In 2014, something like 50 percent of all mobile phones in the United States are smart phones, and the percentage of smart phones there is rising rapidly. Approximately 80 percent of American teenagers have smart phones.

The social media, such as Facebook, Twitter, and YouTube, are also important venues for monetizing—read selling advertisements. One day in March 2010, Facebook actually had more people using it than were using Google. Google makes its money by selling advertisements and bringing people interested in products and services together with the companies that make or offer them. Now Facebook and the other social media sites are making money from advertising in a way that they hope will not turn off people who use them. Between cell phone users, smart phone users, and social media users, there is an enormous market that advertisers are targeting. That, of course, includes you—though you probably don't think of yourself as a target of advertising, but you are.

STUDY QUESTIONS, APPLICATIONS, AND ASSIGNMENTS

1. What was said about direct-to-consumer drug advertising in America?
2. What points did Alexander Eichler make in his analysis of drug advertising and the role of Big Pharma in America?
3. Is advertising dominating the field of medicine in America? What argument can be made to suggest that this is the case? What arguments can be made against this assertion?
4. What interesting statistics did you find from reading the discussion of drug advertising?
5. What data did you learn about children and advertising from Commercial Alert?
6. In some countries, advertising to children is forbidden. Do you think this is a good idea? If so, why? If not, why not? Do a research paper on the effect on children of their exposure to children's advertising. Focus on particular campaigns to the extent possible.
7. What arguments can be made supporting the claim that children's advertising is contributing to the obesity epidemic in America? What arguments can be made to counter this claim?
8. What brand of smart phone do you own (or would you own if you could afford one)? Why did you choose that brand? What

brand will you choose for your next smart phone? What will shape your decision making about the brand to purchase?

9. Monitor your use of your smart phone for one day: How many calls did you make? How many calls did you receive? How many text messages did you send? How many text messages did you receive? How many e-mail messages did you send or receive? How many times did you check your smart phone for e-mail or text messages? What other things did you do with the phone? What are the ten most important apps on your phone? Make a chart that shows the data for all these matters that you can compare with the way your friends use their smart phones.

GLOSSARY

Aberrant Decoding. The notion that audiences decode or interpret texts such as television commercials and print advertisements in ways that differ from the ways the creators of these texts expect them to be decoded. Aberrant decoding is the rule rather than the exception when it comes to the mass media, according to the semiotician Umberto Eco. It has been estimated that about 25 percent of advertisements and commercials are decoded aberrantly, that is, not the way the creators of the texts expected them to be decoded.

Abraham Maslow's Theory of Needs. According to Maslow, there is a ladder of human needs from basic physical needs to self-actualization ones that is found in everyone. Marketers make use of Maslow's theory in designing advertising campaigns.

Advertisement. The word "advert" means "to call attention to something," and thus an advertisement is, for our purposes, a kind of text—carried by electronic or print media—that attracts attention to, stimulates desire for, and in some cases leads to the purchase of a product or service. The convention is that commercial messages in print are called advertisements and those in electronic media are called commercials.

Aesthetics. This involves the way technical matters such as lighting, sound, music, kinds of shots, camera work, and editing affects the way audiences react to commercials or print advertisements.

Alienation. In Marxist theory, capitalist societies can create huge amounts of consumer goods, but they also inevitably generate alienation and feelings of estrangement from oneself and others in the society. Alienation is functional for those who own the means of production and distribution since alienation leads to consumer cultures—ones characterized by endless and frantic consumption, which people use as an escape from their feelings of alienation. In capitalist societies, therefore, advertising plays a central role in maintaining the status quo. See also **Consumer Cultures**.

Archetype. According to Carl Jung, archetypes are images found in dreams, myths, works of art, and religions all over the world. They are not transmitted by culture but are somehow passed on in a collective unconscious. We are not conscious of them directly, but they reveal themselves in our dreams and works of art. One of the most important archetypes is the hero. Archetypal heroes and heroines are commonly used in advertising since they resonate so strongly with people.

Artist. We will consider an artist to be not only someone who writes, paints, sculpts, or plays musical instruments but anyone involved in the creation or performance of a text. The creative people in advertising agencies are copywriters, artists, typographers, designers, and so on. Generally speaking, a creative director in an advertising agency assembles teams of creative artists to work on particular campaigns. Many artists in advertising agencies nowadays do not know how to draw particularly well but are adept at using the computer for finding and creating visual images.

Attitudes. Attitude, as social psychologists use the term, refers to a person's relatively enduring state of mind about some phenomenon or aspect of experience. Attitudes generally are either positive or negative, have direction, and involve thoughts, feelings, and behaviors. I suggest in this book that advertising should be examined in terms of its impact on culture in general rather than being dealt with in terms of attitude change in individuals or groups.

Audience. Audiences are generally defined as collections of individuals who watch a television program, listen to a radio show, or attend a film or some kind of live artistic performance (symphony, rock band, and so on). The members of the audience may be together in one room or, in the case of television, each watching from his or her own set. In technical terms, audiences are addressees who receive mediated texts sent by an addresser. For advertisers, securing the right audiences is crucial because it doesn't pay to advertise to people who either aren't interested in or can't afford the product or service being advertised. The media, in economic terms, can be held to deliver audiences to advertisers.

Blogs. Web logs that individuals use to place their ideas on the Internet. Some blogs are strictly personal and are a form of electronic diary or journal, while others deal with politics and other topics.

Branding. Creating emotional ties between certain products or services and the individuals who will purchase them over the course of their lives. From a semiotic perspective, brands are signs people use to display their taste or wealth and to help them fashion an identity. The fact that certain companies prominently attach their logos to what they make helps users solidify their sense of style and discrimination and their identities.

Broadcast. We use the term "broadcast" to deal with texts that are made available over wide areas via radio or television signals. Broadcasting differs from other forms of distributing texts, such as cablecasting, which uses cables, and satellite transmission, which requires dishes to capture signals sent by the satellites.

Claritas. A market research company that argues that there are sixty-six different kinds of consumers in the United States, each of which tends to be found in certain ZIP codes. They argue that "birds of a feather flock together" and give each of the groupings jazzy names, such as "Blue Blood Estates" and "Shotguns and Pickups."

Class. From a linguistic standpoint, a class is any group of things that have something in common. We use the term to refer to social classes or, more literally, socioeconomic classes: groups of people who share income and lifestyle. Marxist theorists argue that there is a ruling class, which shapes the ideas of the proletariat, the working classes. Advertisers are interested in socioeconomic classes and lifestyles because these phenomena are held to be the key to selling products and services.

Codes. Codes are systems of symbols, letters, words, sounds, and so on that generate meaning. Language, for example, is a code. It uses combinations of letters that we call words to mean certain things. The relation between the word and the thing the word stands for is arbitrary, based on convention. In some cases, the term "code" is used to describe hidden meanings and disguised communications. Audiences have to decode texts correctly, so advertising strives to create print advertisements and commercials that are easy to understand. Despite the best intentions of those who create advertisements, approximately one-quarter of the people decode them aberrantly.

Cognitive Dissonance. Dissonance refers to sounds that clash with one another. According to psychologists, people wish to avoid ideas that challenge the ones they hold, which creates conflict and other disagreeable feelings. Cognitive dissonance refers to ideas that conflict with ones people hold and generate psychological anxiety and displeasure. Advertisers strive to avoid dissonance and to reinforce beliefs people already hold as a means of selling products and services.

Collective Representations. Emile Durkheim used this concept to deal with the fact that people are both individuals pursuing their own aims and social animals guided by the groups and societies in which they find themselves. Collective representations are, broadly speaking, texts that reflect the beliefs and ideals of collectivities. Advertisements are designed, one could say, as collective representations that will appeal to people and help advertisers shape people's behavior.

Communication. There are many different ways of understanding and using this term. For our purposes, communication is a process that involves the transmission of messages from senders to receivers. We often make a distinction between communication using language, or verbal communication, and communication using facial expressions, body language, and other means, or nonverbal communication. In advertisements and television commercials, both verbal and nonverbal communication play very important roles.

Consumer Cultures. Consumer cultures are characterized by widespread personal consumption rather than socially conscious and useful investment in the public sphere. The focus is on private expenditure and leisure pursuits, and this leads to privatism, self-centeredness, and a reluctance to allocate resources for the public realm. Advertising is held by many critics to be a primary instrument of those who own the means of production in generating consumer lust and consumer cultures and distracting people from social and public matters. Social scientists Aaron Wildavsky and Mary Douglas suggest that there are four political cultures and that these also function as consumer cultures: hierarchical or elitist, individualist, egalitarian, and fatalist. See also **Political Cultures**.

CPM. CPM is an acronym for "cost per thousand," the way advertising is traditionally measured. It is the number of viewers reached that is critical, not the absolute cost of running the advertisement. Thus, a print advertisement in a newspaper that costs $10,000 to run and that reaches 500,000 people is much more expensive, on a CPM basis, than a commercial that costs $100,000 to run but that reaches 20 million people.

Critical Research. Critical research refers to approaches to media that are essentially ideological and that focus on the social and political dimensions of the mass media and the way they are used by organizations and others allegedly to maintain the status quo rather than to enhance equality. This contrasts with administrative research. Many books about the advertising industry written by scholars can be described as examples of critical research—including this book.

Cultivation Theory. This theory argues that television dominates the symbolic environment of its audiences and gives people false views of reality. That is, television "cultivates" or reinforces certain beliefs in its viewers, such as the notions that society is permeated by violence, that there are hardly any older people, and that everyone is living in upper-middle-class splendor. Advertising plays a significant role in cultivating the American public.

Cultural Criticism. The term "cultural criticism" refers to the analysis of texts and various aspects of everyday life by scholars in various disciplines who use concepts from their fields of expertise to interpret mass-mediated texts, the role of the mass media, and related concerns. The focus is on what impact these texts and the media that carry them have on individuals, society, and culture. Cultural criticism involves the use of literary theory, media analysis, philosophical thought, communication theory, and various interpretive methodologies.

Cultural Homogenization. When people use the term "cultural homogenization," they mean that the media of mass communication are destroying Third World cultures and regional cultures in specific countries, leading to a cultural sameness, standardization, and homogenization. For example, McDonald's has affected the eating habits of many Asian countries, and McDonald's uses advertising to attract patrons, so advertising plays a role in this cultural homogenization process.

Cultural Imperialism (also Media Imperialism). The theory of cultural imperialism describes the flow of media products (such as songs, films, and television programs) and popular culture from the United States and a few other capitalist countries in Western Europe to the Third World. Along with these texts and popular culture, it is alleged that values and beliefs (and bourgeois capitalist ideology) are also being transmitted, leading to the domination of these people.

Culture. There are hundreds of definitions of culture. Generally speaking, from the anthropological perspective, it involves the transmission from generation to generation of specific ideas, arts, customary beliefs, ways of living, behavior patterns, institutions, and values. When applied to the arts, it generally is used to specify "elite" kinds of artworks, such as operas, poetry, classical music, and serious novels. The argument in this book is that advertising is an important institution and has an enormous impact on our culture.

Defense Mechanisms. Defense mechanisms are methods used by the ego to defend itself against pressures from the id or impulsive elements in the psyche and superego, such as conscience and guilt. Some of the more common defense mechanisms are repression (barring unconscious instinctual wishes, memories, and so on from consciousness), regression (returning to earlier stages in one's development), ambivalence (a simultaneous feeling of love and hate for a person, thing, or concept), and rationalization (offering excuses to justify one's actions). I've explained how the ego mediates between id-dominated desires to purchase products and services and superego attempts to avoid spending money.

Demographics. The term "demographics" refers to similarities found in groups of people in terms of race, religion, gender, social class, ethnicity, occupation, place of residence, age, and so on. Demographic information plays an important role in the creation of advertising and the choice of which media to use to deliver this advertising.

Dysfunctional. In sociological thought, something is dysfunctional if it contributes to the breakdown or destabilization of the entity in which it is found. Some critics of advertising argue that it is dysfunctional in that it diverts the attention of people from public problems to private desires.

Egalitarians. They stress that everyone is equal in terms of certain needs, such as for food, shelter, and access to health care. Egalitarians function as critics of the two dominant political/consumer cultures—elitist and individualist.

Ego. In Freud's theory of the psyche, the ego functions as the executant of the id and as a mediator between the id and the superego (conscience). The ego is involved in the perception of reality and the adaptation to reality. One aspect of the ego, I argue, is in helping the superego to restrain compulsive spending, which the id wishes to do.

Emotive Functions. According to Roman Jakobson, messages have a number of functions. Some of them are emotive functions, which involve expressing feelings by the sender of a message. (Other functions are referential and poetic.) Advertising is an art that makes great use of the emotive functions of actors to generate emotional responses in audiences to convince people to purchase products and services being advertised. See also **Poetic Functions**, **Referential Functions**.

Enclavists. See **Egalitarians**.

Ethical Critics. Ethics involve our sense of what is moral and correct. Ethical critics deal with texts such as advertisements in terms of the moral aspects of what happens in these texts and the possible impact of these advertisements on those exposed to these texts and on others.

False Consciousness. In Marxist thought, false consciousness refers to mistaken ideas that people have about their class, status, and economic possibilities. These ideas help maintain the status quo and are of great use to the ruling class, which wants to avoid changes in the social structure. Karl Marx argued that the ideas of the ruling class are always the ruling ideas in society. Marxists would argue that the belief many Americans have that they are "elites" because they can consume at a relatively high level is an example of false consciousness.

Fatalists. They are at the bottom rungs of society—they have little political or consumer power and can escape their status only as a result of luck or chance.

Feminist Criticism. Feminist criticism focuses on the roles given to women and the way they are portrayed in texts of all kinds, including one of the worst offenders—advertising. Feminist critics argue that women are typically used as sexual objects and are portrayed stereotypically in advertisements and other texts and that this has negative effects on both men and women.

Focal Points. Focal points are the five general topics or subject areas we can concentrate on in studying mass communication: (1) the work of art or text, (2) the artist, (3) the audience, (4) America or the society, and (5) the media.

Formula. A formula in narrative theory refers to a text with conventional characters and actions that audiences are familiar with. Genre texts, such as detective stories, westerns, science fiction adventures, and romances are highly formulaic. Many advertisements and commercials are also formulaic because this facilitates easy comprehension by audience members.

Functional. In sociological thought, the term "functional" refers to the contribution an institution makes to the maintenance of society or an institution or entity. Something functional helps maintain the system in which it is found. Defenders of advertising argue that it is functional in that it facilitates consumption, innovation, and general economic well-being.

Functional Alternative. The term "functional alternative" refers to something that takes the place of something else. For example, professional football can be seen as a functional alternative to religion. I argue in this book that a department store can be seen as a modern functional alternative to medieval cathedrals.

Gender. Gender is the sexual category of an individual: male or female and the behavioral traits connected with each category. Gender is now held to be "socially constructed," which means it is our societies that determine what we think about gender.

Genre. "Genre" is a French word that means "kind" or "class." As we use the term, it refers to the kind of formulaic texts found in the mass media, such as commercials and print advertisements, soap operas, news shows, sports programs, horror shows, and detective programs. I have dealt with this topic at length in my book *Popular Culture Genres* (1992).

Global. Marshall McLuhan suggested, many years ago, that as a result of new developments in technology, the world was becoming a "global" village. The term suggests that as the result of the growth of the Internet and other media of communication, people everywhere are linked together like people in a small village. The advertising industry is now global with giant mega-agencies that own hundreds of other agencies all over the world.

Google. The most important search engine, which has used its technological prowess to become a major force in contemporary American society as far as technology is concerned. By selling advertisements on its search engine, Google has become a very wealthy and powerful company.

Grid–Group Theory. This theory is based on the work of social anthropologist Mary Douglas, who argued that there are four (and only four) consumer cultures or lifestyles in modern societies, based on the degree to which the groups have weak or strong boundaries and whether members have few or many rules and prescriptions to follow.

Hierarchical Elitists. These people are at the top of the economic and power pyramid and believe that hierarchy is needed for society to run smoothly. They have a sense of obligation to those beneath them.

Hypodermic Needle Theory of Media. This theory, generally discredited now, holds that all members of an audience "read" a text the same way and get the same things out of it. Media are seen as hypodermic needles, injecting their messages into one and all. The fact that a relatively high percentage of people decode mass-mediated texts aberrantly suggests that the hypodermic needle theory is too simplistic.

Id. The id in Freud's theory of the psyche (technically known as his structural hypothesis) is that element of the psyche that is the representative of a person's drives. In *New Introductory Lectures on Psychoanalysis*, Freud called it "a chaos, a cauldron of seething excitement." It also is the source of energy, but, lacking direction, it needs the ego to harness it and control it. In popular thought, it is connected to impulse, lust, and "I want it all now" behavior. Many advertisements appeal to id elements in our psyches.

Ideology. An ideology is a logically coherent, integrated explanation of social, economic, and political matters that helps establish the goals and direct the actions of a group or political entity. People act (and vote or don't vote) on the basis of an ideology they hold, even though they may not have articulated it or thought about it. Some critics argue that advertising is an ideological tool that members of the ruling class use to distract people from their problems and convince them that the political order is worth supporting.

Image. Defining images is extremely difficult. In my book *Seeing Is Believing: An Introduction to Visual Communication*, I define an image as "a collection of signs and symbols—what we find when we look at a photograph, a film still, a shot of a television screen, a print advertisement, or just about anything." The term is used for mental as well as physical representations of things. Images often have powerful emotional effects on people and historical significance. Advertisers use the power of images to sell products and services.

Imprints. According to the French psychoanalyst and marketing theorist Clotaire Rapaille, children in all countries are imprinted, by the age of seven, by the culture and country in which they grow up. These imprints then shape their thinking and behavior when they are adults.

Individualists. Individualists believe that the basic function of government is to prevent crime and invasion by foreign powers. They are competitive and stress the importance of individual initiative.

Integrated Marketing Communication. This approach argues that advertising, public relations, and other kinds of messaging must be integrated to achieve the best results.

Intertextuality. This theory argues that texts (works of art) of all kinds are influenced to varying degrees by texts that preceded them. Sometimes, as in the case of parody, the relationship is overt, but in many cases, creators of texts are influenced by stylistic practices or thematic ones from earlier works. We can say, then, that intertextuality involves making allusions to, imitating, modifying, or adapting previously created texts and styles of expression.

Isolates. See **Fatalists**.

Lasswell Formula. Harold Lasswell was a prominent political scientist. Considered by some scholars to be the most famous formula in communication theory, the Lasswell formula goes as follows: Who? Says what? In which channel? To whom? With what effect?

Latent Functions. Latent functions are hidden, unrecognized, and unintended results of some activity, entity, or institution. They are contrasted by social scientists with manifest functions, which are recognized and intended. Some critics suggest that the latent function of advertising is to support the political order, while the manifest function of advertising is to sell goods and services. See also **Manifest Functions**.

Lifestyle. Literally, "style of life," the term "lifestyle" refers to the way people live—to the decisions they make about how to decorate their homes (and where they are located), the cars they drive, the clothes they wear, the foods they eat, the restaurants they visit, and where they go for vacations. Lifestyles tend to be coherent or logically connected, and they play an important part in market research.

Limited Effects (of Media). Some mass communication theorists argue that the mass media have relatively minor effects on the scheme of things. They cite research that shows, for example, that media effects don't tend to be long lasting and argue that mass media's strong effects have not been demonstrated. When they testify before governmental agencies, advertisers argue that advertisements and commercials have limited effects, and when dealing with clients, they argue that they have powerful effects.

Manifest Functions. The manifest functions of an activity, entity, or institution are those that are obvious and intended. Manifest functions contrast with latent functions, which are hidden and unintended. The manifest function of advertising is to sell products and services; the latent function is to sell the political order. See also **Latent Functions**.

Mass. For our purposes, "mass," as in "mass communication," refers to a large number of people who are the audience for some communication. There is considerable disagreement about how to understand the term "mass." Some theorists say that a mass comprises individuals who are heterogeneous, do not know one another, are alienated, and do not have a leader. Others attack these notions, saying they are based not on fact but on theories that are not correct and have not been proven in experiments.

Mass Communication. The term "mass communication" refers to the transfer of messages, information, and texts from a sender (for our purposes, an advertising agency) to a receiver, a large number of people, a mass audience. This transfer is done through the technologies of the mass media—newspapers, magazines, television programs, films, records, computers, the Internet, and CD-ROMs. The sender is often a person in a large media organization, the messages are public, and the audience tends to be large and varied.

Medium (plural: Media). A medium is a means of delivering messages, information, or texts to audiences. There are different ways of classifying the media. One of the most common ways is as follows: print (newspapers, magazines, books, and billboards), electronic (radio, television, computers, CD-ROMs, and the Internet), and photographic (photographs, films, and videos). Various critics have suggested that the main function of the commercial media is to deliver audiences to advertisers and that everything else the media do is of secondary importance.

Metaphor. A metaphor is a figure of speech that conveys meaning by analogy. It is important to realize that metaphors are not confined to poetry and literary works but, according to some linguists, are the fundamental way in which we make sense of things and find meaning in the world. A simile is a weaker form of metaphor that uses either "like" or "as" in making an analogy. Metaphors are an important element in advertising. For example, Fidji perfume had a campaign that was explicitly metaphoric: Woman is an island.

Metonymy. According to linguists, metonymy is a figure of speech that conveys information by association and is, along with metaphor, one of the most important ways people convey information to one another. We tend not to be aware of our use of metonymy, but whenever we use association to get an idea about something (Rolls-Royce = wealthy), we are thinking metonymically. A form of metonymy that involves seeing a whole in terms of a part or vice versa is called synecdoche. Using the White House to stand for the presidency is an example of synecdoche. Metonymy is another important technique used by advertisers to generate information and emotional responses to advertisements.

Mimetic Theory of Art (and Mimetic Desire). This theory, dating from Aristotle's time, suggests that art is an imitation of reality. The term "mimesis" means "imitation." The theory of mimetic desire, developed by René Girard, is that people imitate the desire of others and that advertising uses this mimetic desire to sell people products and services.

Model. Models, in the social sciences, are abstract representations that explain a phenomenon. Theories are typically expressed in language, but models tend to be graphic or statistical or mathematical. Denis McQuail and Sven Windahl define model in *Communication Models: For the Study of Mass Communication* (1993:2) as "a consciously simplified description in graphic form of a piece of reality. A model seeks to show the main elements of any structure or process and the relationships between these elements."

Modernism. The period before postmodernism, from roughly 1900 to 1960, when postmodernism became dominant. Modernism's esthetics and values, its belief in master narratives (like its belief in progress) and grand theories, were rejected by postmodernism.

Motivation Research. Practitioners of motivation research argue that it is necessary to determine and understand people's unconscious and unrecognized attitudes in order to persuade them to purchase products and services. Ernest Dichter was one of the founding fathers of motivation research, which, he argued, could be used also for many socially valuable purposes.

Myth. Myths are conventionally understood to be sacred stories about gods and cultural heroes (and, in more recent years, mass-mediated heroes and heroines) that are used to transmit a culture's basic belief system to younger generations and to explain natural and supernatural phenomena. According to Mark Shorer (1968:355), "Myths are instruments by which we continually struggle to make our experiences intelligible to ourselves. A myth is a large, controlling image that gives philosophical meaning to the facts of ordinary life."

Narrowcasting. A medium, such as radio, with stations that focus on discrete groups of people. It contrasts with broadcasting, which tries to reach as many people as possible. Advertisers use broadcasting, but they aim most of their advertisements at the eighteen- to forty-five-year-old segment of the population.

National Character. This theory argues that people who grow up in a country can be characterized by certain values, beliefs, and behaviors that are distinctive. Thus, there is a big difference between people in different countries—a topic explored by Clotaire Rapaille in his book *The Culture Code*.

Nonfunctional. In sociological thought, something is nonfunctional if it is neither functional nor dysfunctional but plays no role in the entity in which it is found.

Nonverbal Communication. Our body language, facial expressions, styles of dress, and hairstyles are examples of our communicating feelings and attitudes (and a sense of who we are) without words. In advertising, a great deal of the communication is done nonverbally. In some commercials, almost all the information or meaning is communicated nonverbally. You can see this if you turn off the sound and watch commercials. Notice how in many commercials, facial expressions and body language are used to sell the product.

Objective Theory of Art. This theory argues that art is like a lamp and projects a reality (that of the artist) rather than being like a mirror and imitating reality.

Opinion Leaders. People whose opinions affect those of others are opinion leaders. The notion that there are opinion leaders is part of the two-step flow theory of communication. We can adapt this theory and suggest that some people are fashion and lifestyle opinion leaders who can be used to sell products and services. See also **Two-Step Flow**.

Phallic Symbol. An object that resembles the penis either by shape or by function is described as a phallic symbol. Symbolism is a defense mechanism of the ego that permits hidden or repressed sexual or aggressive thoughts to be expressed in a disguised form. For a discussion of this topic, see Freud's book *The Interpretation of Dreams*.

Phallocentric. The term "phallocentric" is used to describe societies that are dominated by males, and the ultimate source of this domination, that which shapes our institutions and cultures, is the male phallus. In this theory, a link is made between male sexuality and male power.

Poetic Functions. In Roman Jakobson's theory, poetic functions are those that use literary devices such as metaphor and metonymy. Poetic functions differ, Jakobson suggests, from emotive functions and referential functions. In this book, I discuss the pseudopoetic aspects of some advertisements meant to convince people that they are having a profound experience. See also **Emotive Functions**, **Referential Functions**.

Political Cultures. According to political scientist Aaron Wildavsky, there are four political cultures in every democratic society: hierarchical or elitist (based on the notion that hierarchy is important and on a sense of obligation of those at the top for those beneath them), individualist (based on the notion that individuals are of primary importance and that government should do as little as possible, except for maximizing individual initiative), egalitarian (based on the notion that everyone has certain needs that have to be taken care of), and fatalist (based on the notion that some people are at the lowest rungs of society, are controlled by those above them, can escape their situation only as a result of chance or luck). See also **Consumer Cultures**.

Popular. "Popular" is one of the most difficult terms used in discourse about the arts and the media. Literally, the term means "appealing to a large number of people." It comes from the Latin "popularis," "of the people." Separating the popular and elite arts has become increasingly problematic in recent years. For example, is an opera shown on television an example of elite or popular culture?

Popular Culture. "Popular culture" is a term that identifies certain kinds of texts that appeal to a large number of people. But mass communication theorists often identify (or should I say confuse?) "popular" with "mass" and suggest that if something is popular, it must be of poor quality, appealing to the mythical "lowest common denominator." Popular culture is generally held to be the opposite of elite culture—arts that require certain levels of sophistication and refinement to be appreciated, such as ballet, opera, poetry, and classical music. Many critics now question this popular culture/elite culture polarity.

Postmodernism. This theory states that a new kind of culture has developed in the United States and elsewhere, since approximately 1960, rejecting the values and beliefs of the modernist society that had been dominant until that time. One theorist of postmodernism argued that it involves "incredulity toward metanarratives," by which he meant the rejection of the overarching religious, social, political, aesthetic, and moral theories of the modernist period that have shaped people's thinking and their lives. Postmodernism is associated with stylistic eclecticism, a rejection of the split between elite and popular culture. The theory is very controversial, and important facets of it are explored in my books *Postmortem for a Postmodernist* (a postmodern mystery) and *The Portable Postmodernist*.

Pragmatic Theory of Art. This theory holds that art must do something and have certain consequences that are held to be desirable. Thus, art should teach or indoctrinate or perform some function. Advertising is a good example of a pragmatic art: It exists to do something, namely, sell goods, services, and, at times, politicians and political parties.

Product Placement. Because so many people are using TiVo and other similar devices to fast-forward through commercials or are avoiding them in other ways, advertising agencies are now paying money to have their products placed in television programs and films, where the audiences for these texts will not or cannot fast-forward them out. In addition, advertisers get a "halo" effect since their products become identified with actors and celebrities.

Psychoanalytic Theory. Sigmund Freud can be said to be the founding father of psychoanalytic theory. He argued that the human psyche has three levels: consciousness, preconsciousness, and the unconscious, which is the largest area of the psyche and an area not able to be accessed by individuals. What is important is that the unconscious shapes and affects our mental functioning and our behavior. Another of his theories posited three forces in the psyche: the id (desire), the ego (reason), and the superego (guilt), which were continually battling with one another for domination. Freud believed that sexuality and what he called "the Oedipus complex" play a dominant role in human behavior, even if their presence is not recognized.

Psychographics. In marketing, the term "psychographics" is used to deal with groups of people who have similar psychological characteristics or profiles. It differs from demographics, which marketers use to focus on social and economic characteristics that people have in common.

Public. Instead of popular culture, we sometimes use the term "public arts" or "public communication" to avoid the negative connotations of "mass" and "popular." A public is a group of people, a community. We can contrast public acts, which are those meant to be known to the community, with private acts, which are not meant to be known to others.

Rationalization. In Freudian thought, a rationalization is a defense mechanism of the ego that creates an excuse to justify an action (or inaction when an action is expected). Ernest Jones, who introduced the term, used it to describe logical and rational reasons that people give to justify behavior that is really caused by unconscious and irrational determinants. We often use rationalizations to justify purchases that are unwise and unnecessary.

Reader Response Theory (also Reception Theory). This theory suggests that readers (a term used very broadly to cover people who read books, watch television programs, go to films, listen to texts on the radio, and so on) play an important role in the realization of texts. Texts such as advertising, then, function as sites for the creation of meaning by readers, and different readers interpret a given text differently.

Referential Functions. In Roman Jakobson's theory, the referential function of speech deals with the way it helps speakers relate to their surroundings. He contrasts it with the emotive and poetic functions of speech. See also **Emotive Functions, Poetic Functions**.

Role. Sociologists describe a role as a way of behavior that we learn in a society and that is appropriate to a particular situation. A person generally plays many roles with different people during the hours of a day, such as parent (family), worker (job), and spouse (marriage). We also use the term to describe the parts that actors have in mass-mediated texts, including commercials.

Sapir-Whorf Hypothesis. This hypothesis argues that language is not something transparent that merely conveys information from one person to another but rather something that affects the way people think and act. Language—for our purposes, language used in print advertisements and radio and television commercials—is not like a windowpane but more like a prism.

Secondary Modeling Systems. Language, according to Yuri Lotman, is our primary modeling system. Works of art, which use phenomena such as myths and legends, function as secondary modeling systems; that is, they are secondary to language. Lotman also argued that every element in a text is important and that texts are so incredibly complex that they can be mined continually for new meanings.

Selective Attention (or Selective Inattention). We have a tendency to avoid messages that conflict with our beliefs and values. One way we do this is through selective attention—avoiding or not paying attention to messages that would generate cognitive dissonance. Thus, we tend to ignore information that would counsel us not to buy something that we want to buy.

Semiotics. Literally, the term "semiotics" means "the science of signs." "Sēmeîon" is the Greek term for "sign." A sign is anything that can be used to stand for anything else.

Sign. The basic concept in semiotics, the science of signs (from the Greek word "sēmeîon," "sign") that deals with how we find meaning in images and other kinds of communication. Ferdinand de Saussure, one of the founding fathers of semiotics, argued that a sign is made up of a signifier (a sound or object) and a signified (a concept). The relation between the signifier and the signified is arbitrary and not natural. C. S. Peirce, another founding father of semiotics, had a different notion. He said a sign is "something which stands to somebody for something in some respect or capacity." His theory of signs is dealt with in the discussion of symbols.

Social Controls. Social controls are ideas, beliefs, values, and mores people get from their societies that shape their beliefs and behavior. People are both individuals with certain distinctive physical and emotional characteristics and desires and at the same time members of societies. And people are shaped to a certain degree by the institutions found in these societies. The question this book considers is, what impact do advertising in general and specific advertising texts have upon societies and individuals?

Socialization. Socialization refers to the processes by which societies teach individuals how to behave: what rules to obey, roles to assume, and values to hold. Socialization was traditionally done by the family, educators, religious figures, and peers. The mass media in general and advertising in particular seem to have usurped this function to a considerable degree nowadays, with consequences that are not always positive.

Socioeconomic Class. A socioeconomic class is a categorization of people according to their incomes and related social status and lifestyles. In Marxist thought, there are ruling classes that shape the consciousness of the working classes, and history is, in essence, a record of class conflict.

Stereotypes. Stereotypes are commonly held, simplistic, and inaccurate group portraits of categories of people. Stereotypes can be positive, negative, or mixed, but generally they are negative. Stereotyping involves making gross overgeneralizations. (All Mexicans, Chinese, Jews, African Americans, WASPS, Americans, lawyers, doctors, professors, and so on are held to have certain characteristics, usually negative.) Stereotypes are used in advertising because they are thought to facilitate understanding by audiences.

Subculture. Any complex society is made up of numerous subcultures that differ from the dominant culture in terms of such matters as ethnicity, race, religion, sexual orientation, beliefs, values, and tastes. Often, members of subcultures are marginalized and victimized by members of the dominant culture. One problem advertisers face is trying to reach and persuade members of these subcultures to purchase products and services designed for members of the dominant culture.

Superego. In Freud's structural hypothesis, the superego is the agency in our psyches related to conscience and morality. The superego is involved with processes such as approval and disapproval of wishes on the basis of their morality, critical self-observation, and a sense of guilt over wrongdoing. The functions of the superego are largely unconscious and are opposed to id elements in our psyches. Mediating between the two and trying to balance them are our egos. The superego, in my application of Freud's theory to advertising, is what tells the ego (and the id) that some product or service that the id longs for is not needed. The id says, "I want to buy it!" The superego says, "Don't buy that!" And the ego helps the superego deal with the id.

Suspension of Disbelief. It was the English critic Samuel Coleridge who first used the phrase "suspension of disbelief" to describe what happens to people when they become involved with works of art and start identifying with characters in these texts. Thus, in plays, films, television shows, and commercials, they forget or "suspend" their recognition of the fact that they are members of an audience and become involved with the characters they are observing.

Symbol. Literally speaking, a symbol is something that stands for something else. The term comes from the Greek word "symballein," which means "to put together." Advertisers use symbols because they have powerful emotional effects on people. Think, for example, of all that is found in three symbols: the cross, the Star of David, and the crescent. In C. S. Peirce's theory of semiotics, there are three kinds of signs: icons, which communicate by resemblance; indexes, which communicate by cause and effect; and symbols, whose meaning must be learned. Advertisers make use of symbols because of their power to affect human emotions.

Taste Cultures. Sociologist Herbert Gans's theory that there are a number of taste cultures in America, "each with its own art, literature, music, and so forth, which differ mainly in that they express different aesthetic standards." Basic to his argument is the idea that all taste cultures are of equal worth.

Teleculture. The concept of teleculture suggests that television has become a dominant influence on society and helps shape both individual behavior and cultural institutions. Our culture used to be passed on through books, parents, teachers, and others, but they have been supplanted by the characters we see on television or in other media.

Text. For our purposes, a text is, broadly speaking, any work of art in any medium. Critics use the term "text" as a convenience—so they don't have to name a given work all the time or use various synonyms. There are problems involved in deciding what the text is when we deal with serial texts, such as soap operas or comics. In this book, I use the term to stand for print advertisements, radio and television commercials, and any other kind of advertising or commercial messages carried by any medium.

Theory. Theories, as I use the term, are expressed in language and systematically and logically attempt to explain and predict phenomena being studied. They differ from concepts, which define phenomena that are being studied, and from models, which are abstract, usually graphic in nature, and explicit about what is being studied.

Two-Step Flow. This refers to a theory of how mass communication reaches and affects people. According to this theory, in the first step the media influence opinion leaders, and in the second step the opinion leaders influence others. Applied to advertising, this suggests that large numbers of people are influenced by certain style and fashion leaders. People identify with others, which is why celebrities, supermodels, and actors are often used in advertising. See also **Opinion Leaders**.

Typology. We will understand a typology to be a system of classification of things that is done to clarify matters.

Uses and Gratifications. This sociological theory argues that researchers should pay attention to the way audiences use the media (or certain texts or genres of texts, such as print advertisements or radio and television commercials) and the gratifications they get from their use of these texts and the media. Researchers of uses and gratifications focus, then, on how audiences use the media and not on how the media affect audiences.

Values. Values are abstract and general beliefs or judgments about what is right and wrong and what is good and bad that have implications for individual behavior and for social, cultural, and political entities. There are a number of problems with values from a philosophical point of view. First, how does one determine which values are correct and good and which aren't? That is, how do we justify values? Are values objective or subjective? Second, what happens when there is a conflict between groups, each of which holds a central value that conflicts with that of another group? Values are part of the VALS—values and lifestyles—marketing system.

Youth Culture. Youth cultures are subcultures formed by young people around some area of interest, usually connected with leisure and entertainment, such as rock music, computer games, hacking, and so on. Typically, youth cultures adopt distinctive ways of dressing and develop institutions that cater to their needs. Youth cultures and young people, though they may have "antiestablishment beliefs," are particularly susceptible to the entrapments of advertising.

ANNOTATED BIBLIOGRAPHY

In this section, I deal with a number of books that offer different approaches to the matter of interpreting advertisements and understanding their social, cultural, and ideological significance. Many of the books use and apply semiotic theory, often in combination with other approaches, since it has become the most important means of deconstructing particular advertising texts and campaigns. There are many books on advertising that I could have cited. I've chosen those that I feel are accessible and that offer a variety of approaches to the subject. The regular bibliography (which follows this section) lists more than a hundred books that students interested in the subject can consult.

Berger, Arthur Asa. *Dictionary of Advertising and Marketing Concepts.* 2013. Left Coast Press.
      This books offers definitions of a number of terms using in advertising and concepts used to understand advertising and marketing, from its first term, "Account Executives," to its last term, "Visual Persuasion." It covers theories and theorists dealing with advertising, marketing and consumer cultures.

Cortese, Anthony J. *Provocateur: Images of Women and Minorities in Advertising.* 2nd ed. 2004. Rowman & Littlefield.
      Cortese deals with important themes such as the semiotics of advertising in social life, postmodernism and advertising, and the representation of marginalized groups in America (such as blacks, women, Latinos, Asians, Native Americans, gays and lesbians). He offers a systematic methodology for a sociological analysis of advertising.

Danesi, Marcel. *Interpreting Advertisements: A Semiotic Guide.* 1995. Legas.
      In this slender volume of 111 pages, Marcel Danesi offers an overview of semiotic theory and then applies it to analyze a number of advertisements, showing how semiotics can be used to "deconstruct" advertisements and find all kinds of interesting things in them.

Ewen, Stuart. *Captains of Consciousness: Advertising and the Social Roots of the Consumer Culture.* 1976. McGraw–Hill.

This important book deals with advertising's impact on social life in America and its functions as an instrument of social control. It has sections on "Advertising as Social Production," "The Political Ideology of Consumption," and "Mom, Dad and the Kids: Toward a Modern Architecture of Daily Life."

Frith, Katherine Toland, ed. *Undressing the Ad: Reading Culture in Advertising.* 1997. Peter Lang.

As the subtitle of this book suggests, it is focused on the relationship between advertising and culture. It contains theoretical chapters on advertising and others that deal with specific advertisements for products such as those for Diesel jeans.

Goldman, Robert, and Stephen Papson. *Sign Wars: The Cluttered Landscape of Advertising.* 1996. Guilford.

The authors of this volume argue that advertising can be seen as involving "sign wars" or "sign competitions," which suggests a semiotic and sociological approach to the industry. They argue that advertising agencies are involved in a brutal war with other agencies to make their signs and advertisements—whether for sneakers or any other product—dominant. The book combines semiotic theory and sociological analysis of the advertising industry and of particular advertising campaigns.

Haug, Wolfang Fritz. *Critique of Commodity Aesthetics: Appearance, Sexuality and Advertising in Capitalist Society.* 1986. University of Minnesota Press.

As the subtitle of the book suggests, Haug offers a Marxist interpretation of the advertising industry and an indictment of its use of sexuality as a means of exploiting those who are exposed to advertising. Haug's focus is on capitalism and its imperatives in "bourgeois" societies as they relate to advertising.

Kern, Montague. *30-Second Politics: Political Advertising in the Eighties.* 1989. Praeger.

An excellent overview and explanation of how political advertising has evolved with a focus on some important and controversial political campaigns in the United States in the 1980s.

Leiss, William, Stephen Kline, and Sut Jhally. *Social Communication in Advertising: Consumption in the Mediated Marketplace.* 3rd ed. 2005. Routledge.

This large volume (683 pages) deals with the relationship that exists between advertising and society and many other topics, such as the communicative strategies employed by advertising. It has chapters on topics such as advertising and the development of communication media, the structure of advertisements, and the mobilization of Yuppies and Generation X.

McLuhan, Marshall. *The Mechanical Bride: Folklore of Industrial Man.* 1967. Beacon.

McLuhan's book was first published in 1951 and can be regarded as a pathbreaking work, a true classic, that focuses attention on the role that popular culture played in American culture. The book deals mostly with advertisements, though it does discuss some comic strips and other aspects of popular culture. What McLuhan does is to use the tools of literary analysis and aesthetics to analyze the cultural significance of several dozen advertisements. His style is jazzy, and his insights are penetrating.

Messaris, Paul. *Visual Persuasion: The Role of Images in Advertising.* 1997. Sage.

This book is useful because it focuses on visual phenomena and the role they play in advertising. Thus, it provides an important theoretical perspective involving applied media aesthetics on how images can be used to persuade people and to affect their emotions.

Myers, Greg. *Ad Worlds: Brands/Media/Audiences.* 1999. Arnold.

Myers covers a wide range of topics, such as how ads work, brands, globalization, the Internet, audience research, and promotional culture. It was written for British readers, but its insights can be adapted to advertising in the United States and other countries.

O'Barr, William M. *Culture and the Ad: Exploring Otherness in the World of Advertising.* 1994. Westview.

O'Barr's book has the same dimensions as McLuhan's *The Mechanical Bride*, and the design of the book and analytical focus suggest a similarity with McLuhan's perspectives on advertising. O'Barr's focus is on the way advertising presents "others" to the world, especially in travel advertising and advertising dealing with people in other cultures, and on explicating the social ideologies found in this advertising. O'Barr describes himself as being heavily influenced by Marxism and semiotic theory.

Vestergaard, Torben, and Kim Schrøder. *The Language of Advertising.* 1985. Basil Blackwell.

The focus of this book is on linguistic communication in print advertising, but the authors are aware of the importance of visual images and deal with them as well. Among the topics covered are verbal and visual messages, the structure of advertisements, strategies for dealing with sex and class differences, and ideological aspects of advertising.

Zaltman, Gerald. *How Customers Think: Essential Insights into the Mind of the Market*. 2003. Harvard Business School Press.

Zaltman offers fascinating insights into new developments in marketing, into the role of metaphors in our thinking and the relationship that exists between the mind and the brain. He is a professor in the Harvard Business School.

BIBLIOGRAPHY

Altstiel, Tom, and Jean Grow. 2005. *Advertising Strategy: Creative Tactics from the Outside In*. Thousand Oaks, CA: Sage.

Ansolabehere, Stephen, and Shanto Iyengar. 1995. *Going Negative: How Political Advertisements Shrink and Polarize the Electorate*. New York: Free Press.

Bakhtin, Mikhail. 1981. *The Dialogic Imagination*. Ed. M. Holmquist. Trans. C. Emerson and M. Holmquist. Austin: University of Texas Press.

Barnouw, Erik. 1979. *The Sponsor: Notes on a Modern Potentate*. New York: Oxford University Press.

Baudrillard, Jean. 1968. *The System of Objects*. Trans. James Benedict. London: Verso.

———. 1998. *The Consumer Society: Myths & Structures*. London: Sage.

Beckett, Jamie. 1989. "Ad Pitches Popping Up in Unusual Places." *San Francisco Chronicle*, July 17.

Berger, Arthur Asa. 1998. *Media Analysis Techniques*. 2nd ed. Thousand Oaks, CA: Sage.

———. 1998. *Seeing Is Believing: An Introduction to Visual Communication*. 2nd ed. Mountain View, CA: Mayfield.

———. 1999. *Signs in Contemporary Culture: An Introduction to Semiotics*. 2nd ed. Salem, WI: Sheffield.

———. 2002. *The Agent in the Agency*. Cresskill, NJ: Hampton.

———. 2011. "The Branded Self." *The American Sociologist* 42, no. 2, 232–39.

Berger, John. 1972. *Ways of Seeing*. London: British Broadcasting System and Penguin Books.

Bilefsky, Dan. 2010. Review of "Galerianka." *New York Times*, March 16, 8.

Bogart, Leo. 1967. *Strategy in Advertising*. New York: Harcourt Brace.

Brennan, Bridget. 2009. *Why She Buys: The New Strategy for Reaching the World's Most Powerful Consumers*. New York: Crown Business.

Breun, Stephen, and Jack Gillum. 2013. "Election 2012 Spending Hits $2 Billion Mark Amid Last-Minute Donations." *Huff Post Politics*, November 23. http://www.huffingtonpost.com/2012/12/07/election-2012-spending-hi_n_2256602.html.

Confessore, Nicholas. 2012. "Total Cost of Election Could Be $6 Billion." *New York Times*. November 1, A14.

Cortese, Anthony J. 2004. *Provocateur: Images of Women and Minorities in Advertising*. 2nd ed. Lanham, MD: Rowman & Littlefield.

Danesi, Marcel. 1995. *Interpreting Advertisements: A Semiotic Guide*. Toronto: Legas.

Diamond, Edwin, with Stephen Bates. 1992. *The Spot: The Rise of Political Advertising on Television.* Cambridge, MA: MIT Press.

Dichter, Ernest. 1960. *The Strategy of Desire.* Garden City, NY: Doubleday.

Douglas, Mary. 1997. "In Defence of Shopping." In *The Shopping Experience.* Ed. Pasi Falk and Colin Campbell. London: Sage.

Dubrow, Joel S. 1984. "Coca-Cola Turns to Pavlov." *Wall Street Journal,* January 19, 34.

Eichler, Alexander. 2013. "Pharmaceutical Companies Spent 19 Times More on Self-Promotion Than Basic Research." *Huff Post Business.* December 5.

Eidelberg, L. 1968. *The Encyclopedia of Psychoanalysis.* New York: Macmillan.

Eisenberg, Lee. 2009. *Shoptimism: Why the American Consumer Will Keep on Buying No Matter What.* New York: Free Press.

Eliade, Mircea. 1961. *The Sacred and the Profane: The Nature of Religion.* Trans. W. R. Trask. New York: Harper and Row.

Elliott, Stuart. 1993. "Advertising." *New York Times,* January 7.

———. 2004. "The Media Business: Advertising." *New York Times,* December 7.

Enzensberger, Hans Magnus. 1974. *The Consciousness Industry: On Literature, Politics, and the Media.* New York: Seabury.

Ewen, Stuart. 1976. *Captains of Consciousness: Advertising and the Social Roots of the Consumer Culture.* New York: McGraw-Hill.

Ewen, Stuart, and Elizabeth Ewen. 1982. *Channels of Desire: Mass Images and the Shaping of American Consciousness.* New York: McGraw-Hill.

Falk, Pasi, and Colin Campbell, eds. 1997. *The Shopping Experience.* London: Sage Publications.

Farrell, Greg. 1999. "Marketers Put a Price on Your Life." *USA Today,* July 7.

Featherstone, Mike. 1991. *Consumer Culture and Postmodernism.* London: Sage.

Foerster, Norman, ed. 1957. *American Poetry and Prose,* Part One. 4th ed. Boston: Houghton Mifflin.

Freud, Sigmund. 1963. "Psychoanalysis." In *Character and Culture.* Ed. Philip Rieff. New York: Collier Books.

———. 1965. *New Introductory Lectures on Psychoanalysis.* Trans. James Strachey. New York: Norton.

Frith, Katherine Toland, ed. 1997. *Undressing the Ad: Reading Culture in Advertising.* New York: Peter Lang.

Frith, Simon. 1981. *Sound Effects: Youth, Leisure, and the Politics of Rock and Roll.* New York: Pantheon.

Gans, Herbert. 1974. *Popular Culture and High Culture: An Analysis and Evaluation of Taste.* New York: Basic Books.

Gibbard, Jeff. 2012. "Using Social Media to Determine Consumer Preferences." *Social Media Philanthropy,* June 27.

Girard, René. 1991. *A Theater of Envy.* New York: Oxford University Press.

Goffman, Erving. 1976. "Gender Advertisements." *Studies in the Anthropology of Visual Communication* 3, no. 2.

Goldberg, Fred S. 2013. *The Insanity of Advertising: Memoirs of Mad Man.* San Francisco: Council Oaks Books.

Goldman, Robert, and Stephen Papson. 1996. *Sign Wars: The Cluttered Landscape of Advertising*. New York: Guilford.

Greer, Germaine. 1971. *The Female Eunuch*. New York: McGraw-Hill.

Hackley, Chris. 2005. *Advertising and Promotion*. Thousand Oaks, CA: Sage.

Hall, Stuart, ed. 1997. *Representation: Cultural Representation and Signifying Practices*. Thousand Oaks, CA: Sage.

Hall, Trish. 1990. "The Young Are Getting and Spending, Too." *New York Times*, August 23.

Hamburger, Tom. 2002. "Drug Industry Ads Aid GOP." *Wall Street Journal*, June 18.

Haug, Wolfgang Fritz. 1986. *Critique of Commodity Aesthetics: Appearance, Sexuality, and Advertising in Capitalist Society*. Trans. Robert Bock. Minneapolis: University of Minnesota Press.

———. 1987. *Commodity Aesthetics, Ideology and Culture*. New York: International General.

Henry, Jules. 1963. *Culture against Man*. New York: Vintage Books.

Herman-Cohen, Valli. 2000. "Primping or Pimping." *San Francisco Chronicle*, September 26.

Hinsie, L. E., and Campbell, R. J. 1970. *Psychiatric Dictionary*. New York: Oxford University Press.

hooks, bell. 1992. *Black Looks: Race and Representation*. Boston: South End.

Howard, Niles. 1981. "A New Way to View Consumers." *Dun's Review*, August 1981.

Huizinga, Johan. 1924. *The Waning of the Middle Ages*. Garden City, NY: Anchor.

Irvine, Martha. 2002. "Survey: More Young People Nagging." Associated Press, June 17.

Itow, Laurie. 1982. "What Your Values Tell Advertisers You'll Buy." *San Francisco Sunday Examiner and Chronicle*, June 27.

Jameson, Fredric. 1991. *Postmodernism, or, The Cultural Logic of Late Capitalism*. Durham, NC: Duke University Press.

Jamieson, Kathleen Hall. 1992. *Dirty Politics: Deception, Distraction, and Democracy*. New York: Oxford University Press.

———. 1996. *Packaging the Presidency*. 3rd ed. New York: Oxford University Press.

Jones, John Philip. 2004. *Fables, Fashions and Facts about Advertising*. Thousand Oaks, CA: Sage.

Jung, Carl. 1968. *Man and His Symbols*. New York: Dell.

Kellner, Douglas. 1988. "Postmodernism as Social Theory: Some Challenges and Problems." *Theory, Culture & Society* 5, nos. 2–3, June.

Kern, Montague. 1989. *30-Second Politics: Political Advertising in the Eighties*. New York: Praeger.

Key, Wilson Bryan. 1973. *Subliminal Seduction*. New York: Signet.

Klein, Melanie, and Joan Riviere. 1967. *Love, Hate, and Reparation*. New York: Norton.

Kotler, Philip, Ned Roberto, and Nancy Lee. 2002. *Social Marketing: Improving the Quality of Life*. Thousand Oaks, CA: Sage.

Kurtz, Bruce. 1977. *Spots: The Popular Art of American Television Commercials.* New York: Arts Communications.

Lakoff, George, and Mark Johnson. 1980. *Metaphors We Live By.* Chicago: University of Chicago Press.

Lefebvre, Henri. 1984. *Everyday Life in the Modern World.* New Brunswick, NJ: Transaction.

Leiss, William, et al. 2005. *Social Communication in Advertising: Consumption in the Mediated Marketplace.* New York: Routledge.

Lotman, Yuri. 1977. *The Structure of the Artistic Text.* Trans. G. Lenhoff and R. Vroon. Ann Arbor: Michigan Slavic Contributions.

Lyotard, Jean-François. 1984. *The Postmodern Condition: A Report on Knowledge.* Trans. Geoff Bennington and Brian Massumi. Minneapolis: University of Minnesota Press.

Marshand, Roland. 1986. *Advertising and the American Dream.* Berkeley: University of California Press.

McAllister, Matthew P. 1996. *The Commercialization of American Culture: New Advertising, Control, and Democracy.* Thousand Oaks, CA: Sage.

McFall, Liz. 2004. *Advertising: A Cultural Economy.* Thousand Oaks, CA: Sage.

McLuhan, Marshall. 1951. *The Mechanical Bride.* Boston: Beacon.

McQuail, Denis, and Sven Windahl. 1993. *Communication Models: For the Study of Mass Communication.* 2nd ed. New York: Longman.

Messaris, Paul. 1997. *Visual Persuasion: The Role of Images in Advertising.* Thousand Oaks, CA: Sage.

Mooij, Marieka de. 2011. *Consumer Behavior and Culture: Consequences for Global Marketing and Advertising.* 2nd ed. Thousand Oaks, CA: Sage.

Moriarty, Sandra, and Shay Sayre. 1991. "A Comparison of Reader Response with Informed Author/Viewer Analysis." Unpublished paper.

Myers, Greg. 1994. *Words in Ads.* London: Edward Arnold.

———. 1999. *Ad Worlds: Brands/Media/Audiences.* London: Arnold.

Nelson, Emily, and Sarah Ellison. 2005. "In a Shift, Marketers Beef Up Ad Spending Inside Store." *Wall Street Journal,* September 25, 1.

Nixon, Sean. 2003. *Advertising Cultures: Gender, Commerce, Creativity.* Thousand Oaks, CA: Sage.

O'Barr, William O. 1994. *Culture and the Ad: Exploring Otherness in the World of Advertising.* Boulder, CO: Westview.

Packard, Vance. 1957. *The Hidden Persuaders.* New York: David McKay.

Pappenheim, Fritz. 1967. *The Alienation of Modern Man.* New York: Monthly Review Press.

Patai, Raphael. 1972. *Myth and Modern Man.* Englewood Cliffs, NJ: Prentice-Hall.

Peterson, Melody. 2002. "Madison Ave. Plays Growing Role in the Business of Drug Research." *New York Times,* November 22.

Pieraccini, Tina, and Robert Schell. 1995. "You're Not Getting Older: You're Getting Better. In *Women and Media: Content/Careers/Criticism.* Ed. C. M. Lont. Belmont, CA: Wadsworth.

Potter, David M. 1954. *People of Plenty: Economic Abundance and the American Character.* Chicago: University of Chicago Press.

Rapaille, Clotaire. 2006. *The Culture Code: An Ingenious Way to Understand Why People around the World Live and Buy as They Do.* New York: Broadway Books.

Riviere, Joan. 1967. "Hate, Greed and Aggression." In *Love, Hate, and Reparation.* Ed. Melanie Klein and Joan Riviere. New York: Norton.

Rothefeld, Michael, and Patrick McGreevy. 2010. "Meg Whitman Sets Spending Record Paces in Campaign for Governor." *Los Angeles Times*, March 10.

Rotzoll, Kim, and James E. Haefner. 1986. *Advertising in Contemporary Society: Perspectives toward Understanding.* Cincinnati, OH: South-Western Publishing.

Saussure, Ferdinand de. 1966. *A Course in General Linguistics.* Trans. W. Baskin. New York: McGraw-Hill.

Scholes, Robert. 1974. *Structuralism in Literature: An Introduction.* New Haven, CT: Yale University Press.

Schwartz, Barry. 2004. *The Paradox of Choice.* New York: HarperCollins.

Sheehan, Kim Bartel. 2014. *Controversies in Contemporary Advertising.* 2nd ed. Thousand Oaks, CA: Sage.

Shorer, Mark. 1968. "The Necessity of Myth." In *Myth and Mythmaking.* Ed. H. A. Murray. Boston: Beacon.

Sides, John, and Lynn Vavreck. 2013. *The Gamble: Choice and Chance in the 2012 Presidential Election.* Princeton, NJ: Princeton University Press.

Solomon, Jack. 1990. *The Signs of Our Time: The Secret Meanings of Everyday Life.* New York: Harper & Row.

Solomon, Michael, Gary Barmossy, and Soren Askegaard. 2002. *Consumer Behavior: A European Perspective.* 2nd ed. Harlow, England: Financial Times/Prentice Hall.

Solow, Martin. 1988. "The Case of the Closet Target." In *Media USA: Process and Effect.* Ed. Arthur Asa Berger. New York: Longman.

Stossel, John. "Teen Spending on the Rise." *20/20.* http://abcnews.go.com/2020/story?id=124346&page=1.

Tellis, Gerard J. 2004. *Effective Advertising: Understanding When, How, and Why Advertising Works.* Thousand Oaks, CA: Sage.

Tharp, Marye C. 2001. *Marketing and Consumer Identity in Multicultural America.* Thousand Oaks, CA: Sage.

Thompson, Michael, Richard Ellis, and Aaron Wildavsky. 1990. *Cultural Theory.* Boulder, CO: Westview Press.

Twitchell, James. 1996. *Adcult USA: Advertising in American Culture.* New York: Columbia University Press.

Underhill, Paco. 2009. *Why We Buy: The Science of Shopping.* New York: Touchstone/Simon & Schuster.

Van Duyn, Aline. 2005. "Bloggers' New Brand Starts to Click with Advertisers." *Financial Times*, March 28.

Vestergaard, Torben, and Kim Schrøder. 1985. *The Language of Advertising.* Oxford, UK: Basil Blackwell.

Walker, Rob. 2008. *Buying In: What We Buy and Who We Are*. New York: Random House.

Walters, Dan. 2002. "A State of Gray." *Wall Street Journal*, October 24.

Weber, Max. 1958. *The Protestant Ethic and the Spirit of Capitalism*. New York: Charles Scribner's Sons.

Weiss, Michael. 1988. *The Clustering of America*. New York: Harper & Row.

Wells, William, Sandra Moriarty, and John Burnett. 2006. *Advertising: Principles and Practice*. 7th ed. Upper Saddle River, NJ: Pearson/Prentice Hall.

Wernick, Andrew. 1991. *Promotional Culture: Advertising, Ideology and Symbolic Expression*. London: Sage.

West, Darrell M. 1997. *Air Wars: Television Advertising in Election Campaigns*. Washington, DC: Congressional Quarterly.

Whiting, Sam. 1998. "Your ZIP Code Tells All about You." *San Francisco Chronicle*, November 23.

Wildavsky, Aaron. 1989. "A Cultural Theory of Preference Formation." In *Political Culture and Public Opinion*. Ed. Arthur Asa Berger. New Brunswick, NJ: Transaction.

Williamson, Judith. 1978. *Decoding Advertisements: Ideology and Meaning in Advertising*. London: Marion Boyars.

Woolf, Virginia. "Mr. Bennett and Mrs. Brown." http://www.columbia.edu/~em36/MrBennettAndMrsBrown.pdf.

Zaltman, Gerald. 2003. *How Customers Think: Essential Insights into the Mind of the Market*. Boston: Harvard Business School Press.

Zukin, Sharon. 2005. *Point of Purchase: How Shopping Changed American Culture*. New York: Routledge.

INDEX

20/20, 157
30-Second Politics: Political Advertising in the Eighties, 126
60 Minutes, 208

Abrams, M. H., 62
Adam, 173
advertising: aesthetic codes and, 21; agony of choice and, 93; Americans annoyed by, 7; battling for people's attention, 211; birds forming Coca-Cola, 92; branding and, 83–84; commercials as mini-dramas, 15–23; emotions and rationality, 43–44; fun and, 19–20; Gans on, 38; global nature of agencies, 28; heroes and heroines in, 16; humor in, 18–19; illusion of control and, 78–79; importance of creatives, 8; Jonathan Edwards and choice, 91; maximizers and satisfizers, 94; money spent on in USA, 76; nonadvertising forms of advertising, 94–96; organization of agencies, 7–8; politics and, 10–11; problem of clutter, 6; pseudopoetic appeal to the illiterati, 114–116; psycho-cultural perspective on, 12–13; race and ethnicity, 17–18; response tendencies in magazine ads, 12; rewards and, 22; salaries in agencies, 8; sexuality and gender, 16–17; smart phones and social media, 211–213; success and, 20; use of terror by cosmetics advertisers, 113–114; way it works, 5–7
Advertising: Principles and Practice, 7
Ad Worlds: Brands/Media/Audiences, 72
Alienation of Modern Man, 88
American Association of Advertising Agencies, 7
American Sociologist, 82
Apple Computer, xiii
Ansolabehere, Stephen, 125
Askegaard, Soren, 42
Atlantic, 155

Bakhtin, M., 188, 202
Barmossy, Gary, 42
Barnouw, Erik, 166
Baudrillard, Jean, 19–20, 24, 25, 58
Baxter, Richard, 10
Beckett, Jamie, 139, 140
Berger, Arthur Asa, 70, 233
Berger, John, 49, 57, 101–102, 122
Bilefsky, Dan, 89
Black Looks: Race and Representation, 17
"Bloggers' New Brand Starts to Click with Advertisers," 158
Botterill, Jacqueline, 4
Bourdin, Guy, 101
"Branded Self," 82
brands: being a "branded" individual, 82; Cortese on, 86; identity and, 83–84; Martin Solow on, 84; selling bodies for, 89
Brennan, Bridget, 116–117, 122

Breun, Stephen, 130
British Broadcasting Company, 49
Brown, Jerry, 133
Bulgari Connection, 95
Burnett, John, 7
Buying In: What We Buy and Who We Are, 211
"Buzz Report," 158

Calvin, John, 9
Campbell, R. J., 14
Cardin, Pierre, 119
"Case of the Closet Target," 84
children and advertising, 209–210
Children's Market Research, Inc., 156
class consumption game, 22
Clinton, Bill, 11
Clow, Lee, 200
Coleridge, Samuel, 230
Commercialization of American Culture: New Advertising, Control, and Democracy, 138
communication theory: focal points, 60–62; Jakobson model, 62–64; Lasswell formula, 59–60; run it up a flagpole, 64–65
"Comparison of Reader Response with Informed Author/Viewer Analysis," 200
Confessore, Nicholas, 130
Consciousness Industry, 126, 140
Consumer Behaviour: A European Perspective, 42
Consumer Culture and Postmodernism, 35
consumer cultures: "branded self" and, 82–83; cultural critique of advertising, 33–34; defined, 34–38; department stores and cathedrals, 47; four kinds, 50–55; lifestyles game, 52; national character and, 55–56; Neiman Marcus and "couthification," 45–46; privatism and, 44–45
Consumer Reports, 84

Consumer Society: Myths and Structures, 19
Cortese, Anthony J., 86, 97, 98, 182, 233
Course in General Linguistics, 54
Critique of Commodity Aesthetics: Appearance, Sexuality, and Advertising in Capitalist Society, 32, 92, 96, 138
Cultural Theory, 50
"A Cultural Theory of Preference Formation," 50
Culture against Man, 114
Culture Code: An Ingenious Way to Understand Why People around the World Live and Buy as They Do, 55

Danesi, Marcel, 233
Davis, Gray, 132
Death of a Salesman, 88
Decoding Advertisements: Ideology and Meaning in Advertising, 100
Dichter, Ernest, 17, 141
Dior, Christian, 101
Douglas, Mary, 50–55, 57, 218, 222
drug advertising, 205–209
"Drug Industry Ads Aid GOP," 208
Dun's Review, 144
Durkheim, Emile, 217

Eco, Umberto, 215
Edwards, Jonathan, 91, 97
Eichler, Alexander, 207, 213
Eidelberg, L., 25, 31
Eisenberg, Lee, 16, 143
Eisenhower, Dwight David, 132
Eisenstein, Sergei, 190
Eliade, Mircea, 67–68, 69
Elliott, Stuart, 154
Ellis, Richard, 50
Ellison, Sarah, 95
eMarketer, 1, 140
Encyclopedia of Psychoanalysis, 25
Enzenberger, Hans Magnus, 126, 136, 140, 141, 164
Essentials of Mass Communication Theory, xxiii

Eve, 173
Everyday Life in the Modern World, 72, xxiv
Ewen, Stuart, 234

Featherstone, Mike, 35
Female Eunuch, 107–108
Fidji perfume advertisement: analyzing Fidji ad, 169–180; analyzing print advertisements, 167–181; feminist interpretation of, 179–180; Lotman's theories, 167–168; Marxist interpretation of, 177–178; myth model and, 178–179; psychoanalytic interpretation of, 173–176; semiotic interpretation of, 171–173; sociological interpretation of, 176; what to analyze in print ads, 168–169
Financial Times, 158
Finn, Bridget, 158
Forbes, xvii
Forester, Norman, 91
Freedom of Will, 91
Freud, Sigmund, 14, 26, 78–80, 86, 97, 135, 175, 181, 222, 226, 228
Frith, Katherine Toland, 204, 234, xxiv

Gamble: Choice and Chance in the 2012 Presidential Election, 128
Gans, Herbert, 37–38, 57, 231
Gauguin, Paul, 172
"Gender Advertisements," 112
Gibbard, Jeff, 158–159
Gillum, Jack, 130
"Global Consumer Hot Buttons," 159
Goffman, Erving, 112, 122
Going Negative: How Political Advertisements Shrink and Polarize the Electorate, 125, 136
Goldberg, Fred, 9, 70, 186, 187
Goldberg Moser O'Neill advertising agency, 8, xi
Goldman, Robert, 234
Goodman, Ellen, 95

"Got Milk" campaign, 2, 3, 8, xxi
Greer, Germaine, 107
Gruber, Selina, 156

Hall, Stuart, 13, 30
Hall, Trish, 156
Harvard Business School, xvii
"Hate, Greed and Aggression," v
Haug, Wolfgang, 32, 92, 138, 234
Henry, Jules, 114–115, 123
Herman-Cohen, Valli, 101, 120, 122
Hidden Persuaders, xvi
Hinsie, L. E., 14
hooks, bell, 17
Howard, Niles, 144
How Customers Think: Essential Insights into the Mind of the Market, 44
"How Teenagers Spend Their Money," 155–156
Huizinga, Johan, 46

"In a Shift, Marketers Beef Up Spending Inside Store," 95
"In Defence of Shopping," 53
"Industrialization of the Mind," 126
Insanity of Advertising: Memoirs of a Mad Man, 187
INSEAD: The European Institute of Business Administration, xxii
integrated marketing communication: defined, 6; Fred Goldberg on, 70
Internet: advertising on, 11; teleculture and, 23
Irvine, Martha, 209
Itow, Laurie, 144
Iyengar, Shanto, 125

Jagger, Bianca, 50
Jakobson, Roman, 62, 63–64, 70, 220, 226, 228
Jameson, Fredric, 41, 43, 57
Jamieson, Kathleen Hall, 132, 136
Jhally, Sut, 4, 234
Jobs, Steve, xiii

Johnson, Mark, 65
Johnson, Philip, 38
Jones, Ernest, 228
Jung, Carl G., 16, 78, 216

Karmarkar, Uma, xvii
Kellner, Douglas, 40–41, 57
Kern, Montague, 126–127, 234
Key, Wilson Bryan, 80–81, 97
Key to the Consumer, 96
Klein, Calvin, 41
Kline, Stephen, 4, 234
Kurtz, Bruce, 75–76, 182

Lakoff, George, 65
Language of Advertising, 204
Laroche, Guy, 177
Lasswell, Harold, 59–60, 64–65, 70, 223
Law and Order, 94
Lawrence, D. H., 172
Lefebvre, Henri, 72, xxiv
Leis, William, 4, 234
Living Proof Cream Hydracel, 111, 113
Lont, C. M., 99
Lotman, Yuri, 167–168, 180, 183
Lutens, Serge, 173
Lyotard, Jean-François, 39, 43

Macintosh "1984" commercial, 183–203; alienated proles, 197–198; analyzing complex commercials, 183–184; background, 186; Big Brother figure, 191; blond as mediator, 196; blond as symbol, 190; brainwasher's message, 191–192; brainwashing scenario, 190–191; clever marketing strategy, 199–200; heroine as mythic figure, 194–195; IBM and, 198–199; image of total institution, 189; levels of analyzing blond heroine image, 196–197; Macintosh announcement, 193–194; Orwell's *1984* and Ridley Scott's "1984," 188–189; prisoner's boots, 189–190; psychoanalytic aspects of commercial, 195; scholarly research and, 200–202; synopsis of text, 183–184; testing the commercial, 186–188
Madison Avenue, 84
Man and His Symbols, 78
Marcus, Stanley, 46
Marketing Power: The Marketer's Reference Library, 115, 157
marketing society: Claritas typology, 151–153; comparison of different typologies, 161–163; demographics and psychographics, 142; illusion of freedom in, 140–142; importance of blogs, 158–159; magazine choice and consumer taste, 153–155; Maslow on needs, 143; problem of self-alienation, 90; selling oneself, 87–88; statistics on advertising, 139–140; types of teenage consumers, 155–158; typology for everyone in world, 159–160; using the VALS 1 typology, 147; VALS 1 typology, 144–147; VALS 2 revision of VALS 1, 147–149; zip codes and kinds of consumers, 149–151
Marx, Karl, 33, 43, 141, 170, 177, 178, 181, 203, 220
Maslow, Abraham, 143, 215
McAllister, Matthew P., 138
McCain, John, 129
McLuhan, Marshall, 26, 27, 62, 161, 221, 235
McQuail, Denis, 60, 225
Mechanical Bride, 26, 161
media: time spent with television, 75; usage in USA, 74
Medusa, 178
Messaris, Paul, 11–12, 103, 122, 124, 166, 235

metaphor: defined, 65–66; role in our lives, 66
Metaphors We Live By, 65
metonymy: defined, 66; relation to metaphor, 67
Miller, Arthur, 88
Moriarty, Sandra, 7, 200, 201
"Mr. Bennett and Mrs. Brown," 42
Murray, Rick, 158
Myers, Greg, 72, 235
myth: defined, 68; marketing and, 67; myth model, 68
Myth and Modern Man, 68, 109

National Public Radio, 208
Nelson, Emily, 95
neuromarketing, xxi
New Introductory Lectures on Psychoanalysis, 14
Newton, Helmut, 101
New York Daily News, 78
New York Times, 104, 129, 130, 156, 207
New York Times Magazine, 212

Obama, Barack, 129, 130
O'Barr, William M., 235
Orwell, George, 188, 201, 202

Packard, Vance, xvi
Pappenheim, Fritz, 88
Papson, Stephen, 234
Paradox of Choice, 92
Patai, Raphael, 68, 109, 122
Pavlov, Ivan, 81, 82,
Peirce, C. S., 171, 181, 231
Perseus, 178
"Pharmaceutical Companies Spent 19 Times More on Self-Promotion Than Basic Research," 207
Pieraccini, Tina, 99
political advertising, 125–137; California campaign for governor in 2010, 132–133; changes in, 126–128; cost

of presidential campaigns, 129–130; emotional basis of partisan politics, 134; FiveThirtyEight predictions, 129; four stages in campaigns, 127–129; positive appeals and their negations, 134; questions raised by campaigns, 132–132
Popular Art of American Television Commercial, 182
postmodernism: advanced form of capitalism, 41; de-differentiation and, 42; definitions of, 38–39; eclecticism and, 39; "incredulity toward metanarratives," 39; pastiche and, 40
"Postmodernism as Social Theory: Some Challenges and Problems," 40
Postmodernism or, The Cultural Logic of Late Capitalism, 41
Potter, David, 34, 56
"Primping or Pimping," 120
Promotional Culture: Advertising, Ideology and Symbolic Expression, 124
Protestant Ethic and the Spirit of Capitalism, 9
Provocateur: Images of Women and Minorities in Advertising, 86, 98, 182
"Psychoanalysis," 79
psychoanalytic theory: four stages of sexual development, 25–26; iceberg model of psyche, 80; id, ego, and superego, 14; role of the unconscious in consumption, 44; structural hypothesis, 14

Rapaille, Clotaire, 55–57, 57, 222, 225
Reiman, Arnold S., 207
Representation: Cultural Representations and Signifying Practices, 13
Riviere, Joan, v
Romney, Mitt, 130, 131
Roslaniec, Katarzyna, 89
Rowland, Greg, 106
Ruskin, Gary, 76

San Francisco Chronicle, 101

San Francisco Sunday Examiner and Chronicle, 144

Saussure, Ferdinand de, 54–55, 163, 171, 172, 181, 229

Sayre, Shay, 200, 201

Schell, Robert, 99

Scholes, Robert, 63

Schroder, Kim, 204, 2535

Schwartz, Barry, 93–94

Scott, Ridley, 186, 187, 202

sexuality and gender in advertising: analysis of BONBON advertisement, 104–107; Berger on use of sex in, 101–102; exploitation of female body, 99; preference for slender models, 103; sex and problem of clutter, 118–120; sex appeal and gender appeal, 116–118; sexploitation and anxiety, 107–109

Shoptimism: Why the American Consumer Will Keep On Buying No Matter What, 16, 143

Shorer, Mark, 225

Sides, John, 128, 129, 136

Signs of Our Time: The Secret Meanings of Everyday Life, 41, 58, 118, 100

Silver, Nate, 129

Social Communication in Advertising: Consumption in the Mediated Marketplace, 4

Solomon, Jack, 58, 100, 118, 122

Solomon, Michael, 42

Solow, Martin, 84, 97

Spider-Man 2, xvi

Sponsor: Notes on a Modern Potentate, 166

Spots: The Popular Art of American Television Commercials, 75

Stossel, John, 157, 165

Strategy of Desire, 141

Structuralism in Literature: An Introduction, 63

Structure of the Artistic Text, 167–168

Subliminal Seduction, 80

Super Bowl, xviii; audience in 2014, 27; showcase advertisements, 27

"Suspension of Disbelief as a Bridge between Media and Consumption," 85

System of Objects, 24, 58

taste cultures: and advertising, 37–38; all of equal worth, 37; Gans on advertising, 38

Teen-Age Research Unlimited, 155

television: exposure to commercials, 75–76; "hauls," 77

Theory, Culture and Society, 40

Thompson, Derek, 155

Thompson, Michael, 50

"Total Cost of Election Could Be $6 Billion," 130

Twitchell, James, 4

Underhill, Paco, xix, 48, 57, 142, 210

Undressing the Ad, 204, xxiv

Ungaro, Emmanuel, 101

"Using Social Media to Determine Consumer Preferences," 158

Vavreck, Lynn, 128, 129, 136

Vestegaard, Torben, 204, 235

Vilkeviciute, Edita, 104

Visual Persuasion: The Role of Images in Advertising, 11, 103, 124, 166

Walker, Rob, 212

Wall Street Journal, 81, 95, 98

Wanamaker, John, 1

Waning of the Middle Ages, 46

Warner, W. Lloyd, 20

Ways of Seeing, 49, 101

Weber, Max, 9, 10, 30, 57

Wegner, Daniel, 141

Weiss, Michael, 149, 151

Weldon, Fay, 95

Wernick, Andrew, 124

Weston, Drew, 134–135, 137

"When It's All Too Much," 93

Whitman, Meg, 133, 136

Why She Buys: The New Strategy for Reaching the World's Most Powerful Consumers, 116

Why We Buy: The Science of Shopping, 48, xix

Wildavsky, Aaron, 50–53, 135, 218

Wiley, Norbert, 85–86

Williamson, Judith, 100, 122

Windahl, Sven, 60, 225

Wise Up to Teens: Insights into Marketing and Advertising to Teenagers, 115

Women and Media: Content/Careers/Criticism, 99

Woolf, Virginia, 42–43

"Young Are Getting and Spending, Too," 156

Zaltman, Gerald, 44, 57, 141, 235

Zollo, Peter, 115

ABOUT THE AUTHOR

Arthur Asa Berger is professor emeritus of broadcast and electronic communication art at San Francisco State University, where he taught from 1965 until 2003. He attended the University of Massachusetts, the University of Iowa, and the University of Minnesota, where he received a PhD in American studies in 1965. He wrote his dissertation on the comic strip "Li'l Abner." During the 1963–1964 school year, he had a Fulbright scholarship to Italy and taught at the University of Milan. He spent a year as visiting professor at the Annenberg School for Communication at the University of Southern California in Los Angeles in 1984 and taught a short course on advertising in 2002 as a Fulbright senior specialist at the Heinrich Heine University in Düsseldorf, Germany.

Berger is the author of numerous articles, book reviews, and books on the mass media, popular culture, humor, and everyday life. Among his recent books are *Video Games: A Popular Culture Phenomenon*, *Jewish Jesters: The Art of Comedy Writing*, and *The Portable Postmodernist*. He also wrote a number of mysteries: *Die Laughing*, *The Hamlet Case*, *Postmortem for a Postmodernist*, *The Mass Comm Murders: Five Media Theorists Self-Destruct*, and *Durkheim Is Dead: Sherlock Holmes Is Introduced to Social Theory*. His books have been translated into German, Swedish, Italian, Korean, Indonesian, Arabic, Turkish, and Chinese. He has lectured in more than a dozen countries in the course of his career.

Married with two children and four grandchildren, Berger lives in Mill Valley, California. His wife teaches philosophy at Diablo Valley College.